a cost accounting handbook
for colleges and universities

a cost accounting handbook

for colleges and universities

james a. hyatt

nacubo

Copyright © 1983 by the National Association of
  College and University Business Officers
One Dupont Circle
Washington, DC 20036

Library of Congress Cataloging in Publication Data

Hyatt, James A.
  A cost accounting handbook for colleges and
universities.

  Bibliography: p.
  1. Universities and colleges—United States—
Accounting.   I. Title.
LB2342.H9   1983   378′.1′00681   82-18840
ISBN 0-915164-16-7

contents

(**Note:** All right-hand pages in exhibit sections have a vertical color bar.)

acknowledgments

This handbook was developed under a grant from the Carnegie Corporation of New York, with supervision by members of the Cost Accounting Handbook Task Force. The members of the task force were:

Catherine H. Briel
Controller
Boston College

Edward W. Doty
Vice President for Finance and Management
State University of New York at Buffalo

Roger J. Fecher
Senior Vice President
Kalamazoo College

A. W. Flowers
Executive Vice Chancellor
Maricopa County Community College

E. Leroy Knight
Treasurer and Business Manager
Connecticut College

Rudolph E. Koletic
Vice President for Financial Affairs
University of Tampa

James R. Topping
Financial Services Manager
National Center for Atmospheric Research

G. Richard Wynn
Vice President for Business Affairs
Earlham College

Keith W. Mathews, controller at Ohio Wesleyan University, served as a consultant to the project. Exhibits and case studies in the handbook were developed by A. W. Flowers, Peter M. Forman, cost analyst at Fairleigh Dickinson University, and Keith W. Mathews.

The project director and principal author of the handbook was James A. Hyatt, associate director of the financial management center, NACUBO. Other project staff included Stephen D. Campbell and Laurel J. Radow. NACUBO's committees for financial management, programs for small colleges, two-year colleges, and minority institutions provided valuable assistance in developing the handbook.

Four regional review sessions were held in March 1982 in order to solicit comments from college and university business officers regarding the utility and applicability of the costing procedures described in the handbook. The sessions were as follows:

Region	Date	Host	Number of Attendees
West	3/11/82	Alan B. Holloway Saint Mary's College of California Moraga, CA	16
East	3/16/82	Joseph F. Canney College of the Holy Cross Worcester, MA	25
South	3/23/82	Robert D. Flanigan, Jr. Spelman College Atlanta, GA	13
Central	3/26/82	Roger J. Fecher Kalamazoo College Kalamazoo, MI	14

A total of 68 persons, representing 58 colleges and universities, attended the sessions. Approximately 70 percent of the participants were from independent four-year institutions and about 22 percent were from public two-year institutions. Other participants represented four-year public institutions and state boards of higher education. During April 1982 the handbook was revised to incorporate suggestions and comments from session participants.

Members of the cost accounting handbook task force and staff hereby express appreciation to Alan B. Holloway, Joseph F. Canney, Robert D. Flanigan, Jr., and Roger J. Fecher for hosting the review sessions and to the college and university business officers who attended.

In addition to the regional review sessions, the field review edition of the handbook was reviewed by many college and university business officers and other persons knowledgeable in the areas of cost accounting and financial management. Comments and suggestions from those reviewers were also used in revising the handbook. The project task force and staff wish to express appreciation for the contributions of those persons to the handbook. The task force and staff also recognize the support and assistance provided by D. F. Finn and M. J. Williams of NACUBO.

preface

Evidence of cost studies for colleges and universities can be traced to the late nineteenth and early twentieth centuries. The pioneering work in the field was conducted by Reeves and Russell in the 1930s at the University of Chicago. Several national studies in the 1950s attempted to compare unit costs of instruction across institutional and state boundaries. Because these efforts were largely unsuccessful, there was an increased emphasis in the 1960s and 1970s on standardization of cost terminology and procedures (for example, by NACUBO, the National Center for Higher Education Management Systems, and the National Commission on the Financing of Postsecondary Education). With the 1980s bringing reduced resource bases and dwindling student populations, the use of cost analysis is now focused on improving the internal management of the institution. This provided the major impetus for NACUBO to seek a grant from the Carnegie Corporation of New York to produce *A Cost Accounting Handbook for Colleges and Universities.*

The task force had several goals in guiding the development of the handbook:

1. The handbook should be based on sound case study material prepared by college and university business officers. To accomplish this, the task force polled 40 business officers and collected 7 case studies.

2. The handbook is directed to the small college business officer. Most of the earlier costing work had been geared to major research universities or central offices of large public systems of higher education. A "small college," in the context of this book, is one whose primary function is instruction.

3. This book focuses on noninstructional areas, in contrast to most of the earlier costing literature, which focused almost exclusively on the instructional

function to the exclusion of the academic, student, and institutional support functions. While a chapter on instructional costing is included here, it is not the principal topic of the handbook. The chapters on each functional area may be used independently. Certain fundamental concepts outlined in chapters 1 and 2 are repeated elsewhere to facilitate such use.

4. This book is intended for use in a series of separate costing applications, for example, the motor pool or the print shop. The book is not a comprehensive costing system for all institutional functions. Again, in an effort to keep the applications simple and relatively straightforward, the task force avoided the temptation to develop a total "systems" approach. Also, certain sections of the handbook, such as exhibit 2-A on OMB Circular A-21, may be more applicable to certain types of institutions than to others. Those sections should be used as references for readers interested in various applications and aspects of costing.

5. Cost analysis should be conducted with a definite purpose in mind. While this may appear to be self-evident, members of the task force have too often observed that cost accounting is performed for the sake of cost accounting. All potential users of the handbook are urged to define the purpose of a possible cost study and to identify potential users of the data before beginning the study.

Earlier drafts of the handbook were reviewed extensively through a series of regional review sessions attended by 68 business officers and through direct mail reviews coordinated with NACUBO committees for financial management, programs for small colleges, minority institutions, and two-year colleges. The task force sincerely hopes that this document will assist in developing cost information for institutions of higher education, throughout the 1980s and beyond.

part 1

introduction to cost accounting
for colleges and universities

1
a general approach

Cost accounting is the branch of accounting that is concerned with accumulating, classifying, allocating, summarizing, interpreting, and reporting the cost of personnel, goods and services, and other expenses incurred during a specific period. The primary difference between cost accounting and financial accounting is that the former involves obtaining unit cost information while the latter involves the reporting of costs by organizational unit and function. According to Horngren (1977): "The field of financial accounting is concerned mainly with how accounting can serve *external* decision makers, such as stockholders, creditors, governmental agencies, and others. The field of managerial (cost) accounting is concerned mainly with how accounting can serve *internal* decision makers, such as managers."[1]

The purpose of this handbook is to describe procedures for collecting and analyzing cost information at single-purpose colleges and universities. In the context of this book, single-purpose institutions are defined as those institutions whose primary activity is instruction. The handbook is specifically oriented to the use of cost information for internal decision making. It illustrates how to collect cost information for the institution as a whole and how to conduct cost studies of specific functional areas, such as plant operation and maintenance, instruction, auxiliary enterprises, and support and service activities. While it may be possible for two institutions using the same costing methodology to exchange and compare data, that is not the principal objective of this handbook.

The costing procedures described in the book are consistent with those in NACUBO's *College & University Business Administration (CUBA), A Management Reporting Manual for Colleges,* and the *Administrative Service.* These publications, as well as others on accounting, are cited throughout the text.

Costing Considerations

As stated in the preface, cost analysis should be conducted with a purpose in mind. To determine the type and amount of cost information that should be collected, it is necessary to conduct the following analysis.

- Identify the purpose for collecting the data.

- Determine who will use the cost information. For example, will it be used by senior administrators, department chairpersons, directors of auxiliary services, a combination of these, or all of them?

- Define the area or areas of study, such as auxiliary enterprises, instruction, and plant operation and maintenance.

- Decide on the level of cost data that will satisfy the information needs of the users.

- Assess the adequacy of accounting, budgeting, facility utilization, and inventory data, not only in their current form but also in terms of historical data.

- Compare the potential benefit of collecting cost data with the cost of collecting and analyzing the data.

---

[1]Charles T. Horngren, *Cost Accounting—A Managerial Emphasis,* 4th ed. (Englewood Cliffs, N.J.: Prentice-Hall, 1977), p. 4.

Other factors to be considered in designing and implementing cost procedures are described in NACUBO's "Fundamental Considerations for Determining Cost Information in Higher Education" (see appendix A).

Purposes for Collecting Institutional Cost Data

Frequently cost data are collected to answer a specific question, such as whether it is more effective to contract with an external vendor for a service or to provide the service in-house. In this instance, the collection of cost data is a one-time-only proposition and need not involve the implementation of an ongoing cost accounting system. In the last few years, however, many institutional administrators have felt an increasing need for a set of cost accounting procedures to assist them in the decision-making processes of planning, budgeting, control, and evaluation. The uses of cost data in these areas are discussed below.[2]

Planning and budgeting. The process of planning and budgeting is designed to formulate an institution's method for achieving its long-term mission and short-term goals and objectives. In planning and budgeting, cost information is one factor used in examining alternatives. By determining the cost requirements of each alternative, decision makers can select those that make the most effective use of available resources. Cost information may be used in modifying the budget plan during the operating period by indicating the cost consequences of proposed actions in view of changes in priorities or economic conditions, and other circumstances that were not foreseen during the planning and budgeting process.

The costing procedures described in this book are concerned with the collection and analysis of historical full cost. These data are useful in determining the cost of activities for a particular period of time and in serving as a base for planning and budgeting. If the user wishes to determine the future cost of activities for the purpose of planning, budgeting, and pricing, it is important to consider the effect of certain environmental, volume, and decision factors on cost. For a detailed discussion on how these factors relate to cost analysis, refer to NACUBO's *Costing for Policy Analysis* (1980) or "Cost Behavior Analysis for Planning in Higher Education" (1977), by Robin-son, Ray, and Turk [NACUBO *Professional File*, vol. 9, no. 5 (May 1977)].

Control. In controlling current operations, cost information is a valuable indicator for identifying areas in which current budgeting adjustments may be required or corrective actions needed. The control process involves the comparison of incurred cost to budgeted cost, and any variances are examined to determine appropriate action.

Evaluation. Cost information is important in the evaluation of performance. Evaluation involves an after-the-fact examination of results and assists in determining whether the educational and related activities conducted were as effective as anticipated. Evaluation also involves an analysis of current institutional funding levels to determine whether they are providing appropriate support and whether certain activities should be reduced or eliminated. By comparing the results of operations to the original plan, areas can be identified in which adjustments may be needed in future planning and budgeting.

Pricing. Cost information is important in evaluating and setting prices for institutional goods and services, for example, in evaluating the cost of evening division courses or summer sessions, and in setting tuition and fees. Cost information is also used in determining interdepartmental charges in the financial accounting system. In auxiliary enterprises, cost data can be used in establishing prices for student housing, food service, and others.

Other purposes. At those institutions that have sponsored research projects, cost information can be used to establish indirect cost recovery rates on federal grants and contracts. Though this handbook is oriented toward institutions that do not have extensive research programs, a discussion of indirect cost recovery rates is described in exhibit 2-A, which follows chapter 2.

Prior to collecting cost data for any purpose, it is necessary to identify potential data users in order to determine the level of aggregation of data. For example, if the data are to be used by the chairperson of an academic department or directors of service or support operations, a greater level of detail may be required than if the data are to be used solely by senior administrators for institutional policy formulation and long-range planning. The level of aggregation of data, therefore, depends on the specific information requirements of particular users. The needs of individual users also determine the type of cost reports required by administrators at different management and organizational levels.

---

[2]NACUBO/NCHEMS, *Procedures for Determining Historical Full Costs, Technical Report 65,* 2nd ed. (Washington, D.C., 1977), pp. 1.8-1.10.

Data Requirements

To collect cost information, it is necessary to have an accounting system that generates financial data in an accurate, consistent, and timely manner. For the purposes of this handbook, an adequate accounting system is defined as one that is in general compliance with the accounting guidelines presented in Part 5 of NACUBO's *College & University Business Administration* (1982).

In addition to an accounting system, several other types of data may be needed to conduct cost analysis. These can include student information, such as student credit hours and student contact hours; facilities and equipment inventories; personnel data; and budget data. Other data sources, such as library utilization studies, can also be useful in allocating support costs to benefiting cost centers (see chapter 2).

The Tiered Approach to Cost Accounting

This book employs a three-tiered approach to cost accounting. The tiered approach is a method of collecting and analyzing institutional costs by groupings and levels of cost. Below is a detailed description of the three tiers; an illustration of the tiered approach is provided at the end of this chapter.

Tier one costs encompass all direct costs that are readily identifiable with a specific cost objective or cost center. They include the costs associated with salaries and wages, employee benefits, supplies and office expenses, travel, contractual services, and non-capitalized equipment. Costs identified through an institutional chargeback system should also be included as tier one costs of the cost center. Examples of these types of costs are printing costs, costs of using a vehicle in a motor pool, or computing costs charged directly to the cost center. Chapter 2 includes a discussion of institutional chargeback systems.

Tier one costs are usually identified in the financial records of an institution and/or in the budgets of cost objectives or centers. A cost objective is any activity to which costs can be attributed. A cost objective can be a service provided by an organizational unit, a project, a responsibility center, a function, a program, or any other identifiable activity. A cost center is the smallest unit of activity or area of responsibility into which an operating organization is divided for control and accountability purposes and to which costs are assigned or allocated. For the purposes of this handbook, the major program areas of an institution, such as instruction, institutional support, and auxiliary enterprises, have been designated as cost objectives. Each of the various departments within these program areas, such as academic departments and support and service departments, and individual auxiliary enterprises, such as housing and food services, have been designated as cost centers.

Tier two costs consist of all tier one costs plus indirect costs that are attributable to a cost objective or center. Indirect costs are those costs not readily identifiable with a specific cost objective or center. Indirect costs occur when support services are provided to benefiting cost objectives and centers. They include the cost of providing support services, such as plant operation and maintenance, accounting, purchasing, and computing.

Indirect costs should be allocated through the use of consistent allocation or proration methodologies. Specific bases for allocating indirect costs are presented in chapter 2.

Tier three costs include all tier two costs plus a depreciation or use charge on facilities and capitalized equipment. Tier three costs represent the full costs attributable to a cost objective or center. Depreciation is that portion of the cost of limited-life capital assets (building and equipment) that expires during a specified period. Whether a depreciation or use charge is made for the use of facilities or capital equipment, these costs must be included in tier three costs in order to obtain the full cost associated with a cost objective or cost center.

The value of collecting tier three costs depends on the purpose for which the cost information is to be used. Tier three costs, for example, can be used in the auxiliary enterprise area to determine the extent to which auxiliary enterprises are self-supporting. The methodology for allocating or prorating tier three costs can vary among institutions, but the one used should be supported by sufficient background material to justify its use.

A number of other costs should be considered in determining the full costs associated with a cost objective. These costs include the value of any contributed goods and services attributable to a cost objective or center that is *not* reflected in the institution's financial statements. Contributed goods can consist of donated supplies and equipment. Contributed services can range from instructional services donated by members of religious orders at church-affiliated institutions to the employee pension expenses incurred by the state for faculty and staff at public higher education institutions.

Another cost that may be considered in conducting cost analysis is imputed cost. Imputed cost is the value of potential resources that would have been available to an institution had one alternative been chosen instead of another. Imputed costs do not consider the past, present, or future disbursements of cash or its equivalent but rather are concerned with measuring the cost of alternative opportunities. An example of imputed cost is the revenue lost by failing to fill most class sections to capacity.

The decision to collect cost at any tier depends upon the purpose for which costs are being collected and the institutional resources available to conduct cost analysis. For many single-purpose institutions, the collection of only tier one costs may provide sufficient information for many types of decisions. At other institutions the collection of tier two or tier three costs may be more desirable, especially in the evaluation of new and existing academic programs or in the setting of prices for housing and food services. In the chapters that follow, procedures are described for collecting and analyzing multiple tiers of cost data for each of the functional or program areas of the institution. Whether direct or full costing procedures should be applied at an institution is left to the discretion of its administrators.

A Five-Step General Procedure for Cost Accounting

A major purpose of this handbook is to provide a basic set of procedures for collecting and arraying cost data. Figure 1.1 presents a five-step general cost accounting procedure.

Figure 1.1
A Five-Step General Cost Accounting Procedure

1. Designate specific cost objectives and cost centers.
2. Select consistent categories of cost.
3. Assign all tier one costs to designated cost objectives and centers. (These data should be available directly from the institution's accounting system.)
4. Assign all tiers two and three costs to designated cost objectives and centers as desired.
5. Develop unit costs or output measures.

The tiered approach to cost accounting, discussed in the previous section, is used in conjunction with the five-step general procedure. Specific steps in the procedures are described below. In reviewing steps 1 through 3, it should be noted that the information generated by following these steps is normally available from an institution's financial accounting system.

1. *Designate specific cost objectives and cost centers.* Develop a standard set of accounts that sep-

arates the functions of the institution into specific cost objectives or cost centers. At colleges and universities, cost objectives or cost centers are derived from the institution's chart of accounts. This handbook uses the chart of accounts in *College & University Business Administration,* chapter 5:6. The relevant portion of that chapter has been reproduced as exhibit 1-A and follows this chapter. This exhibit will be referred to throughout the handbook. At those institutions with a chart of accounts that differs from the NACUBO structure, the institution's own charts of accounts should be used to designate cost objectives and cost centers. Depending on the purpose for which cost data are being collected, cost centers can relate to a function, such as logistical services, or to specific activities, such as purchasing, printing, or motor pool.

2. *Select consistent categories of cost.* Once institutional cost centers have been designated, it is necessary to select a standard set of cost categories. These cost categories should be based on the institution's current classification of expenditures by object. The object-of-expenditure classification identifies that which is received in return for the expenditures. The three major object-of-expenditure classifications found in most colleges and universities are personnel compensation, supplies and operating expenses, and capital expenditures. Breakdowns within these major categories will depend on how useful the detail is to individual decision makers. For example, personnel compensation includes all salaries, wages, and employee benefits. This object can be further broken into personnel compensation for groups of faculty, staff, and student employees and for full-time and part-time personnel. For a more detailed description of object-of-expenditure classifications, refer to NACUBO's *A Management Reporting Manual for Colleges* and *College & University Business Administration,* chapter 5:6 (see exhibit 1-A).

3. *Assign all tier one costs to designated cost objectives and centers.* Tier one or direct costs are those expenses that are readily identifiable with a specific cost center. Tier one costs for specific cost centers are contained in the financial records of the institution. For example, if the cost center is the chemistry department, identifiable chemistry faculty and staff compensation and supplies are tier one costs of the department. For the institutional support area, tier one costs of the business office would include staff compensation, supplies, and other objects of expenditure identified in the unit's budget. Figure 1.2 presents typical tier one costs.

Figure 1.2
Typical Tier One Costs

- Compensation
  Salaries
  Wages
  Employee benefits
- Supplies and operating expenses
  Consumable supplies and materials
  Communications, e.g., telephone, telegraph, postal, printing, binding, and duplicating services
  Academic and administrative computing services
- Travel
- Contractual services
- Noncapitalized equipment

If a decision is made to account for cost at a lower level of detail than the accounting system will provide, such as the costs associated with upper-division and lower-division chemistry, some method of distributing tier one costs between these activities must be used, for example, a faculty activity reporting system, which is described in chapter 6.

4. *Assign all tiers two and three costs to designated cost objectives and centers as desired.* Tier two costs include all tier one costs plus indirect costs that are attributable to a cost objective or center. Indirect costs reflect the cost of support services provided to benefiting cost centers and cost objectives. Indirect costs of a chemistry department could include an allocated portion of the expenses of plant operation and maintenance, institutional support, and academic support. For the business office these costs could include an allocation of the costs associated with plant operation and maintenance, data processing services, campus security, and other institutional support services. Methods for allocating indirect costs are described in chapter 2.

Tier three costs include all tier two costs plus a depreciation or use charge on facilities and capitalized equipment. Depreciation charges should be based on the useful life of the assets and should take into consideration such factors as type of construction, potential obsolescence, and the institution's renewal and replacement policies.

In the NACUBO/NCHEMS document cited earlier, *Procedures for Determining Historical Full Costs,* an alternative to depreciation is presented in the form of an annual use charge on buildings and land improvements. The use charge may be one overall rate that an institution can apply to the total cost of all its buildings and land improvements, or it may be a combination of rates that reflects the remaining lives of capital assets and the institution's policy toward the maintenance of its capital assets. An important difference between the use-charge rate and depreciation is that a use-charge rate can be applied to a particular building or group of buildings as long as that building is in existence, while under the depreciation method the time period is limited to the estimated useful life of the building. In *Procedures for Determining Historical Full Costs,* NACUBO recommends an overall annual rate of 2 percent, based on an estimated useful life of 50 years for buildings and land improvements. For capital equipment a 10 percent rate reflecting an estimated useful life of 10 years is recommended, although this can vary by type of equipment.[3] Figure 1.3 illustrates the application of an annual use charge on buildings and land improvements.

Figure 1.3
Application of Annual Use Charge on Buildings and Land Improvements

Original cost of all buildings and land improvements		$10,000,000
Multiply by: Annual use factor		.02
Annual use charge for buildings and land improvements		$ 200,000

Depreciation expenses for program areas and for the institution as a whole are described throughout the book.

5. *Develop unit cost or output measures.* Once the desired cost data have been collected, the final step in costing is an analysis of the data. Frequently, comparative analysis of tiers one, two, and three costs for different time periods is helpful in assessing the efficiency of the institution's operations. In other instances, cost data can be combined with other statistical data to produce unit costs. A unit cost is the cost of a single item or unit of service provided by a cost objective or center. When the costs associated with plant operation and maintenance, for example, are divided by the square footage assigned to each cost center, the cost per assignable square foot can be determined.

---

[3]Office of Management and Budget Circular A-21, Section J9, sets the use allowance for buildings at 2 percent of acquisition cost and the use allowance for equipment at 6⅔ percent. No limits are set on useful life, but estimates of useful life should be based on the institution's own experience.

An Illustration of the Five-Step General Procedure And Tiered Approach to Cost Accounting

The following example illustrates the use of the five-step general procedure and tiered approach to cost accounting. Institution A operates a motor pool. For the purpose of this illustration, the motor pool has been designated a cost center. Figure 1.4 highlights general information on the motor pool for one fiscal year.

Figure 1.4
General Information on the Motor Pool

Number and Type of Vehicles	Miles per Gallon for Each Type of Vehicle	Estimated Annual Mileage for Each Type of Vehicle
1 bus	7 miles/gallon	20,000 mi/yr.
3 vans	11 miles/gallon	15,000 mi/yr.
8 sedans	18 miles/gallon	20,000 mi/yr.

Note: Fuel consumption and annual mileage figures can vary from institution to institution depending on the location of the institution and its role and mission.

Steps one through three of the five-step general procedure for cost accounting involve the assignment of all tier one or direct costs attributable to designated cost objectives or centers. The tier one costs assigned to the motor pool are outlined in figure 1.5. The tier one costs for each type of vehicle are also shown. The method used to distribute tier one costs by vehicle type is based on actual usage data, such as vehicle service records, and on the number of vehicles of each type. The total tier one costs for the motor pool come from Institution A's financial records.

Step four of the general procedure for cost accounting requires the assignment of all tiers two and three costs attributable to the motor pool cost center. Figure 1.6 shows all tier two costs attributable to the motor pool cost center. Only those tier two costs that are significant or material to the operation of the motor pool, such as purchasing and accounting, have been included. The costs associated with executive management or the president's office, for example, have not been included since the motor pool's share of the cost of these activities is not significant or

Figure 1.5
Tier One Costs of the Motor Pool Cost Center

Tier One Costs (obtained from Institution A's financial records)		By Type of Vehicle		
		1 Bus	3 Vans	8 Sedans
Staff salaries and employee benefits				
1 FTE motor pool manager	$14,000			
Distributed by type of vehicle based on number of vehicles of each type		$ 1,167	$ 3,500	$ 9,333
.25 FTE secretary	3,000			
Distributed by type of vehicle based on number of vehicles of each type		250	750	2,000
1.5 FTE licensed student bus drivers	3,500			
Distributed only to the bus[1]		3,500	—	—
Total staff salaries and benefits	20,500			
By type and number of vehicles		4,917	4,250	11,333
Contractual service on vehicles	15,300			
Distributed by type of vehicle based on service records		2,200	3,050	10,050
Gasoline[2]	19,700			
Distributed by type of vehicle based on actual usage		3,500	5,100	11,100
Supplies and expenses, such as postage and telephone	600			
Distributed by type of vehicle based on number of vehicles		50	150	400
Insurance on vehicles[3]	5,300			
Distributed by type of vehicle based on annual insurance premium		750	1,250	3,300
Total tier one costs	$61,400			
Total tier one costs by type of vehicle		$11,417	$13,800	$36,183

[1]Student bus drivers work on a part-time basis during the school year.
[2]Estimated price of gasoline: $1.25 per gallon.
[3]Insurance is for basic liability only. (This figure can vary from institution to institution depending on region, locality (rural or urban), and insurance experience rating.)

material. The method used to allocate the cost of support activities, such as purchasing, personnel, and accounting, to the motor pool is indicated in figure 1.6. Chapter 2 includes a more complete description of these allocation methods.

To determine the tier three costs attributable to the motor pool cost center, it is necessary to include a depreciation charge on all motor pool facilities and capitalized equipment. The depreciation charges on all capitalized equipment in the motor pool cost center are listed in figure 1.7. Note that the vehicle purchase price, salvage value, and useful life listed in figure 1.7 can vary from institution to institution. Tier three costs attributable to the motor pool cost center are shown in figure 1.8.

Based on the cost data in figure 1.5, the tier one or direct costs of operating the motor pool are $61,400 per year. If indirect costs and the depreciation on capitalized equipment and facilities are included, the tier three cost of operating the motor pool is $82,424 per year. Under step five of the general procedure for cost accounting, these cost data can be combined with related data, such as the number of vehicles in the motor pool by type (buses, vans, sedans) and the total mileage logged during the year, to yield a number of unit cost or output measures. An example of unit costs is shown in figure 1.8. These output measures are useful in preparing future plans and budgets for the motor pool.

If the indirect portion of the motor pool costs is adjusted to reflect only avoidable indirect costs, or those indirect costs that would be eliminated if the motor pool operation was discontinued, output measures, such as cost per vehicle per mile by type, can be constructed. These measures can then be contrasted with industrial standards for auto-leasing companies. If these costs are adjusted to take into consideration future costs due to environmental factors such as inflation and volume factors such as estimated annual mileage, it is then possible to evaluate whether it is more efficient to operate the motor pool or to lease a fleet of vehicles. In reviewing the costs in figure 1.8 it is important to note that avoidable indirect costs usually *include* those costs, such as accounting services and plant operation and maintenance costs, that could be reduced if the motor pool were to be discontinued. Avoidable indirect costs usually *do not include* the cost of activities, such as executive management, that would continue regardless of whether the motor pool continued or ceased operation.

Figure 1.6

Tier Two Costs of the Motor Pool Cost Center

		By Type of Vehicle		
		(Distributed on the basis of number of vehicles of each type)		
		1 Bus	3 Vans	8 Sedans
Tier Two Costs				
Operation and maintenance charges allocated on the basis of assignable square footage of the motor pool garage	$ 800	$ 67	$ 201	$ 532
Various institutional support charges allocated by such measures as:				
Purchasing based on number of purchase orders processed	300	25	75	200
Personnel based on total direct costs of the motor pool cost center	325	27	81	217
Duplicating based on job orders	350	29	87	234
Accounting based on total direct costs of the motor pool cost center	425	35	105	285
Attributable indirect costs	2,200	183	549	1,468
Plus tier one costs (see figure 1.5)	61,400	11,417	13,800	36,183
Total tier two costs	$63,600			
Total tier two costs by type of vehicle		$11,600	$14,349	$37,651

Figure 1.7
A. Annual Depreciation Charge on Motor Pool Capitalized Equipment by Type of Vehicle

Type of Vehicle	(a) Average Purchase Cost	−	(b) Salvage Value	(a − b = c) Depreciable Portion	(d) Useful Life	(c ÷ d = e) Annual Depreciation Charge (using straight-line depreciation)
Bus	$60,000		$5,000	$55,000	8 years	$\frac{\$55,000}{8} = \$6,875$
Van	8,500		2,000	6,500	6 years	$\frac{6,500}{6} = 1,083$
Sedan	6,000		1,500	4,500	5 years	$\frac{4,500}{5} = 900$

B. Total Annual Depreciation Charge by Type of Vehicle

Type of Vehicle	Annual Depreciation Charge (see (e) above)	×	Number of Vehicles	=	Total Annual Depreciation Charge
Bus	$6,875		1		$ 6,875
Van	1,083		3		3,249
Sedan	900		8		7,200
Total annual depreciation charge on capitalized equipment in the motor pool cost center					$17,324

Figure 1.8
Tier Three Costs of the Motor Pool Cost Center

		By Type of Vehicle		
		1 Bus	3 Vans	8 Sedans
Tier Three Costs				
Total annual depreciation charge on capitalized equipment (from figure 1.7)	$17,324			
Distributed to all vehicles on the basis of depreciation schedule (from figure 1.7)		$ 6,875	$ 3,249	$ 7,200
Total annual depreciation charge on facilities based on assignable square feet of motor pool	1,500			
Distributed by type of vehicle based on number of vehicles		125	375	1,000
Total annual depreciation charge	18,824			
Total annual depreciation charge by type of vehicle		7,000	3,624	8,200
Total tier two costs (from figure 1.6)	63,600	11,600	14,349	37,651
Total tier three costs	$82,424			
Total tier three costs by type of vehicle		$18,600	$17,973	$45,851
Unit Costs				
Estimated cost per mile for each type of vehicle	$82,424	$18,600	$17,973	$45,851
(see figure 1.4 for estimated annual mileage data by type of vehicle)	225,000 mi. = $0.37/mi.	20,000 mi. = $0.93/mi.	45,000 mi. = $0.40/mi.	160,000 mi. = $0.29/mi.

exhibit 1-a

chart of accounts: current funds expenditures and transfers accounts*

Current funds expenditures accounts should bear identifying codes and symbols that will identify functions, such as Instruction, Institutional Support, and Scholarships and Fellowships; identify organizational units, such as Department of Physics, Controller's Office, and Registrar's Office; and identify the object of expenditures, such as Personnel Compensation, Supplies and Expenses, and Capital Expenditures. If desired, interdepart-

mental purchases, as contrasted with purchases from external sources, also may be identified by code or symbol. The object coding and symbols should be designed to provide for common usage of the objects throughout the entire chart of accounts, although, of course, there will be individual object codings that will be used only for particular functional categories.

Educational and General

Instruction

Accounts by divisions, schools, colleges, and departments of instruction following the administrative organization of the institution. The five functional subcategories are:

General Academic Instruction
Occupational and Vocational Instruction
Special Session Instruction
Community Education
Preparatory and Adult Basic Education
  Adult Basic Education
  Compensatory Education
  Doctoral Language Requirements Courses
  English for Foreign Students
  General Educational Development (GED)
  High School Completion
  Manpower Development Training (MDTA)
  Reading—Study Skills
  Remedial Instruction
  Speed Reading

Research

Accounts by individual projects, classified by organizational units. The two functional subcategories are:

Institutes and Research Centers
Individual or Project Research

Public Service

Accounts by activities, classified by type of activity, such as:

Community Service
Conferences and Institutes
Cooperative Extension Service
Public Lectures

---

*From *Administrative Service*.

Radio
Regional Medical Program
Television
Testing Services

Academic Support

Accounts by activities, classified by type of activity, such as:

Libraries
Museums and Galleries
Audiovisual Services
Ancillary Support
  Demonstration School
  Departmental Stores
  Dramatic Art Productions
  Educational Television
  Elementary School
  Herbarium
  Optometry Clinic
  Photographic Laboratory
  Psychology Clinic
  Shop Services
  Veterinary Medical Teaching Hospital
  Vivarium
Academic Administration and Personnel Development
  Dean's Office
Computing Support *excluding administrative data processing*
Course and Curriculum Development *if separately budgeted*

Student Services

Accounts by activities, classified by type of activity, such as:

Student Services Administration
Social and Cultural Activities
  Cultural programs
  Intramural Athletics
  Housing Services
  Intercollegiate Athletics *if operated as an integral part of department of physi-
    cal education and not essentially self-supporting*
  Public Ceremonies
  Recreational Programs
  Student Organizations
Counseling and Career Guidance
  Counseling
  Placement
  Foreign Students' Program
Financial Aid Administration
  Financial Aids Office
  Loan Records and Collection
Student Admissions and Records
  Admissions Office
  Registrar's Office
Health and Infirmary Services *if not an integral part of a hospital nor operated
  as an essentially self-supporting operation*

Institutional Support—*detailed as needed, for example:*

Executive Management
  Governing Board
  Chief Executive Office
  Chief Academic Office
  Chief Business Office
  Academic Senate

Planning and Budgeting
Investment Office
Legal Counsel
Fiscal Operations
 Accounting
 Cashiers
 Contract and Grant Administration
General Administrative Services
 Administrative Data Processing *(computer center for administrative services)*
 Administrative Information Systems
 Auditing, Internal and External
 Commencements
 Convocations
 Employee Personnel and Records
 Environmental Health and Safety
Logistical Services
 Business Management
 Material Management
  Inventory
  Receiving
  Storehouse
 Purchasing
 Service Departments
  Duplicating
  Motor Pool
  Mail and Messenger
 Security *(police, etc.)*
 Telephone and Telegraph *unless charged to departmental budgets*
 Transportation *including motor pool, unless operated as a service department*
 Printing.
 Space Management
Community Relations
 Development Office
 Public Information
 Publications
  Catalogues and Bulletins
 Relations with Schools
 Alumni Office
 Fund Raising
General
 General Insurance Other than Property Insurance
 Interest on Current Funds Loans
 Memberships
 Provision for Doubtful Accounts and Notes

Operation and Maintenance of Plant

Accounts for all organizational units and functions, such as:

Physical Plant Administration
Building and Equipment Maintenance
Custodial Services
Utilities
Landscape and Grounds Maintenance
Major Repairs and Renovations
Other Services
 For subaccounts under each of the major accounts listed above, see Administrative Service supplement 3:4:2.

Scholarships and Fellowships

Accounts as needed and desired for scholarships, fellowships, grants-in-aid, trainee stipends, prizes, and awards.
Tuition and Fee Remissions *other than those properly classified as staff benefits*

Accounts may be set up for instructional divisions and departments, such as:

School of Medicine
Department of Physics

Mandatory Transfers, Educational and General—*detailed to show subcategories, such as:*

Provision for Debt Service on Educational Plant
Loan Fund Matching Grants

Nonmandatory Transfers, Educational and General *(to and from)—detailed to show significant subcategories, such as:*

Loan Funds
Quasi-Endowment Funds
Appreciation on Securities of Endowment and Similar Funds
Plant Funds
    Renewals and Replacements of Plant Assets
    Additions to Plant Assets
    Voluntary Payments on Debt Principal

Auxiliary Enterprises, Hospitals, and Independent Operations

Auxiliary Enterprises

Accounts as needed and desired for such enterprises as included in the Current Funds Revenues accounts.
Provision should be made for identification of mandatory and nonmandatory transfers—to and from—by significant subcategories.

Hospitals

Accounts as needed and desired. Provision should be made for identification of mandatory and nonmandatory transfers—to and from—by significant subcategories.

Independent Operations

Accounts as needed and desired for organizational units.
Provision should be made for identification of mandatory and nonmandatory transfers—to and from—by significant subcategories.

("Classification of Expenditures by Object" is on following page.)

Classification of Expenditures by Object

The object classification of expenditures identifies that which is received in return for the expenditures. Object classification has importance as a tool for internal management, but should be considered complementary to the classification of expenditures by function and organizational unit and should not replace these classifications in the various schedules of current funds expenditures. The value of object classification will depend on the usefulness of the information it provides to management. The classifications may be omitted from published financial reports or they may be used to any degree considered desirable by the institution. The use of object classifications and the related identifying codes and symbols should not be carried to an extreme; the number of categories should be limited to those that will be of significant value to management.

Three major object classifications are found in most colleges and universities: Personnel Compensation, Supplies and Expenses, and Capital Expenditures. Breakdowns of objects within these major categories may be necessary or desirable in some situations.

Personnel Compensation

This classification includes salaries, wages, and staff benefits. In the various salary and wage expense accounts, it may be desirable to distinguish between groups of faculty and other staff members, such as full-time and part-time personnel; student and nonstudent workers; and professional, secretarial, clerical, skilled, and nonskilled employees. Appropriate code numbers and symbols within this category will aid in identifying, collecting, and summarizing information.

Supplies and Expenses

Because of their general significance to nearly all organizational units within an institution, it may be beneficial to identify significant categories of these expenditures, such as supplies, telephone, travel, and contractual services.

Capital Expenditures

The following object categories within this classification (which includes both additions to and renewals and replacements of capital assets) may prove helpful in the accounting and reporting systems of educational institutions: scientific equipment, laboratory apparatus, office machines and equipment, library books, furniture and furnishings, motor vehicles, machinery and tools, building remodeling, minor construction, and livestock.

indirect cost allocation procedures

The preceding chapter described a five-step general cost accounting procedure for colleges and universities. The first part of the fourth step in that approach involves the allocation of all indirect costs to designated cost centers. This chapter examines procedures for identifying and allocating the indirect costs associated with the provision of support services to benefiting cost centers. These procedures are based on previous studies in the area of cost accounting.

This chapter and exhibit 2-B also examine the use of chargeback systems as a means of assigning the cost of support activities to benefiting cost centers.

Support Activities

Institutions of higher education have many support and service activities that are essential to effective operation. Such activities include plant operation and maintenance, institutional support, academic support, and student services. Specific support activities range from libraries to fiscal operations, such as accounting, and logistical services, such as purchasing, print shop, and motor pool. A complete list of support and service activities is presented in exhibit 1-A.

Support activities provide services to some or all areas of an institution, but frequently the costs of providing these services are not assigned to benefiting cost objectives or centers. However, if the purpose for collecting cost data is to determine the full cost of a cost objective or center, some basis must be developed for allocation of support costs to benefiting cost objectives and centers. The bases used to allocate support costs can differ among institutions, but they should be consistently applied within an institution and in all instances should be good measures of benefits received. A list of alternative allocation bases appears later in this chapter.

Institutional Chargeback Systems

Many institutions use chargeback systems to assign certain support costs to benefiting cost objectives and centers. Chargeback systems differ from indirect cost allocation procedures in that: (1) costs are tied to specific requests for service; (2) costs are used to establish a rate for services; and (3) charges for services are reflected in the institution's accounting and budgeting systems. Support costs identified through a chargeback system are allocated direct costs and should be treated as tier one costs for the purpose of cost analysis.

Ideally, a chargeback system would establish rates that cover the full costs of the support activity. Frequently, however, rates are established that reflect only direct costs of providing support activities, and indirect costs are not recognized. As a result, many service operations are subsidized by the institution. Since many support activities, such as print shop, motor pool, and duplicating, can be provided by external vendors, it is necessary to know both the direct and avoidable indirect costs of providing services in order to assess whether or not it is better to provide these services in-house or through contracts with vendors. A detailed example of a chargeback system for physical plant is presented in exhibit 4-A. In addition, an example of a chargeback system currently in place at an institution is included in exhibit 2-B.

Indirect Cost Allocation Procedures

There are two commonly used methods of allocating indirect costs: (1) the direct allocation method; and (2) the recursive or step-down method.

The *direct allocation method* is based on the premise that the services produced by all support activities contribute directly only to the final cost objectives of instruction, research, public service, and auxiliary enterprises.[1] Under the direct allocation method the costs of support activities are *not* allocated to other support activities as an intermediate step. Thus, while it is true that plant operation and maintenance costs are associated with the provision of student services, academic support, and institutional support, no recognition is made of this relationship under the direct allocation method. Instead, the costs of each support activity are allocated only to each of the final cost objectives of instruction, research, public service, and auxiliary enterprises. The basis for allocating support costs is described later in this chapter.

The second method of allocating indirect costs is the recursive or *step-down method.* The step-down method, which is the method used in this handbook, makes allowances for the contribution of costs of support activities to other support activities. A necessary requirement for the step-down method is to identify and order all support activities according to the sequence in which allocations should occur. Those support activities assumed to provide the broadest support (such as plant operation and maintenance) are allocated first; those that provide the next broadest support are allocated second, and so on. An illustration of this procedure is presented in chapter 3. The step-down allocations continue until the costs of all support activities have been completely allocated to the primary functions of instruction, research, and public service as well as to auxiliary enterprises.[2] Note that once the cost of a support activity has been allocated, no further allocations are made to that activity.

The costing procedures described in OMB Circular A-21 provide an illustration of the step-down method. Under these procedures, indirect costs are grouped into cost pools of similar items. The cost pools are then allocated to the primary programs of the institution on the basis of units of service provided. A detailed discussion of this procedure is included in exhibit 2-A.

The step-down method has been chosen for use in this handbook because it permits the generation of cost data for support activities as well as for the final cost objectives of instruction, research, public service, and auxiliary enterprises. In addition, since the step-down method is similar to the costing procedures in OMB Circular A-21, it is familiar to many

college and university administrators. Note that if cost information is to be used only to determine costs of the final cost objectives of instruction, research, public service, and auxiliary enterprises, the direct method of allocating indirect costs can yield results quite close to those of the step-down method.[3]

Indirect Cost Allocation Bases

As noted in chapter 1, indirect costs are those costs not readily identifiable with a specific cost objective or center. The indirect costs of the business office, for example, could include a portion of the costs associated with plant operation and maintenance, administrative data processing, campus security, and other institutional support services.

Ideally the costs of support activities should be allocated to benefiting cost objectives on the basis of actual usage. The cost of providing computer services, for example, could be allocated to cost objectives and specific cost centers on the basis of computer records or job orders. In practice, however, records are often not maintained for many support activities. As a result, the costs of support activities usually must be allocated on the basis of certain parameters or proxy measures. Allocation parameters should be good measures of benefits received. They should use data that can be identified with specific cost objectives and centers and that are readily obtainable from the institution's student records, personnel, and financial data systems.

The allocation bases used in this book are derived from the experiences of individual colleges and universities and from allocation bases outlined in several cost accounting manuals, including *Cost Analysis Manual* and *Procedures for Determining Historical Full Costs.* A list of alternative allocation bases is presented in figure 2.1. An "x" in a column in figure 2.1 indicates the alternative allocation base that can be used to allocate the cost of support activities to benefiting cost objectives. For example, building and equipment maintenance can be allocated to all benefiting cost objectives, such as instruction, research, public service, and auxiliary enterprises, on the basis of actual usage data, such as work orders, or on the basis of the direct costs of benefiting cost objectives, or on the basis of the assignable square feet of benefiting cost objectives. In reviewing figure 2.1, note that no one allocation base is recommended for all institutions; instead, the allocation base selected

---

[1] James R. Topping, *Cost Analysis Manual* (Boulder: NCHEMS at WICHE, 1974), pp. 194, 204.

[2] Ibid., p. 150.

[3] Ibid., p. 152.

should be the one that is most compatible with the organizational structure and data systems of the institution. In addition, allocation bases can be modified to reflect the outcomes of direct cost studies of specific support activities. To assist in understanding and applying the allocation bases outlined in figure 2.1, descriptions of the most frequently used bases are as follows:

Figure 2.1
Alternative Bases for Allocating Support Costs

Support Activities		Actual Usage Data: -job orders processed -purchase orders -requests for service -voucher count	Total Direct Costs	Assign. Square Feet	Total Comp.	Instr./ Res./ Public Service Comp.*	Student Head-counts	Total Hours of Use	Student Credit Hours	Cost Objectives Receiving Support Costs
Academic Support	Libraries	X	X			X		X	X	Instruction, Research, and Public Service
	Museums and Galleries		X					X		Instruction and Public Service
	Audiovisual Services	X				X				Instruction
	Ancillary Support	X	X							Instruction, Research, and Public Service
	Academic Admin. and Personnel Development	X	X							Instruction, Research, and Public Service
	Academic Computing	X	X							Instruction, Research, and Public Service
	Course and Curriculum Development		X			X				Instruction
Student Services	Student Services Administration		X						X	Instruction
	Social and Cultural Activities		X				X		X	Instruction
	Counseling and Career Guidance		X				X	X	X	Instruction
	Financial Aid Administration	X				X			X	Instruction
	Student Admissions and Records	X				X			X	Instruction
	Health and Infirmary Services		X			X		X		Instruction
Institutional Support	Executive Management		X		X					All cost objectives eligible to receive support costs
	Fiscal Operations	X	X		X					
	General Administrative Services	X	X		X					
	Logistical Services	X	X							
	Community Relations		X					X		
Plant Operation and Maintenance	Physical Plant Administration	X	X	X						
	Building and Equipment Maintenance	X	X	X						
	Custodial Services	X	X	X						
	Utilities	X	X	X						
	Landscape and Grounds Maintenance	X	X	X						
	Major Repairs and Renovations	X	X	X						

* = Compensation of individuals, such as faculty, involved in the areas of instruction, research, and public service.

1. *Usage.* In the case of certain support activities, such as computer services and print shop, job orders may provide a general indication of the level of service provided to benefiting cost objectives or centers. If vouchers or purchase orders are used as a basis for allocating support costs, they must be identified with specific cost centers and be traceable through an institution's financial records. A useful technique for identifying users of support services is to assign blocks of purchase order numbers to specific cost centers. Figure 2.2 describes how to allocate the direct cost of the purchasing office to benefiting cost centers, and in particular to the auxiliary enterprises area, on the basis of purchase orders processed for each area.

Figure 2.2
Usage Data as an Allocation Base

1. Number of purchase orders processed by area for fiscal year: (identified with specific areas on the basis of blocks of purchase order numbers)

Operation and maintenance of plant	1322
Institutional support	494
Academic support	653
Student services	582
Instruction	776
Public service	61
Research	148
Auxiliary enterprises	1164
Total purchase orders	5200

2. Total auxiliary enterprise purchase orders as a percentage of total purchase orders $\dfrac{1164}{5200} = 22.4\%$

3. Total direct cost of the purchasing office $35,000

4. Direct costs of the purchasing office allocated to the auxiliary enterprise area on the basis of purchase orders processed

$35,000
× 22.4%
$7,840

---

2. *Total direct costs.* Include those categories of expenditures assigned to a specific cost center. As specified in chapter 1, these include:

Personnel compensation (salaries, wages, and employee benefits);

Supplies and operational expense;

Travel;

Contractual services; and

Noncapitalized equipment.

Total direct costs should be identified in the institution's financial records. The use of total direct cost as a basis for allocating the direct costs of fiscal operations to the public service cost objective is described in figure 2.3. Note that direct cost may not be the most accurate method of allocating support costs.

Figure 2.3
Use of Total Direct Costs as a Basis for Allocating Fiscal Operations Costs to Final Cost Objectives

1. Direct costs of final cost objectives

Instruction	$4,600,000
Public service	60,000
Research	150,000
Auxiliary enterprises	1,400,000
Total direct costs	$6,210,000

2. Direct costs of public service as a percentage of total direct costs. $\dfrac{\$60,000}{\$6,210,000} = 0.97\%$

3. Direct costs of fiscal operations, e.g., accounting, cashiers, and grant and contract administration $200,000

4. Direct costs of fiscal operations allocated to the public services cost objective

$200,000
× 0.97%
$1,940

---

3. *Assignable square feet.* This allocation parameter is based on the sum of the areas in all rooms that can be used by the building occupants to carry out their functions. Excluded are circulation, custodial, mechanical, and structural areas. A more detailed description of space assignment data is contained in Leonard Romney's *Higher Education Facilities Inventory and Classification Manual* (Boulder: NCHEMS at WICHE, 1972). The use of assignable square feet as an allocation base presupposes a facilities inventory. Figure 2.4 illustrates the use of assignable square feet as a base for allocating plant operation and maintenance direct costs to a college bookstore at Institution A. If a facility inventory is not available, total square footage may be substituted for assignable square footage.

Figure 2.4
Use of Assignable Square Feet as an Allocation Base

1. Total assignable square footage at Institution A — 400,000 asf*

2. Total assignable square footage of the college bookstore — 3,000 asf

3. Assignable square footage of college bookstore as a percentage of total assignable square footage at Institution A $\dfrac{3,000 \text{ asf}}{400,000 \text{ asf}} = 0.75\%$

4. Total direct costs of plant operation and maintenance activities — $1,100,000

5. Direct costs of plant operation and maintenance activities allocated to the college bookstore on the basis of assignable square feet

$1,100,000
× 0.75%
$8,250

*asf = assignable square feet

4. *Total compensation.* This allocation base uses the total dollar amount, including gross salaries and employee benefits, paid directly to or on behalf of all exempt and nonexempt personnel. Figure 2.5 illustrates the use of total compensation as a basis for allocating the direct costs of logistical services (see exhibit 1-A for a definition of logistical services) to the cost objective of instruction. Under the simplified method described in OMB Circular A-21, an institution can combine allowable indirect costs in one pool and calculate a single indirect cost rate based on direct salaries and wages (see exhibit 2-A).

Figure 2.5
Total Compensation as a Basis for Allocating the Direct Costs of Logistical Services*

1. Compensation of final cost objectives

Instruction	$3,900,000
Public service	45,000
Research	95,000
Auxiliary enterprises	750,000
Total compensation of final cost objectives	$4,790,000

2. Compensation of instruction as a percentage of total compensation
$$\frac{\$3,900,000}{\$4,790,000} = 81.4\%$$

3. Total direct costs of logistical services $ 306,900

4. Direct costs of logistical services assigned to the instructional cost objective

	$ 306,900
	× 81.4%
	$ 249,817

*Logistical services include such support services as materiel management, purchasing, duplicating, and security (see exhibit 1-A).

---

5. *Student headcount.* This allocation base involves the number of students, both part-time and full-time, as of an official census date. Student headcount frequently can be a better method of allocating the cost of student services to benefiting cost objectives than FTE students, because part-time students frequently require as many student services as full-time students. For an illustration of the use of student headcount in assigning costs to student service activities, refer to *Costing for Policy Analysis* (1980).[4]

6. *Student credit hours.* This allocation base represents one student engaged in an activity for which one hour of credit is granted toward a degree or a certificate. Total student credit hours for a course are calculated by multiplying the course's credit hour value by the number of students enrolled in the course.[5] Student credit hours are useful in allocating the cost of academic support activities to academic departments.

In the chapters that follow, procedures are described for determining institutional costs and the cost of specific program areas. In presenting these procedures, a number of the allocation bases discussed in this chapter are used. In implementing cost accounting procedures, however, college administrators should not feel restricted to using only these allocation bases, but instead should use bases that best reflect the relationship between the cost of support activities and the benefits received by cost centers at their particular institutions.

---

[4]*Costing for Policy Analysis* (Washington, D.C.: NACUBO, 1980), pp. 52-67.

[5]Sherrill Cloud, comp., *A Glossary of Standard Terminology for Postsecondary Education, 1979-80* (Boulder: NCHEMS).

exhibit 2-a

cost accounting and omb circular a-21

Mention cost accounting to many college and university business officers and they will think immediately of Office of Management and Budget Circular A-21, *Cost Principles for Educational Institutions.* Some may equate Circular A-21 with cost accounting theory. In reality, the circular represents a special case, an application of cost concepts to a particular purpose—cost determination for sponsored agreements with the federal government. The circular contains a mixture of cost accounting principles and special purpose rules. Because of its prominence in college and university business administration, Circular A-21 merits special consideration in this handbook.

The purpose of this exhibit is to relate the content of Circular A-21 to cost accounting theory and practice. The reader should consult the circular itself to study its detailed provisions. Interpretive and explanatory materials are also available from the government and from NACUBO. The government revises Circular A-21 periodically.

The stated objective of Circular A-21 is to "provide principles for determining the costs applicable to research and development, training, and other sponsored work performed by colleges and universities under grants, contracts, and other agreements with the Federal Government. These agreements are referred to as sponsored agreements." (Section A1). The government reimburses the institution for all or part of the costs of a project, according to the terms of the sponsored agreement. The circular does not apply to student financial aid grants or loans, capitation awards, or any other award under which the institution does not account to the government for actual costs incurred.

Full Costing

The circular prescribes a form of full costing for sponsored agreements. Federal reimbursement of costs can include both the direct costs of the project and an appropriate share of indirect costs incurred by the college or university.

The terms direct cost and indirect cost as used in the circular have the same meaning as in general cost accounting literature. Direct costs are those readily identifiable with a product or service, in this case the service covered by a sponsored agreement. Indirect costs are not readily identifiable with a product or service, and in a college or university setting they consist primarily of the various categories of support—academic support, student services, institutional support, and plant operation and maintenance.

In the institution's accounting system, each sponsored agreement can have a separate ledger account, classified as instruction, research, or public service, depending on the nature of the project. Accounting documents representing direct costs of the project include the appropriate account number. These documents—such as payroll distributions, requisitions, petty cash vouchers, travel reports, service department invoices—cause the direct costs to be charged to the sponsored agreement account. The only practical way to charge the sponsored agreement with support costs, however, is the use of a predetermined indirect cost rate. The calculation of this rate is a primary theme of Circular A-21.

Indirect costs of sponsored agreements include much of the cost found in the various categories of support expenditures mentioned previously. They also include some expenditures found in the instruction category and some costs not recognized in the formal accounting system at all.

Indirect Cost Rates

To calculate indirect cost rates, the institution must first group the indirect costs into pools of similar items. Circular A-21 specifies certain cost pools that must be used as a minimum. These pools do not correspond exactly to the generally accepted expenditure categories used in college and university accounting, so some regrouping is necessary. The following list shows the required cost pools and the related expenditures categories.

A-21 Indirect Cost Pools	Expenditure Categories
Academic departmental administration	Instruction
	Academic support (dean's offices, administrative portion)
Sponsored projects administration	Instruction
Library	Academic support
Student administration and services	Student services
	Institutional support (catalogs, commencement, convocations)
General administration and general expenses	Institutional support
Plant operation and maintenance	Operation and maintenance of plant
Depreciation and/or use allowances	None

Generally accepted accounting principles for colleges and universities do not require but do permit recognition of depreciation. The cost pool for depreciation and use allowances will contain figures typically not found in the financial statements. Use allowances are an optional substitute for depreciation. They are based on fixed rates specified in Circular A-21 rather than on estimated useful lives of buildings or equipment.

After the institution has established indirect cost pools, it allocates the cost in each individually to what Circular A-21 calls the "major functions" of the institution. The major functions are instruction, organized research, other sponsored activities, and other institutional activities. Other sponsored activities are those from the financial statement expenditure category of public service that are financed through government or private grants and contracts. The remaining public service expenditures are classified as other institutional activities, as are auxiliary enterprises and museums and galleries.

The allocation of the indirect cost pools may be based on institutional cost studies if such studies are available and if they meet certain standards of reliability. Any of the indirect cost pools mentioned can be subdivided for allocation purposes if that improves the reasonableness of the allocation. The allocation should reasonably reflect the use of the various support services by the major functions. Figures allocated are actual costs for a full fiscal year, usually the last year preceding the calculation.

If an institution does not have its own cost studies, it must allocate the indirect cost pools using common denominators specified in Section F of Circular A-21. Section F requires some rather detailed and complex calculations, but basically it makes use of denominators that represent units of service performed. Denominators mentioned include the following:

Denominator	Indirect Cost Allocated
Usable square feet occupied	Depreciation and use allowances, buildings and equipment
	Operation and maintenace of plant, buildings and equipment
Salaries and wages	Depreciation and use allowances, shared space or equipment
	Operation and maintenance of plant, shared space or equipment
FTE students and employees	Depreciation and use allowances, land improvements
	Operation and maintenance of plant, land improvements
Modified total direct cost (salaries, wages, benefits, materials, supplies, services, travel, and subgrants and subcontracts up to $25,000 each)	General administration and general expense
	Academic department administration
	Sponsored projects administration
Users	Library

Section F further specifies that any indirect cost that benefits only one major function be allocated solely to that function. Student services and administration benefit only the instruction function. Certain buildings may also be used solely for one function.

Circular A-21 requires the step-down method of allocation. The allocation of the indirect cost pools follows a specific sequence. Allocations of Pool 1 costs go to the other indirect cost pools as appropriate based on the denominator used, as well as to the major functions. Pool 2 follows, with its total now including costs allocated from Pool 1. The sequence continues until all pools are allocated. Once a pool has been allocated, it no longer receives costs from other pools. See Illustration 1 at the end of this exhibit for a condensed example of the step-down method.

The circular specifies that depreciation and use allowances, plant operation and maintenance, and general administration and general expenses, in that sequence, be the first pools distributed. The institution can establish the remaining sequence.

When the allocation process is complete, the institution calculates indirect cost rates for each major function. The rate base is the modified total direct cost of the major function. (Again, modified total direct cost includes salaries, wages, benefits, materials, supplies, services, travel, and certain subgrants and subcontracts.) The indirect cost rate equals allocated indirect cost divided by modified total direct cost. The institution calculates a single indirect cost rate for each major function, using the total of all indirect costs allocated to that function. It also calculates separate rates for each of the pools allocated to the function. See Illustration 2 for a condensed example of these calculations.

To compute the indirect costs of a sponsored agreement, the institution multiplies the modified total direct cost of the agreement by the indirect cost rate for the appropriate major function. If the activity covered by the agreement does not benefit from the full range of support services, the institution would use the rates for the individual supporting pools rather than the total rate.

The provisions of Circular A-21 discussed to this point are well grounded in cost accounting theory. Most cost accounting textbooks offer a similar series of steps to be followed in allocating indirect costs to products or services.

Following is an example of what most textbooks state:

1. Establish pools or groupings of indirect costs.

2. Distribute indirect cost pools individually to production departments (or major functions) using common denominators that reasonably represent support services provided. Frequently used denominators include direct labor hours or dollars, direct cost, number of employees, and square feet of space occupied.

3. Calculate an indirect cost rate for each production department (major function) using an appropriate rate base. The rate base is usually direct cost or labor hours.

4. Use the indirect cost rate for each production department (major function) to apply indirect costs to the products or services (sponsored agreements) produced in that department.

Unallowable Activities and Costs

Circular A-21 includes other provisions that do not represent general cost accounting theory or practice. The purpose of the circular is to provide a means of calculating costs to be reimbursed by the federal government; the government will not reimburse certain types of costs, whether direct or indirect. Thus, the circular introduces an additional set of cost classifications: *allowable* and *unallowable*.

Section J of the circular discusses these classifications. Activities and costs described as unallowable, and the related section numbers, are listed below. The dollar amount of these items can be significant.

J2. Bad debts
J4. Commencement and convocation costs
J7. Contingency provisions
J10. Donated services and property
J12. Entertainment costs
J13. Equipment and other capital expenditures (cost recovered through depreciation and/or use allowances)
J14. Fines and penalties
J17. Interest, fund raising, and investment management costs
J19. Losses on other sponsored agreements or contracts
J25. Preagreement costs
J27. Profits and losses on disposition of plant equipment or other capital assets
J39. Special services costs
J40. Student activity costs

The institution may not include any of these items in the indirect cost pools. Unallowable activities, items that include salaries and wages, become part of other institutional activities, one of the major functions. Other unallowable costs are eliminated from the computation.

Because of this requirement, the indirect cost rates calculated under Circular A-21 do not represent the complete indirect costs of the institution. Rather, they represent that portion that the federal government will consider for reimbursement under sponsored agreements.

Accounting Rules

Section J of the circular also contains some procedural rules that must be followed in accounting for certain items. The most complex rules pertain to employee compensation. Others cover depreciation and use allowances, employee benefits, materials, and specialized service facilities, such as computer centers. The rules specify accounting and computational methods, records to be maintained, and procedures to be followed. Generally, they reflect good accounting practice. However, many business officers think the record-keeping requirements for employee compensation are excessive.

Simplified Method

The calculation of indirect cost rates using the procedures just described can be a difficult and time-consuming task. The effort involved might seem excessively burdensome to business officers at institutions with a relatively low dollar volume of government grants and contracts. The low level of indirect cost reimbursements might not justify the amount of staff time required to calculate the rates. Circular A-21 provides an alternative for such cases. At institutions where the total direct cost of covered sponsored agreements does not exceed $3,000,000 in a fiscal year, business officers may elect to use a simplified method described in Section H of the circular.

Under the simplified method, the institution combines allowable indirect costs into one pool and calculates a single indirect cost rate based on direct salaries and wages. This avoids the step-method allocation of seven or more separate indirect cost pools and the calculation of individual rates for each major function. The reduction in staff time devoted to the rate calculation is substantial.

In exchange for simplicity, the institution gives up a degree of precision in the indirect cost rate calculation. The single rate equals total allowable indirect costs divided by direct salaries and wages. Not used are the other common denominators listed previously—usable square feet occupied, FTE students, FTE employees, library users, and modified total direct costs. The simplified method does not relate an indirect cost to the denominator that best measures the related support service. It associates all allowable indirect costs with direct salaries and wages.

Other simplifying (and arbitrary) rules govern the accumulation of allowable indirect costs into a single pool. These rules deal with student administration and services, academic department administration, plant operation and maintenance, and depreciation and use allowances.

Institutions using the simplified method cannot include student administration and services in the in-direct cost pool. The regular procedure specifies that student administration and services must be allocated entirely to instruction. The government will not allow these indirect costs in association with organized research, other sponsored activities, or other institutional activities. This becomes a problem with the simplified method, as it provides only one rate for use with all four major functions.

The simplified method specifies academic department administration to be 20 percent of the salaries and expenses of deans and heads of departments. Many deans and heads of academic departments teach and do research in addition to administrative work. In fact, teaching and research may be their principal duties, with administration being secondary. The regular procedure requires personnel time and effort reports to separate the administrative costs associated with such persons. The simplified method avoids this time and effort reporting by specifying the arbitrary 20 percent.

Those using the simplified method can include only the educational and general portion of plant operation and maintenance and of depreciation and use allowances. This limit seems to represent a tacit admission that direct salaries and wages are a poor denominator for these costs. The institution must make a preliminary allocation between educational and general and other institutional activities (including auxiliary enterprises). This preliminary allocation can be based on institutional cost studies or on square feet occupied. Only the educational and general portion goes into the indirect cost pool.

The more imprecise and arbitrary features of the simplified method may cause it to produce a rate that is not equitable, either to the institution or to the government. If so, the institution can elect to use the regular procedure, and the government can require it to do so.

Conclusion

Circular A-21 provides procedures for determining costs allowable under certain U.S. government grants and contracts. Many procedures found in the circular represent sound cost accounting theory and practice. It does, however, require the exclusion from the indirect cost pools of significant dollar amounts representing unallowable activities and costs. The single rate developed under the simplified method is influenced by other arbitrary provisions and exclusions. Therefore, the indirect cost rates developed using the circular may not be useful for internal analysis or management.

Illustration 1
Step Method of Allocating
Indirect Cost Pools
(Condensed)

	Indirect Costs			Major Functions		
	Pool 1	Pool 2	Pool 3	A	B	C
Denominators converted to % for:						
Pool 1	100%	7%	14%	44%	14%	21%
Pool 2	100		27	45	18	10
Pool 3	100			53	29	18
Dollar totals in millions	$14	$10	$12			
Allocations of dollar totals based on denominators above						
Pool 1	(14)	$1	$2	$6	$2	$3
Pool 2		(11)	3	5	2	1
Pool 3			(17)	9	5	3

The denominators are usable square feet occupied by benefiting functions, salaries and wages of benefiting functions, modified total cost of benefiting functions, etc. They are reasonable measures of service received, converted to percentage form.

Alternative allocation methods found in cost accounting literature include the following:

Direct method. Allocations from indirect cost pools go only to major functions, not to other indirect cost pools.

Matrix algebra method. Each indirect cost pool receives allocations from all other indirect cost pools through use of simultaneous equations.

Illustration 2
Calculation of Indirect Cost Rates
(Condensed)

	Major Functions					
	A		B		C	
	Amount	Rate	Amount	Rate	Amount	Rate
Allocated indirect costs— dollars in millions, from Illustration 1						
Pool 1	$6	20%	$2	12%	$3	20%
Pool 2	5	16	2	12	1	7
Pool 3	9	29	5	32	3	20
Totals	$20	65%	$9	56%	$7	47%
Base Modified total direct costs	$31		$16		$15	

The rates equal the allocated indirect costs divided by the base.

exhibit 2-b

case study: ohio wesleyan university the chargeback system

Certain departments within a college or university exist to perform requested and measurable services for other departments. An example at Ohio Wesleyan University is a central duplicating department that prepares copies of materials brought in for that purpose. A type composition department is a similar example. Others are a mailroom that meters postage on outgoing mail, an audiovisual aids department that prepares and shows instructional material on request, an office supplies storeroom that fills requisitons from user departments, telephone switchboard operators who place long-distance toll calls, and a motor pool that makes vehicles available as needed.

Common characteristics of these departments are that they act only upon request and they provide services measurable in terms of materials used or hours worked for each individual customer order. These characteristics enable the service departments to charge user departments for the specific services they provide. Ohio Wesleyan processes these charges in its general accounting system as tier one costs of user departments. The services directly further the operations of the user departments and their budget performance reports reflect the related costs.

This treatment differs from that of other support departments where the service is more indirect, not readily measurable, or based on specific requests. User departments receive no direct charges for that work.

Charging for service department work helps to control volume. If services were free to users, there would probably be little restraint in demands for services and volume would tend to reach unmanageable levels. However, if users must give up budget funds to obtain services, this circumstance limits their demands. Conversely, an institution might avoid charging for a particular service in order to encourage its use, if that seemed desirable from a policy point of view. Ohio Wesleyan presently charges for all the services previously mentioned, but not for computer services, since the university has wanted to encourage computer use for both instruction and administrative work. Computer operations are treated as a final cost objective, separately budgeted and accounted for.

Rates

Ohio Wesleyan establishes rates for services at a level designed to cover the budgeted direct costs of the service departments. There is no markup for indirect costs or profit. Rates are reviewed annually. Routine revisions take effect at the beginning of the fiscal year, July 1. Announcements of these come earlier, in time for consideration in departmental budgeting.

Budgeted rather than actual costs are the basis for rate calculations. Budget variances, either favorable or unfavorable, are the responsibility of the service departments. Users have no control over the management of the service departments, so they should not have to share budget variances. Similarly, rate calculations presume normal use of equipment, after allowances for normal "down" time for repairs and maintenance. The service departments themselves bear the cost of any excessive down time or underuse.

Rate adjustments during a fiscal year are rare. They occur only when unusual circumstances, such as a sudden increase in supply costs, require a revision in a service department's budget. When this happens, the budgets of user departments are also revised.

The following paragraphs contain more information about the rates of individual service departments.

Duplicating. The principal direct costs of the duplicating department are the salary of the manager, hourly wages, employee benefits, paper, equipment rental or depreciation charges, and equipment maintenance. User charges depend on the number of copies made. The rate per copy declines as the number of copies increases. This reflects actual costs, because set-up and most handling costs are the same for each job, regardless of the number of copies. Use of colored paper or card stock and special services, such as folding, cutting, and binding, carry extra charges. Department personnel patterned the overall rate structure on that used by commercial printers in the community, adjusting the rates downward to the level of their own costs and volume.

Composition. Charges for type composition include recovery of hourly wages, employee benefits, paper, and equipment maintenance and depreciation. The department uses a single hourly rate, which it calculates by dividing budgeted costs by estimated annual hours available after allowing for normal down time.

Postage. Mailroom employees batch outgoing mail by sending department. They charge each department for the amount of postage metered and for assistance in preparing a mailing. A piece rate is used for work such as assembling, folding, inserting, and stuffing; the piece rate is based on compensation costs and standard time allowed for particular operations. The department does not charge for handling outgoing envelopes that are ready for mailing or for handling incoming mail.

Audiovisual Aids. The audiovisual department charges separately for services and for materials provided to other departments. An hourly rate covers services such as preparation of tapes, cassettes, slides, and transparencies, as well as the showing of films and repairing of equipment owned by other departments. The hourly rate reflects budgeted compensation costs. Charges for materials represent approximate invoice cost. Located in the library, the department also develops and maintains materials for general use. The cost of this work, including related equipment, remains in the department's account, classified as academic support.

Office Supplies Storeroom. The university obtains lower prices by purchasing large quantities of paper, envelopes, pencils, pens, file folders, scissors, glue, paper clips, and other materials for inventory. Bookstore personnel operate the storeroom and issue these items to individual departments. The prices include invoice cost and an allowance for estimated freight, spoilage, and handling. The bookstore does not earn a profit on storeroom business.

Telephone. Telephone switchboard operators charge calling departments for long-distance tolls but not for local service.

Motor Pool. The motor pool has the most complicated pricing structure of the services. Different rates are appropriate for each of its classes of vehicles—sedans, wagons, and vans—reflecting different levels of gasoline usage, repair costs, insurance, and depreciation. To establish such rates, it is necessary to group these costs by class of vehicle. Labor costs associated with operation of the motor pool itself must be apportioned among the vehicle classes. Rates represent budgeted costs per class of vehicle divided by normal usage. The rates are stated as an amount per mile plus an amount per day. The relationship between the mileage and daily rates is similar to the billing structure of car rental companies.

Procedures

The computerized general ledger file has a separate account record for each service department. Each account contains debits for all of the direct costs of the department and credits for charges to users. The account balances, usually debits, represent costs not covered by user charges. These net costs include budget and usage variances and, in the cases of the mailroom, audiovisual aids department, and telephone switchboard, costs not intended to be charged out.

All debits and credits in each account are further classified by object code. Object codes used for costs include salaries, hourly wages, employee benefits, supplies, equipment depreciation, equipment rentals, equipment maintenance, postage, telephone tolls, fuel and lubricants, and insurance. Separate object codes identify credits resulting from user charges. Budget amounts exist for all object codes, including user charges.

Although generally accepted accounting principles for colleges and universities do not call for depreciation, Ohio Wesleyan does depreciate equipment used by service departments, in order to get the cost of this equipment into the user rates.

The accounting system provides two types of monthly reports for service department managers. One lists all transactions for the month, showing date, document reference, object code, description, and debit or credit amount. The other summarizes results by object code, giving expenditure and user charge balances for the current month and the year to date, open purchase orders, the budget, and unused budget remaining. (Reports of this nature are furnished to all university department heads.) Managers are thus informed about their direct operating costs as well as their user charges and net results.

A department manager with financial problems does not have to wait for a monthly report, however. He or she can go to the accounting office at any time to get up-to-date figures. Accounting office personnel can display all transactions up through the previous day's business on a computer terminal screen.

A separate object code number exists for user charges from each service department. Such charges are then adequately identified in the monthly reports of using departments. The report of the economics department, for example, might contain separate line items for audiovisual services, office supplies, and motor pool.

For example, the object code number for duplicating charges is 92. A $100 job for the economics department would result in the following accounting entry:

01116.92 Economics Department—
  Duplicating Charges   100.00
    01315.92 Duplicating Department—
    Duplicating Charges   100.00

Each service department has its own form for processing user charges, but the forms have certain common characteristics. Each contains the name and account number of the using department, a description of the service or item provided, any special directions or specifications, the quantity (copies reproduced, miles driven, hours worked), the rate, and the expended dollar amount. (Sample forms are provided at the end of this exhibit.)

Each service department forwards its documents to the accounting office in daily batches. Accounting office personnel establish batch control totals and enter the data onto the computer transaction file at their terminals. Computer processing and reporting technique depends on volume. Individual documents for audiovisual services and materials, office supplies, motor pool, and composition are carried on the computer file as separate transactions; the computer lists them individually on monthly reports. However, the volume of documents for postage, toll calls, and duplicating is so great that these individual charges are totaled by department on the computer. They are carried and reported as a single item. Since individual charges in these areas tend to be low, this procedure has not provoked any complaints from department heads. Listing such charges individually would create lengthy transaction reports and the detail would not be particularly meaningful.

Authorized Users

Authorized users of service departments include only university personnel and certain student groups. The duplicating department performs personal work for employees on a low priority basis, at the same rates as for university business. Payment is by cash or through employee receivables.

Summary

Ohio Wesleyan has departments that exist to perform requested, measurable services for other departments. These departments charge users for the work performed and materials supplied; the charges cover budgeted direct costs of providing a normal level of service. Thus, users bear these amounts as tier one costs, while the service departments bear budget variances and costs of excessive down time or underuse. Charging also serves to control the level of demand for services.

The university's accounting system accommodates service department charges to users. The computerized general ledger file has a separate account record for each service department. These accounts contain debits for direct costs and credits for user charges, both classified by object code. Each service department uses appropriate forms to generate user charges. The system provides a fair and equitable method of distributing these costs to benefiting departments and functions.

Sample Form

OFFICE SUPPLIES IN DUPLICATING

Dept._____
Acct. No._____
Date_____
Signature_____

OWU Rag Content Letterheads, 2-color
  Executive_____   Regular_____
  (7¼ x 10½)   (8½ x 11)
OWU Rag Content Envelopes, 2-color
  Executive_____   Regular_____

Campus Envelopes_____
Postage-Paid Return Envelopes_____
Campus Maps_____
Plain white paper (500 per)_____
  25% rag content_____
  Typing paper_____
Envelopes, plain white, #10_____
Desk Trays: Legal_____   Letter_____
Copy Sets: White (500 per)_____
OWU Brown Ink Memo Pads_____
While-you-were-out Pads_____
Scratch Pads: Size_____
OWU (fine) Pens_____
Staplers: Bates_____
Staples: Bates_____   Swingline_____
OWU Name Tags_____
IBM Ribbons: 1136108 (6)_____
              1136182 (6)_____
              1136136 (3)_____
              1136137 (3)_____
              1136138 (3)_____
   Tech III   1136391 (1)_____
Correctable Film:
              1299095 (1)_____
Lift-Off Tapes 1136433 (6)_____
Cover-Up Tapes 1136435 (6)_____
Duplicating Fluid (one gal.)_____
Masters (100 per box)_____
Stamp Pad_____
Stamp Pad Ink_____
Tape Dispenser_____
Scotch Tape Refill_____
File Folder Labels_____

OWU Printed Mailing Labels
  (minimum order 99)_____
Transparencies (Savin copier)_____
Labels (Savin copier)_____
Masking Tape (1"-2" rolls)_____

Sample Form

WORD PROCESSING CENTER
COMPOSITION ORDER FORM

Date Received _____ Account Number _____

Department _____

Job Name _____

Type Style(s) _____

Type Size(s) _____ Leading _____

Page Size _____

Pica Width _____ Depth _____

Mode Identification:
  JUSTIFICATION   _____
  RAGGED RIGHT   _____
  FLUSH LEFT   _____
  FLUSH RIGHT   _____
  CENTERED   _____
  DOT LEADER   _____

Number of Lines _____ Number of Hours _____

Date Needed _____

Comments: _____

_____

_____

_____

TOTAL COST _____

Sample Form

OHIO WESLEYAN UNIVERSITY
MOTOR POOL ORDER

ORDER NUMBER N⁰ 2910

Date of trip _____ Time _____ M   Date of Return _____ Time _____ M

Ordered by _____ Dept. _____ For _____

To _____ Driver's Name (printed) _____

Special Instructions _____

Vehicle assigned _____
Speedometer - End of Trip _____
Speedometer - Start of Trip _____
Miles _____ Rate _____ = _____
Driver's Time _____ Rate _____ = _____
Meals, toll, etc. _____ _____

Total Cost _____

_____

Accounting Data

Charge Account No. _____   Credit Account No. _____
Charge Account No. _____   Credit Account No. _____
Date forwarded to Accounting _____

Signed _____

3

a cost accounting system

This handbook is divided into two parts, each of which reflects a different application of cost accounting procedures. The first application, described in this chapter, focuses on determining full institution-wide costs associated with the final cost objectives of instruction, public service, research, and auxiliary enterprises. The second application, presented in part 2 (chapters 4-7), involves the use of cost studies to determine full costs of specific functional areas, such as plant operation and maintenance, institutional support, instruction, and specific auxiliary enterprises, such as housing and food service. Both applications use the tiered approach and the five-step general cost accounting procedure described in chapter 1.

An Institutional Cost Accounting System

This chapter contains a step-by-step process for collecting tier three or full cost data for the final cost objectives of instruction, public service, research, and auxiliary enterprises. Figures 3.1 and 3.2 present an overview of the costing process.

Step 1. *Designate specific cost objectives and/or cost centers.* The cost objectives in figure 3.1 are based on the chart of accounts in *College & University Business Administration,* chapter 5:6 (see exhibit 1-A). If an institution's chart of accounts differs from *CUBA,* then the cost objectives should be modified to reflect the institution's structure. For the purpose of illustration, figure 3.1 lists only the major

Figure 3.1

An Institutional Cost Accounting System

Step 1: *Designate specific cost objectives and/or cost centers;*

Cost Objectives

Tier One Cost Categories	Support Activities				Final Cost Objectives			
	Plant Operation and Maintenance	Institutional Support	Academic Support	Student Services	Instruction	Public Service	Research	Auxiliary Enterprises

Step 2. *Select consistent cost categories;* and Step 3. *Assign all tier one costs to designated cost objectives.*

Tier One Cost Categories								
a. Personnel compensation	$650,000	$525,000	$275,000	$400,000	$3,900,000	$45,000	$95,000	$750,000
b. Supplies	399,879	355,000	175,000	150,000	600,000	10,000	50,000	600,000
c. Other expenditures	50,000	50,000	50,000	50,000	100,000	5,000	5,000	50,000
Total Tier One Costs	$1,099,879	$930,000	$500,000	$600,000	$4,600,000	$60,000	$150,000	$1,400,000

Figure 3.2
An Institutional Cost Accounting System

| | Cost Objectives | | | | | | | | |
| | Support Activities | | | | | Final Cost Objectives | | | |
	Plant Operation and Maintenance	Institutional Support	Academic Support	Student Services	Instruction	Public Service	Research	Auxiliary Enterprises	Total
(i)	$1,099,879	$930,000	$500,000	$600,000	$4,600,000	$60,000	$150,000	$1,400,000	$9,339,879
(ii)	24,000	18,000	10,000	12,000	90,000	2,000	4,000	40,000	200,000
(iii)	1,812	1,359	755	906	6,795	151	302	3,020	15,100
(iv)	$1,125,691	949,359	510,755	612,906	4,696,795	62,151	154,302	1,443,020	9,554,979
4b (i)	($1,125,691)	112,569	67,541	78,798	574,103	11,257	22,514	258,909	
4b (ii)		$1,061,928							
4c (i)		($1,061,928)	74,335	84,954	669,015	10,619	21,239	201,766	
4c (ii)			$652,631						
4d (i)			(652,631)		626,526	6,526	19,579	-0-	
				$776,658					
4e (i)				(776,658)	776,658	-0-	-0-	-0-	
4f					$7,343,097	$90,553	$217,634	$1,903,695	$9,554,979
5					(a) cost/ student credit hour (b) cost/ student contact hour	(a) cost/ scheduled events	(a) indirect cost recovery rate on grants and contracts	(a) cost/resident in student housing (b) cost/product line for student bookstore	

Step 4. *Assign all tiers two and three costs to designated cost objectives.*

Step 4a. *Allocate annual use charge on buildings, land improvements, and capital equipment to all cost objectives.*

(i) Tier one costs of all cost objectives (from figure 3.1)

(ii) Use charge on buildings and land improvements allocated on basis of assignable square feet (from figure 3.5)

(iii) Use charge on capital equipment allocated on basis of assignable square feet (from figure 3.6)

(iv) Total tier one costs + buildings, land improvements, and equipment usage costs

Step 4b. *Allocate all plant operation and maintenance costs to all benefiting cost objectives.*

(i) Allocate all plant operation and maintenance costs on the basis of assignable square feet (from figure 3.7)

(ii) Total tier one costs + depreciation + equipment usage + plant operation and maintenance costs

Step 4c. *Allocate all institutional support costs to all benefiting cost objectives*

(i) Allocate all institutional support costs on the basis of total direct costs (from figure 3.8)

(ii) Total tier one costs + depreciation + equipment usage + plant operation & maintenance costs + institutional support costs

Step 4d. *Allocate all academic support costs to all benefiting cost objectives.*

(i) Allocate all academic support costs on the basis of total direct costs (from figure 3.9)

Step 4e. *Allocate all student service costs to all benefiting cost objectives.*

(i) Allocate all student service costs to the instruction cost objective (if instructional cost center detail is required, allocate to cost centers on the basis of SCH.)

Step 4f. *Calculate tier three costs for all final cost objectives.*

Step 5. *Develop unit costs or output measures.*

cost objectives of an institution, such as plant operation and maintenance, instruction, and auxiliary enterprises. These objectives, of course, can be disaggregated into a number of smaller cost centers. For specific detail on the cost centers encompassed by each cost objective, refer to part 2 of this book.

Step 2. *Select consistent categories of costs.* The cost categories in figure 3.1 are based on the major object-of-expenditure classifications found in most colleges and universities and are consistent with the categories in NACUBO's *A Management Reporting Manual for Colleges* (1980) and *College & University Business Administration.* Breakdowns within these major categories depend on the level of detail found in the institution's financial records and the usefulness of the detail to decision makers.

Step 3. *Assign all tier one costs to designated cost objectives.* The tier one, or direct, costs associated with specific cost objectives are obtained directly from the institution's accounting system and are arrayed in a format similar to that outlined in figure 3.1. Depending on the purpose of the cost study, each category of tier one costs can be broken into its component parts, such as salaries and wages for full-time and part-time personnel, employee benefits, and specific supply and expense items.

Step 4. *Assign all tiers two and three costs to designated cost objectives.* As noted in chapter 1, tier two costs include all tier one costs plus indirect costs that are attributable to a cost objective or center. Tier three costs include all tier two costs plus a depreciation or use charge on facilities and capital equipment. Tier three costs represent the full costs attributable to each cost objective. In order to determine the tier three costs associated with each of the final cost objectives, it is necessary to combine the tier one costs identified in step 3 with the indirect costs and depreciation, or facilities and equipment use charges, attributable to each cost objective. The tier one costs for plant operation and maintenance (as presented in figure 3.1), for example, become part of the tier two costs for instruction, public service, research, and auxiliary enterprises.

As noted in chapter 2, this handbook uses the step-down method for allocating support costs to benefiting cost objectives. A necessary requirement of this method is that the sequence for allocating these costs be clearly identified prior to beginning the allocation process. The sequence used in this illustration is as follows: (1) annual use charge on facilities and capital equipment, (2) plant operation and maintenance, (3) institutional support, (4) academic support, and (5) student services. The costs of support activities are allocated to the final cost objectives of instruction, public service, research, and auxiliary enterprises. Note that the allocation of academic support and student services does not have to follow any specific sequence. Figure 3.2 presents an overview of the allocation process.

Step 4a. *Allocate annual use charge on all buildings, land improvements, and capital equipment to all benefiting cost objectives.* The amount of depreciation on facilities and equipment can be calculated on each individual capital asset or an annual use factor can be calculated for all buildings, land improvements, and capital equipment. In *Procedures for Determining Historical Full Costs* (1977), NACUBO recommends an overall annual use charge of 2% on the original cost of all buildings and land improvements (based on an estimated useful life of 50 years) and a 10% charge on all capital equipment purchases made within the last 10 years. In this illustration, the annual use charge technique has been adopted. Note that replacement value is normally a more valid indicator than original cost in arriving at an annual use charge factor on building and land improvements. Whenever possible, therefore, replacement value should be used in calculating the annual use charge; unfortunately, figures on replacement

---

Figure 3.3

Calculation of Annual Use Charge on Buildings and Land Improvements

Original cost of all buildings and land improvements	$10,000,000
Multiply by: Annual use factor	.02
Annual use charge on buildings and land improvements	$ 200,000

---

value often are not readily available, and the original cost is used. Figure 3.3 indicates how to calculate the use charge on all buildings and land improvements, and figure 3.4 presents the way to calculate the total usage charge on capital equipment.

Once the total cost of buildings, land improvements, and capital equipment usage has been determined, it is necessary to allocate these costs to benefiting cost objectives. The base used to allocate the annual use charge on buildings and land improvements is assignable square feet, as illustrated in figure 3.5. The base for allocating capital equipment usage costs is also assignable square feet, as shown in figure 3.6.

Step 4b. *Allocate all plant operation and maintenance costs to all benefiting cost objectives.* After allocating all building and equipment usage costs, it is necessary to allocate the cost of plant operation and maintenance to all benefiting cost objectives. The costs of plant operation and maintenance are allocated at this time because the support activities that provide the broadest support to all activities should be allocated first. Plant operation and maintenance costs are allocated on the basis of assignable square feet, as illustrated in figure 3.7.

Step 4c. *Allocate all institutional support costs to all benefiting cost objectives.* As noted in chapter 2, it is preferable to allocate institutional support costs on the basis of actual usage data, such as number of work orders or computer runs. At most institutions, however, actual usage data is not readily available. As a result, proxy measures are used to allocate institutional support costs. Figure 3.8 uses direct costs as the basis for allocating institutional support costs.

Step 4d. *Allocate all academic support costs to all benefiting cost objectives.* It is preferable to allocate academic support costs on the basis of actual use studies. In the case of libraries or museums and galleries, this could involve studies of the number of users of each service by type of user, for example, student, faculty member, visiting scholar, and researcher. Frequently, however, studies of actual use are not available and the costs of academic support must be allocated on a basis that best approximates actual use. In this chapter, academic support costs have been allocated to the benefiting cost objectives of instruction, public service, and research on the basis of direct costs, as shown in figure 3.9.

Figure 3.4

Calculation of Annual Use Charge on Capital Equipment

Year*	Capital Expenditures for Equipment
1971	$ 20,000
1972	10,000
1973	15,000
1974	10,000
1975	22,000
1976	14,000
1977	10,000
1978	25,000
1979	15,000
1980	10,000
Total	151,000
Multiply by: Annual use factor	.10
Annual use charge on equipment	$ 15,100

*In the following year, the 1971 figure will be dropped and the 1981 figure added. The use charge will then be recalculated for the most recent 10-year period.

Figure 3.5

Allocation of Annual Use Charge on Buildings and Land Improvements to Benefiting Cost Objectives

Cost Objective	Assignable Square Feet (ASF)*	Percentage of Total ASF	×	Annual Use Charge on Buildings and Land Improvements (see figure 3.3)	=	Annual Use Charge on Buildings and Land Improvements Allocated to Benefiting Cost Objective
Plant operation and maintenance	48,000	12%	×	$200,000	=	$ 24,000
Institutional support	36,000	9		200,000		18,000
Academic support	20,000	5		200,000		10,000
Student services	24,000	6		200,000		12,000
Instruction	180,000	45		200,000		90,000
Public service	4,000	1		200,000		2,000
Research	8,000	2		200,000		4,000
Auxiliary enterprises	80,000	20		200,000		40,000
Total	400,000	100%		$200,000		$200,000

*Assignable square feet (ASF) includes the sum of areas in all rooms that can be used by building occupants to carry out their functions. Excluded are circulation, custodial, mechanical, and structural areas.

Figure 3.6

Allocation of Equipment Use Charges to Benefiting Cost Objectives

Cost Objective	Assignable Square Feet (ASF)	Percentage of Total ASF	×	Annual Equipment Use Charge (see figure 3.4)	=	Equipment Use Charge Allocated to Cost Objective
Plant operation and maintenance	48,000	12%	×	$15,100	=	$1,812
Institutional support	36,000	9		15,100		1,359
Academic support	20,000	5		15,100		755
Student services	24,000	6		15,100		906
Instruction	180,000	45		15,100		6,795
Public service	4,000	1		15,100		151
Research	8,000	2		15,100		302
Auxiliary enterprises	80,000	20		15,100		3,020
Total	400,000	100%		$15,100		$15,100

Figure 3.7

Allocation of Plant Operation and Maintenance Costs to Benefiting Cost Objectives

Cost Objective	Assignable Square Feet (ASF)	Percentage of Total ASF	×	Plant Operation and Maintenance Costs (see figure 3.2, step 4a (iv))	=	Plant Operation and Maintenance Costs Allocated to Benefiting Cost Objectives
Institutional support	36,000	10%	×	$1,125,691	=	$ 112,569
Academic support	20,000	6		1,125,691		67,541
Student services	24,000	7		1,125,691		78,798
Instruction	180,000	51		1,125,691		574,103
Public service	4,000	1		1,125,691		11,257
Research	8,000	2		1,125,691		22,514
Auxiliary enterprises	80,000	23		1,125,691		258,909
Total*	352,000	100%		$1,125,691		$1,125,691

*Total ASF is less the square footage assigned to P.O.& M in figure 3.5, or 400,000 ASF – 48,000 ASF = 352,000 ASF.

Step 4e. *Allocate all student service costs to benefiting cost centers.* In figure 3.2 all student services costs are allocated to the instruction cost objective. If cost information for specific academic departments is desired, then student services costs should be allocated on the basis of student credit hours or contact hours produced by each department or by other methods appropriate to the institution. For a more detailed discussion of this procedure, refer to chapter 6.

Step 4f. *Calculate tier three costs for all final cost objectives.* After the costs associated with all support activities have been allocated to benefiting cost objectives, the tier three costs of the final cost objectives can be determined. As noted in chapter 1, tier three costs enable administrators to examine the full

costs associated with a cost objective as well as its tier one (see figure 3.1) and indirect cost components. Tier three costs of instruction, for example, include the following:

1) Tier one costs (see figure 3.1) $4,600,000

2) Annual use charge on buildings and land improvements   90,000

3) Equipment use   6,795

4) Support costs associated with:
     Plant operation and maintenance   574,103
     Institutional support   669,015
     Academic support   626,526
     Student services   776,658

5) Tier three costs of instruction (see figure 3.2). $7,343,097

Step 5. *Develop unit cost or output measures.* The cost information developed in steps 1 through 4 can be combined with data from other information systems, including student records, inventory, and personnel, to produce a number of unit cost measures, such as cost of instruction per student credit hour (SCH); cost per resident in student housing; cost per public service event, for example, lectures and conferences; or the cost per product line, for example, textbooks or clothing sold in the college bookstore.

The cost accounting procedures described in this chapter are useful in determining the institutional costs associated with the cost objectives of instruction, public service, research, and auxiliary enterprises. This chapter represents one of the two applications of cost accounting procedures in this handbook. The second application of cost accounting procedures, in part 2, helps determine the costs associated with specific functional areas, including plant operation and maintenance, institutional support, instruction, and specific auxiliary enterprises such as housing and food service.

It is important to remember that, prior to implementing cost accounting procedures, the purpose for collecting the cost information must be clearly identified. The purpose for collecting cost information will determine whether the cost accounting procedures presented in this chapter or those described in part 2 should be used.

Figure 3.8
Allocation of Institutional Support Costs to Benefiting Cost Objectives

Cost Objective	Direct Costs of Cost Objective (see figure 3.1)	Percentage of Total Direct Costs	×	Institutional Support Costs (see figure 3.2, step 4b (ii))	=	Institutional Support Costs Allocated to Benefiting Cost Objectives
Academic support	$ 500,000	7%	×	$1,061,928	=	$ 74,335
Student services	600,000	8		1,061,928		84,954
Instruction	4,600,000	63		1,061,928		669,015
Public service	60,000	1		1,061,928		10,619
Research	150,000	2		1,061,928		21,239
Auxiliary enterprises	1,400,000	19		1,061,928		201,766
Total Direct Costs	$7,310,000	100%		$1,061,928		$1,061,928

Figure 3.9
Allocation of Academic Support Costs to Benefiting Cost Objectives

Cost Objective	Direct Costs of Cost Objective (see figure 3.1)	Percentage of Total Direct Costs	×	Academic Support Costs (see figure 3.2, step 4c (ii))	=	Academic Support Costs Allocated to Benefiting Cost Objectives
Instruction	$4,600,000	96%	×	$652,631	=	$626,526
Public service	60,000	1		652,631		6,526
Research	150,000	3		652,631		19,579
Total Direct Costs	$4,810,000	100%		$652,631		$652,631

part 2

selected program areas

4

plant operation and maintenance

The efficient operation and maintenance of buildings, grounds, and other physical facilities is essential to the health of educational institutions. Often, however, members of the governing board, faculty, staff, and students are unaware of the full cost of providing these services. Moreover, plant operation and maintenance is frequently among the first institutional areas to experience budget reductions during periods of fiscal stringency. Thus, it is important that adequate cost information be available for making informed decisions about this important area.

Assessing the Need for Cost Data

The need for cost information must be assessed prior to collecting data. Cost information on plant operation and maintenance is frequently used to evaluate the efficiency of existing services and to assess the impact of providing alternative levels of service. Cost data are also used in conducting limited comparisons with similar institutions, and in submissions to national organizations, such as the Association of Physical Plant Administrators of Universities and Colleges (APPA) and the National Center for Education Statistics (NCES). For a more comprehensive discussion on the uses of cost data, refer to chapter 1.

Plant Operation and Maintenance Costs and Cost Centers

According to the chart of accounts in NACUBO's *College and University Business Administration* (see exhibit 1-A), the plant operation and maintenance area encompasses the following activities:

Physical plant administration
Building and equipment maintenance

Custodial services
Utilities
Landscape and grounds maintenance
Major repairs and renovations

For the purpose of this handbook, the area of plant operation and maintenance is viewed as a cost objective and the activities listed above as cost centers within this objective. At many small colleges and universities, two or more of the activities listed above are combined. When this occurs, the procedures for designating cost centers can be modified to reflect the institution's own chart of accounts.

Once cost centers have been designated, it is necessary to select consistent categories of cost. A useful source document in establishing cost categories for the plant operation and maintenance area is supplement 3:4:2 (formerly 3:3:2 and dated June 1975) to NACUBO's *Administrative Service*. That document outlines in detail a classification of accounts for physical plant. At a minimum, cost categories should include personnel compensation, supplies and expenses, and other objects of expenditure identified in the cost center's budget. Based on the institution's cost categories, all tier one, or direct, costs associated with each cost center can be identified and collected directly from the institution's financial records.

The assignment of all tier one costs to designated cost centers provides institutional and cost center administrators with a general idea of the cost of providing plant operation and maintenance services. There are, however, additional indirect costs associated with providing these services. Custodial services, for example, can incur indirect costs from services provided by the accounting and cashier's office, administrative data processing, and employee personnel and records services. Physical plant administration is also a source of indirect costs for custodial services since it provides administrative support to the custodial area. Methods for allocating indirect costs to plant operation and maintenance cost centers are similar to those outlined in chapter 2. Later in this chapter, the procedures for allocating indirect costs to cost centers will be highlighted through the use of an illustration. The combination of tier one costs plus attributable indirect costs represents the tier two costs associated with plant operation and maintenance cost centers.

In order to determine the tier three or *full* costs of providing plant operation and maintenance services, the costs associated with the depreciation of facilities and capital equipment used in the plant operation and maintenance area must be considered. As noted in chapters 1 and 2, these costs can be calculated either individually for each capital item or by the use of a uniform annual use charge for all facilities and capital equipment. The combination of direct and indirect costs plus depreciation represents the tier three costs associated with plant operation and maintenance cost centers.

Cost Accounting Procedures for the Plant Operation and Maintenance Area

Methods for collecting cost data for plant operation and maintenance can vary among institutions. *Administrative Service* supplement 3:4:1 (formerly numbered 3:3:1 and dated April 1975) provides an example of a system for accounting for physical plant costs. The primary objective of this system is that each cost center will "sell" or credit its services in an amount equal to its operating expenses so that at the end of a period all cost center budgets will net to zero and all physical plant charges will be charged and recorded as expenditures of benefiting activities. A description of this system is included in exhibit 4-A, which follows this chapter. In addition, an institutional case study highlighting the use of the specific service or job order method of cost accounting for plant operation and maintenance is described in exhibit 4-B.

The cost accounting approach in this chapter is one in which the costs of the plant operation and maintenance area are attributed to specific cost centers. The total costs associated with the plant operation and maintenance area are then allocated to other program areas either through the use of indirect cost allocation procedures or on the basis of a chargeback system.

In the illustration that follows, a procedure for collecting cost data for a specific cost center, landscape

and grounds maintenance, is described. Similar procedures are applicable to other cost centers in plant operation and maintenance.

The first step in implementing cost accounting procedures is to designate specific cost centers. In this instance, landscape and grounds maintenance has been designated as a cost center. The second step in the costing process is to select a consistent set of cost categories. In this example, the three major object of expenditure categories—personnel compensation, supplies and operating expenses, and capital expenditures—are used. Once categories of cost have been established, all tier one, or direct, costs can be assigned to the cost center. Tier one costs should be readily obtainable from the institution's financial records. Figure 4.1 presents the tier one costs for the landscape and grounds maintenance cost center.

In addition to the tier one costs outlined in figure 4.1, landscape and grounds maintenance receives services from a number of other support areas of the institution, such as fiscal operations, general administrative services, and logistical services. In order to determine the indirect costs associated with the landscape and grounds maintenance cost center, some method must be used to allocate the cost of these support services to the cost center. Some suggested allocation bases are:

Sources of Indirect Costs	Allocation Bases
Fiscal operations, for example, accounting and cashier's office.	Actual use data, such as number of accounting transactions, or total direct costs.
General administration, for example, administrative data processing and personnel.	Actual use data, such as job orders or requests for service; or total direct costs.
Logistical services, for example, business management, materiel management, and service departments.	Actual use data, such as vouchers or purchase orders; or total direct costs.

Whenever possible, actual usage data, such as the number of work or purchase orders, should be used to allocate support costs to benefiting cost centers. Figure 4.2 highlights the use of purchase orders as a basis for allocating a portion of the cost of the purchasing office to the landscape and grounds maintenance cost center. The use of the number of purchase orders as an allocation base assumes that purchase orders can be identified with specific cost centers either on the basis of blocks of purchase order numbers assigned to each cost center or through some other means of identification.

Figure 4.1
Tier One Costs for the Landscape and Grounds Maintenance Cost Center

Tier One Costs

Personnel compensation	
Salaries and wages	$ 76,500
Employee benefits	13,500
Supplies	15,000
Insurance	1,000
All other items in cost center budget, for example, travel and postage	1,300
Total tier one costs	$107,300

Figure 4.2
Actual Use Data as a Method for Allocating Purchasing Direct Costs to the Landscape and Grounds Maintenance Cost Center

1. Number of landscape and grounds maintenance purchase orders processed for fiscal year — 40
2. Total institutional purchase orders — 5,200
3. Landscape and grounds maintenance purchase orders as a percentage of total purchase orders — $\frac{40}{5200} = 0.8\%$
4. Total direct costs of purchasing office — $35,000
5. Direct cost of purchasing office allocated to the landscape and grounds maintenance area on the basis of purchase orders processed — $\begin{array}{r} 35,000 \\ \times\ 0.8\% \\ \hline \$\ \ 280 \end{array}$

Frequently data on the actual use of many support activities are not readily available. In these instances, a proxy measure, such as total compensation, may be used. Figure 4.3 illustrates the use of total compensation as a basis for allocating the direct cost of physical plant administration to the landscape and grounds maintenance cost center.

Indirect costs allocated to the landscape and grounds maintenance cost center are indicated in figure 4.4. Note that figure 4.4 includes only those indirect costs that have a material effect on the cost

center. For example, the costs associated with the purchasing office have been included as attributable indirect costs while the costs associated with the president's office have not. The combination of tier one costs (from figure 4.2) with indirect cost represents the tier two costs described in chapter 1.

In order to determine the tier three, or full, costs of providing landscape and grounds maintenance, the costs associated with depreciation of facilities and equipment must be considered. In this illustration, straight-line depreciation is calculated for all facilities and equipment used in landscape and grounds maintenance. When depreciation is added to the direct and indirect costs of figures 4.1 and 4.4, the tier three costs associated with the cost center can be determined. The tier three costs associated with the landscape and grounds maintenance cost center are highlighted in figure 4.4.

Figure 4.3
Use of Total Compensation as a Basis for Allocating Physical Plant Administration Direct Costs to Benefiting Physical Plant Cost Centers

1. Total compensation of benefiting cost centers:

Cost Center	Compensation	Percentage of Total Compensation Costs
Building and equipment maintenance	$120,000	20%
Custodial services	390,000	65
Landscape and grounds maintenance	90,000	15
Total compensation	$600,000	100%

2. Compensation of landscape and grounds maintenance as a percentage of total compensation — 15%
3. Direct costs of physical administration — $65,000
4. Direct cost of physical plant administration allocated to landscape and grounds maintenance — $\begin{array}{r} 65,000 \\ \times\ 15\% \\ \hline \$\ 9,750 \end{array}$

Based on the cost information presented in figures 4.1 and 4.4, the tier one costs of providing landscape and grounds maintenance services are $107,300. If depreciation and indirect costs are taken into consideration, the tier three, or full, costs of providing these services are $130,330.

Figure 4.4
Tiers Two and Three Costs for the
Landscape and Grounds Maintenance Cost Center

Tier Two Costs

Indirect costs

Physical plant administration (see figure 4.3)	$ 9,750
Fiscal operations	300
General administrative services (employee personnel, admin. data processing)	350
Logistical services	
1. Purchasing (see figure 4.2)	280
2. Other logistical services	350
Attributable indirect costs	11,030
Total tier one costs (see figure 4.1)	107,300
Total tier two costs	$118,330

Tier Three Costs

Depreciation on facilities	$ 2,000
Depreciation on equipment	10,000
Total depreciation on facilities and equipment	12,000
Total tier two costs (see above)	118,330
Total tier three costs	$130,330

Unit Cost Data

If the cost figures in figure 4.4 are combined with related data, a number of unit cost or output measures can be derived. These cost data can be used in comparing the institution's landscape and grounds maintenance costs with other programs of similar institutions, private industry, and local, state, and federal governments. For a more complete description of physical plant unit costs and their utility in conducting interinstitutional comparisons, refer to NACUBO's *Administrative Service* supplement 3:4:3 (formerly numbered 3:3:3 and dated November 1978).

Case Study on Cost Accounting for Plant Operation and Maintenance

This chapter has described procedures for collecting cost data in plant operation and maintenance. This cost information can be useful in helping administrators understand the cost of providing plant operation and maintenance services. It is also important to understand the effect of plant operation and maintenance costs on other areas of the institution. In the case study (exhibit 4-B) that follows, a method of allocating the plant operation and maintenance costs to other areas of the institution is described.

exhibit 4-a

a system for accounting for physical plant costs*

THE SYSTEM DESCRIBED HERE is presented as one approach to complete, planned physical plant cost accounting for a college or university, and one that may be modified according to differences among institutions. Depending on individual circumstances such as size and/or complexity of the operation, an institution may require cost information that is more detailed or less detailed than indicated in this system. This system is designed to accommodate modifications that may be required or desired to satisfy changing requirements for specific plant cost information or the requirements of an integrated, institutional management information system. Regardless of size or complexity of an institution, the concepts of this system may be helpful in evaluating or modifying an institution's current system or in installing a new system.

This system provides cost reports for shop supervisors and project superintendents as well as summary reports for the director of physical plant and for other levels of institutional management. The system is sufficiently flexible to prepare any type of desired summary report from information captured in the institution's data base. Reports for management by exception, for example, can be programmed easily from detailed information recorded in the data base. The system also provides for the establishment of standards against which performance can be measured.

OBJECTIVES OF THE SYSTEM

A cost accounting system for physical plant should accomplish at least four objectives:

1. Financial Accountability — Satisfy such needs as controlling expenditures within budgeted allocations and accounting for expenditure transactions, purchasing transactions, personnel and payroll obligations, materials inventories, and funding requirements.

2. Unit Cost Information—Provide information at points where costs can be measured and compared, historically and laterally, such as physical plant cost centers, work orders, physical facilities (structures and vehicles), and benefiting activities.

3. Management Reporting—Create labor utilization reports, vehicle utilization reports, job status reports, budget versus actual labor hours reports, and budget versus actual work order funding reports.

4. System Integration—Integrate data (payroll and operating expense) from, and feed data (charges to institutional budgetary units—benefiting activities) into, the central accounting system of the institution.

DEVELOPMENT OF THE SYSTEM

A prerequisite to any effective operation is a clear understanding of organizational responsibilities. The physical plant organizational structure must provide its director with the capability to plan, budget, and manage, in addition to providing operational and maintenance services. Many kinds of cost and budget information needed for physical plant management are not provided by a conventional accounting and budgeting system; therefore, it is necessary to develop a separate system to receive and process data and to produce information tailored for the management of physical plant. Developing a system for any purpose begins with documentation of policies and procedures that define the authority and rules within which an operation is to be conducted, and systems processing should facilitate operating procedures. The director of physical plant should identify long-term

---

*From *Administrative Service.*

48

goals and shorter-term objectives within institutional goals and objectives; this system is designed to simplify such identification and to facilitate the attainment of goals and objectives.

Weekly staff meetings and progress reports are two ways in which physical plant managers can utilize information to monitor progress toward goals and objectives. Monthly progress reports should identify accomplishments, problems, and needed action. Annual reviews of achievements can be documented to provide a perspective for the governing board and others.

BASIC COMPONENTS OF THE SYSTEM

This cost system has three basic components: cost centers, work orders, and benefiting activities.

Cost centers represent units of activity, usually physical plant offices and shops to which all physical plant operating costs are charged and from which production or services are measured. Each cost center operates almost as a separate business or subcontractor, such as paint shop, electrical shop, engineering and estimating offices, and physical plant offices. Each has its own operating costs and its own production or services. Costs are accumulated by cost centers, and production or services are treated like "sales," which are charged to work orders. Finally, there are benefiting activities, which receive physical plant services and "pay" for charges made to work orders established for each job. The relationships among cost centers, work orders, and benefiting activities can be demonstrated by a summary cost flow chart (Figure 1).

OVERALL COST FLOW

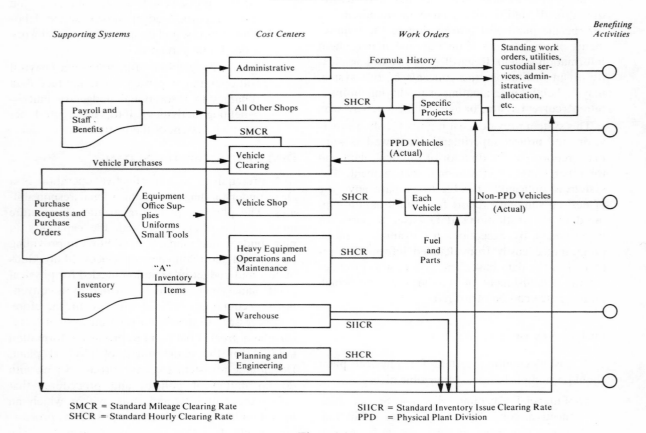

SMCR = Standard Mileage Clearing Rate
SHCR = Standard Hourly Clearing Rate

SIICR = Standard Inventory Issue Clearing Rate
PPD = Physical Plant Division

Figure 1

Charging Operational Expenses

Expenses of physical plant operation are charged to cost centers through the institution's central accounting systems—payroll, vehicle equipment, fuel and repairs, insurance, shop equipment, supplies that are not identifiable with specific projects (work orders), and other plant overhead expenses. Each organizational cost center is charged with payroll and with supplies that are purchased for the operation of the shop, such as sandpaper, nails, hammers, power saws, and with use of vehicles. Materials and other expense incurred in connection with specific work order projects, such as renovation materials, steel beams, roofing, generators, and wall cabinets, are charged directly to a work order established for the project and not to a cost center. They are purchases for a job and not for the operation of a shop. Inventory issues are charged either to a shop or directly to a work order, depending on whether the issue is for a shop or is material chargeable to one project.

The end result is that all physical plant costs are charged to work orders: materials that can be identified with specific jobs are charged directly to work orders, and general shop operating costs are charged to cost centers; then all cost center costs are charged to work orders. Shop labor and miscellaneous shop supplies are expended for many different projects and can best be captured as shop costs when incurred, then charged to work orders as service is provided.

Distribution of Costs to Work Orders

Distribution of cost center costs to work orders can be accomplished on the basis of a standard hourly clearing rate multiplied by the number of direct labor hours accumulated against a work order (for most physical plant shops), miles driven (for vehicle shops), inventory issues (for warehouses), or a formula (for physical plant administration). In the case of vehicles, actual costs are accumulated to work orders; a work order is established for each vehicle. All work orders for physical plant vehicles are charged to a vehicle clearing cost center and from there to a particular shop on the basis of a standard rate per mile as driven. All vehicle acquisitions are charged directly to the cost center clearing account. (In small insti-

tutions, which may not purchase vehicles on a periodic basis, this procedure could cause rates to vary widely from year to year.) By charging all vehicle work orders to a vehicle clearing cost center, it is possible to utilize a standard rate for each type of vehicle, whereas otherwise it would be necessary to charge one rate for a 1967 quarter-ton and another rate for a 1973 quarter-ton. Acquisition and maintenance costs for vehicles that do not belong to physical plant can be charged directly to the owning department.

As noted, all physical plant costs are charged either directly or by a cost center clearing rate to work orders. There are two kinds of work orders: (1) standing—for ongoing, repetitive, and routine expenditures to maintain or serve an activity on a more or less permanent basis, such as custodial service of a facility, utility charges, or maintenance of a vehicle; and (2) specific—for jobs that are begun, accomplished, and concluded, such as a major or minor renovation project, large equipment construction or installation, or alteration of space.

In addition to regular work orders, provision may be made for *special service* orders, which can be used for minor operating repair or maintenance requiring immediate attention, or for an emergency situation that has developed through an unforeseen situation (such as accident, fire, or storm) and requires immediate attention to save life or property. Charges can be made against accounts designated by the originator.

Work order numbers are assigned by the director of physical plant according to the general nature of work to be performed. A work order numbering scheme consisting of five digits could be assigned as follows:

Number	*Work Order Description*
	Specific work orders (projects):
0XXXX	Minor
1XXXX	Major
	Standing work orders:
	Maintenance and repairs:
	Buildings and facilities:
21XXX	Janitorial (building number is in three low-order positions)
22XXX	Routine maintenance and repairs

Number	Work Order Description
40XXX	Equipment (movable)
51XXX	Grounds
52XXX	Landscape
53XXX	Pavement
	Utility operations and maintenance:
61XXX	Purchased services
	Distribution systems:
62XXX	Electricity
63XXX	Natural gas
64XXX	Water
65XXX	Steam
66XXX	Sewage
	Vehicle operations and maintenance:
91XXX	Vehicles (vehicle number is in three low-order positions)
92XXX	Charter vehicles
99XXX	Administration

When a work order number is assigned, responsibility code numbers also are assigned. A responsibility code is a two-digit number representing the individual responsible for the project or work order. A work order responsibility report is prepared, based on this code. The five-digit code could be increased to seven digits to include the last two digits of the year of the work order.

A cost account code also is assigned to each work order. One use of a cost account code is to accumulate costs by building and thereby calculate costs per square foot; another is to accumulate mileage information and costs of a vehicle, which the system is designed to receive, to provide cost-per-mile information.

Benefiting Activities

Each work order is established as a project or service for an institutional budgetary or other funding source designated as a "benefiting activity." Each work order number is related to the account number of a benefiting activity in the general accounting system. A benefiting activity is a final funding source for charges made through the work order process. It may be a chemistry laboratory for which the physical plant division installs scientific equipment, or it may be a contract or grant which requires the services of the division in instal-lation or maintenance. It may be a plant fund that provides for new construction in which the physical plant division is involved, it may be an outside contractor, or it may be an auxiliary unit that is maintained or repaired. It may be the physical plant budget itself in the form of maintenance to a resident instruction facility, custodial service, or other typical physical plant service.

The system provides for two instances in which charges may be made directly to benefiting activities rather than through work orders: inventory issues (from other than the physical plant warehouse) and physical plant warehouse issues. If charges are made directly to benefiting activities and do not involve physical plant work or work orders, they are not considered physical plant expenses. An example would be the direct purchase of a chemical from the warehouse by the chemistry department. But if a warehouse issue is made to a project accomplished by the physical plant department, then the issue is a physical plant expense.

A primary objective of the system is that each cost center will "sell" or credit its services in an amount equal to its operating expenses, so that at the end of a period all cost center budgets will net to zero and all physical plant charges will be charged and recorded as expenditures of benefiting activities. "Sales" of a cost center are termed "service credits" in the system. In order to break even, each cost center prepares two budgets, one for the cost of its operations and one for charging its production to work orders and, in turn, to benefiting activities.

Cost Center Production Budget

The cost center operating budget can be prepared in the traditional way; it is the preparation of the production budget that is unique to the system. In most cases, preparation of a cost center's production budget begins with an estimate of chargeable direct labor hours, miles driven (for vehicle cost centers), or inventory issues (for warehouses). Estimated direct labor hours include actual time chargeable to work orders and exclude all indirect hours such as vacation, holidays, sick leave, and idle shop time. Indirect hours are considered and recovered as shop overhead.

Standard Clearing Rate

The next step is to develop a standard clearing rate for each cost center. A standard clearing rate is the basis for distributing physical plant costs to benefiting activities through the work order system. A cost center clearing rate includes payroll and staff benefit costs, vehicle costs, equipment and supply costs, hand tools, and other expenses of operating a cost center. A single, standard clearing rate eliminates the need for individual labor rates in a cost center, although there may be other types of clearing rates that are based on individual labor rates.

Direct Hours Charged

The following steps may be used in computing a standard clearing rate for a cost center that distributes its costs on the basis of direct hours charged:

1. Calculate the total available (budgeted) labor hours by multiplying the total full-time equivalent (FTE) positions by 2,080 hours. Supervisors should be excluded.

2. Determine the total number of indirect labor hours (sick leave, vacation, holidays, etc.) or labor hours not chargeable to work orders.

3. Calculate the chargeable direct labor hours by deducting the total indirect labor hours from the total available labor hours. The experience of previous years and projected workloads should be considered in judging the reasonableness of the estimate of direct labor. Variances occurring during the budget year should be charted, and estimated direct labor hours should be adjusted accordingly.

4. Determine the total salaries and wages for all budgeted FTE positions, including shop supervisors and project superintendents. Staff benefits may be added to this total on a percentage basis or included in other expenses discussed in Item 5 below.

5. Add the remaining budgeted expenses to Item 4 above. This sum should represent the total budgeted operating expenses for a cost center.

6. Compute the cost center standard clearing rate by dividing the total budgeted operating expenses in Item 5 above by the total chargeable direct labor hours in Item 3 above.

Costs of bus operations cost centers and heavy equipment operations and maintenance cost centers are distributed on the basis of operators' chargeable hours. Mechanics' wages are treated as indirect costs and not as direct labor. Some institutions have a separate cost center for heavy equipment, but the physical plant cost center often provides its own operator, and therefore pays only the hourly rate for the item of equipment.

Vehicle Cost Centers

Standard clearing rates for vehicle cost centers (motor pool operations) are based on vehicle mileage. Cost center clearing accounts are designed to collect and distribute all costs of operating physical plant vehicles. They are not operating units and do not have assigned staff. Costs charged to the vehicle cost centers flow from vehicle work orders and purchases of vehicles. Each cost center has one standard rate per mile to provide equitable distributions of cost. It has been indicated that by charging all vehicle costs to a vehicle clearing account, one rate can be calculated so that a benefiting activity using an old vehicle is not charged for the cost of excessive repairs, and an activity using a new vehicle is not charged for expensive insurance.

The following steps may be used in computing a standard clearing rate for vehicle cost centers:

1. Estimate the total miles to be driven by all vehicles in the cost center; all miles should be accounted for and charged to a cost center or benefiting activity.

2. Determine the total budgeted expense for the vehicle clearing cost center.

3. Compute the cost center standard clearing rate by dividing the total budgeted expense, Item 2 above, by the estimated total miles, Item 1 above.

Other methods of computing standard clearing rates for vehicle cost centers might also be appropriate in certain situations, such as (1) the amount of time the vehicle is used, (2) a combination of mileage and time, or (3) the greater of mileage or time.

At some institutions the vehicle cost center may not be a part of the physical plant cost accounting system, but rather serves the physical plant cost centers and all other units of the institution. However, the vehicle cost center is typically an integral part of the physical plant cost accounting system.

Administrative and Warehouse Costs

Depending on whether an institution chooses to charge or not to charge physical plant administration cost center costs, they may or may not be included in the overhead of other cost centers or distributed on a percentage of a direct cost formula basis. In full costing, all costs are charged out, and in direct costing, not all costs are charged out. Not every institution will elect to charge all costs, and there are degrees of full cost in all cost systems.

The basis for distributing costs of the warehouse cost center is the dollar amount of each inventory issue. The clearing rate provides for distributing the costs of operating the warehouse cost center by adding an allocable portion of the operating costs to the cost of each warehouse issue. The issue price of an inventory item, therefore, includes the cost of the inventory issue and a loading factor computed by applying a clearing rate percentage. The clearing rate, or loading factor, is computed as follows:

1. Estimate the total cost of inventory issues for the year.
2. Determine the total budgeted expense for the warehouse cost center.
3. Compute the clearing rate, or the loading factor, by dividing the total budgeted expense, Item 2 above, by the estimated total cost of inventory issues, Item 1 above.

BUDGETING

Once the standard clearing rate has been calculated, the production budget can be completed. It is prepared in terms of estimated direct labor hours to be charged or miles to be driven, and also in dollars as the product of the total estimated direct labor hours or miles driven multiplied by the standard clearing rate. Service credits, mentioned above, are used to represent the charges of a production budget to a benefiting activity. As the year progresses, the variance between actual service credits produced and service credits budgeted represents the difference between actual and planned direct labor charged.

To budget for charging all costs to benefiting activities, each cost center budget should show a net zero between budgeted expenditures and budgeted service credits. Analyses of the variance of budgeted expenditures versus actual expenditures and the variance of budgeted service credits versus actual service credits provide a basis for evaluating the performance of a cost center. The system also provides comparisons between actual and estimated costs for each work order and actual and estimated work-hours by cost center. Since every physical plant service is costed on a work order basis, the costs of all types of physical plant work can be compared to a budget plan.

Controls are maintained between the physical plant cost accounting system and the institution's central accounting system to insure that the former is balanced with the latter. Cutoff periods and the frequency of processing for both systems are the same, although this may not be possible or desirable for some institutions. If the central system does not include full encumbrances, the physical plant system provides for payroll accruals and purchase encumbrances on a memorandum, reconcilable basis only. Charges to the physical plant accounting system generally originate with the central accounting system, and distributions of costs usually originate with the physical plant accounting system. Most cost distributions originate with daily labor reports; distributions of vehicle costs begin with vehicle mileage reports, and inventory charges come from "Issue/Return of Materials" tickets.

DISTRIBUTING COSTS BY LABOR HOURS

For most cost centers, personal services (payrolls and staff benefits) constitute a major portion of total costs. Labor hours, therefore, are perhaps the most equitable basis on which to distribute costs from a cost center, and it is essential that they be reported accurately. Each cost center prepares a daily labor summary preprinted with the name of the cost center, cost center number, names of employees, and budget position numbers (Form 1).

A daily time card completed by the employee is the source document for the daily summary. Labor hours are recorded daily as direct hours or indirect hours; direct hours are entered by work order number. Payroll costs for cost center super-

PHYSICAL PLANT DIVISION

DAILY LABOR SUMMARY

COST CENTER Plumbing   COST CENTER NO. **51**   DATE   PAGE **79**   **01**

NAME		BUDGET POSITION	BUD-GET	TO-TAL	1	2	3	4	5	6	7	8	9	10	11	12	13	14	15	16	19	20	TOTAL DIRECT	HOLI-DAY	VACA-TION	SICK LEAVE	PAID ABST	OTHER
BELL	A	17-14	8	8							8																	
BARDLEY	T	17-9	8	8					8																			
BROOKS	R	17-23	8	8							8																	
BRUCE	T	17-6	8	8									2	2	3	1												
BRYANT	J	17-8	8	8		7						1																
HANCOCK	H	17-23	8	8									2	2	3	1												
HARRIS	B	17-4	8	8	8																							
MCCURLEY	R	17-5	8	8	8																							
MEADOWS	J	17-7	8	8				8																				
ROA~~...~~			8	8																								
~~...~~HAN	Z	17-00																										
ROACH	H	17-20	8	8						5								3										
ROACH	P	17-12	8	8																								
TEASLEY	G	17-19	8	8													8											
THORNTON	L	17-15	8	8			8																					
TUCKER	F	17-1	8	8		7						1																
YOUNG	I	17-25	8	8							8																	
SIGNATURE **NO. ATTACHED FORMS** —	COST CTR. 5 1		208.0	208.0	30.0	23.0	28.0	34.0	24.0	5.0	25.0	2.0	4.0	4.0	6.0	2.0	16.0	3.0					205.0					3.0
			00001	00011	11024	11048	11056	11058	11060	11121	11145	22048	22081	22111	22134	22176	6300	6680					00010	00004	00005	00006	00009	00007

Form 1

visors are included as a part of shop overhead in figuring the cost center standard clearing rate; time spent in overall supervision is not easily chargeable to work orders.

Shop supervisors are responsible for the accuracy of the daily labor summary reports for their shops. Either they directly enter the work-hour utilization each day and total the direct labor hours by work order, or they carefully review a clerk's preparation of the form. Each day following a workday, daily labor summaries are submitted to a control clerk who verifies clerical accuracy, establishes control totals, and prepares the forms for processing. If data processing equipment is used, cost center totals by work order number may be keypunched, but labor utilization information for each employee is not. Work order numbers are assigned by the physical plant division according to the general nature of work to be done. If a computer system is used, the program should be written to reject direct labor charges to invalid work order numbers.

Weekly processing of labor data includes:

1. Shop charges to work orders at standard clearing rates.
2. Distribution of costs to benefiting activities.
3. Record of service credits to cost centers.

Three weekly reports concerning labor utilization are provided from the daily labor summary, as follows:

1. *Weekly shop summary.* This report summarizes labor utilization for each day by displaying the total labor hours paid as direct and indirect. The types of indirect hours also are indicated, such as holiday, vacation, sick leave, and other. The direct hours and their percentage to the total hours paid are indicated, thereby providing an easily readable analysis of the efficiency in which total shop labor hours are utilized, a basis for evaluating the need for overtime, and a basis for determining the reasonableness of standard clearing rates.

2. *Labor time report, by shop within work order.* This report shows total labor hours estimated for each shop within each work order, labor hours expended to date, and labor hours remaining to be expended, based on estimated hours. The report enables project superintendents to determine the status of projects and to evaluate job performance by comparison of expended hours to estimated hours for each shop. Since labor hours for work to be accomplished by shops within each work order are assigned by estimators external to the shops, the effect is the establishment of standards against which work performance can be measured.

3. *Labor time report, by work order within shop.* This report shows work orders within a shop, indicating hours estimated to be worked for each work order, hours expended, and hours remaining to be worked.

INVENTORIES

Inventories are an important part of physical plant operations, both as a supply point and as a chargeable cost to a work order when utilized. The physical plant division may maintain large inventories for its own use and for that of other departments. Therefore, the physical plant division will have a warehouse cost center. It has been indicated that the warehouse cost center is charged for payroll and other expenditures necessary in the operation of the warehouse, and the calculation of a warehouse clearing rate is derived by dividing the estimated dollars of warehouse issues into the warehouse operating budget. The quotient, expressed as a percentage, is added to the direct cost of issues as a loading factor and recorded as a service credit to the warehouse cost center.

A selective inventory control system may contain the following categories:

Category	Description
A	Regularly stocked items subject to perpetual recordkeeping; represents major portion of inventory investment.
C	Regularly stocked items having a low unit cost and low usage value (expendables such as nuts, bolts, and sandpaper); physical controls are used in-

stead of perpetual records to reduce handling costs for items having a relatively low value.

O	Obsolete and slow-moving items.
S	Nonstocked items purchased and held for a specific work order and warehoused until delivery to a job site.

An "Issue/Return of Materials" ticket is used to record issuances and returns of "A" inventory items only. "C" and "O" inventory issues and returns are not recorded in the physical plant cost accounting system, and "S" items are charged directly to a work order without going through an inventory account. Issues are charged to a cost center, to a work order, or directly to an outside department if purchased for departmental use not in connection with a physical plant project; the issue price includes the loading factor. Issue price of an inventory item, including the loading factor, is computed as follows:

1. Estimate the item's unit cost (which may change during the period).

2. Estimate the total cost of all "A" inventory issues for the year.

3. Divide Item 2 into the warehouse cost center's operating budget. The quotient is the loading factor, which is multiplied by Item 1.

4. Add Item 1 to Item 3 to determine the unit issue price.

VEHICLE COSTS

Vehicle costs are incurred by physical plant in (1) motor vehicle pool, (2) maintenance and repair of vehicles, (3) campus transit system, and (4) charter bus service.

Figure 2 is a flow chart of vehicle costs. The items indicated by a circled number are explained below:

1. *Vehicle repair shop.* Payroll, staff benefits, and other operating expenses not identifiable with specific vehicles are charged to the vehicle repair shop cost center. Costs flow from the repair shop to vehicle work orders at a standard hourly rate.

2. *Bus operations.* This cost center is charged for payroll, staff benefits, and other operat-

VEHICLE TRANSACTIONS COST FLOW

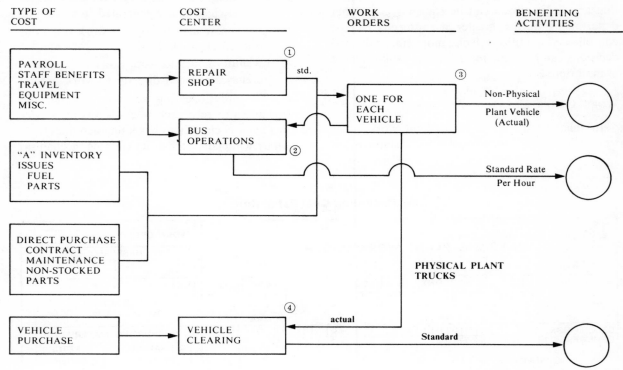

Figure 2

ing expenses not identifiable with specific vehicles. Bus purchases are charged to the bus operations cost center and a standard hourly rate is used to distribute costs directly to benefiting activities. Fuel, repairs, and other costs identifiable with specific buses are charged to individual bus work orders and these costs are distributed to the bus operations cost center through the work order clearing account. In institutions in which there are only a few buses, bus operations may be considered a part of the motor pool rather than a separate cost center.

3. *Work orders.* A standing work order should be established for each institutional vehicle. Costs identifiable with specific vehicles, such as fuel, replacement parts, and direct purchases, are charged directly to individual vehicle work orders. Costs are accumulated in work orders and distributed in three different ways: to bus operations cost center, to benefiting activities for non-physical plant

vehicles, and to vehicle clearing accounts for physical plant vehicles.

4. *Vehicle clearing accounts.* Vehicle clearing accounts collect vehicle operating costs for physical plant vehicles from vehicle work orders and acquisition costs of physical plant trucks and automobiles from vehicle purchase transactions. Costs are distributed at a standard clearing rate per mile to other physical plant cost centers.

A standing work order is established for each vehicle. The system provides for the recording of speedometer readings and a motor vehicle work order status report at the end of each month, which displays current month and year-to-date costs, mileage, and costs per mile for each vehicle. Another report prepared by the system is a vehicle utilization report, which shows monthly, year-to-date, and cumulative average mileage driven for each vehicle within an institutional department or other unit.

This report is particularly useful to management

in the review and evaluation of requests from departments to purchase additional vehicles. Vehicles that are underutilized can be transferred to other departments having greater need; needs can be consolidated to utilize vehicles more efficiently, and decisions can be made regarding the establishment of motor pools.

WORK ORDER CLEARING ACCOUNT

In this system, all physical plant work order transactions are processed and summarized through a work order clearing account, which operates in many ways like a cost center. Charges to work order clearing are generated from:

1. Cost center distributions to work orders at standard clearing rates.
2. Inventory issues to work orders.
3. Purchases charged directly to work orders.

The work order clearing account automatically self-balances to zero each week—costs in, service credits out (as charges to benefiting activities).

A physical plant work order clearing mechanism

WORK ORDER
(Including Cost Estimate)

PHYSICAL PLANT WORK ORDER

WORK ORDER [1][1][1][4][5]

PURCHASE REQUEST

| NUMBER | BUDGET AMENDMENT | DATE |

DATE	ACCOUNT	COST ACCT.	RESP.	TYPE
[7][4] [0][8] [2][3]	[P][1][0][0][7][0][0][6]	[4][2][1]	[1][0]	[2]
DATE REQUIRED	ACCOUNT TITLE ENTOMOLOGY INSTALL LAB EQUIP	DEPARTMENT ENTOMOLOGY		

LOCATION OF WORK
BIO-SCIENCES
RM 411-419-424

DESCRIPTION OF WORK [B][I][O][S] [I][N][S][T][L] [L][A][B] [E][Q][U][I][P]
CONNECTION OF LAB FURNITURE

SUPPORTING MATERIALS
[X] DRAWINGS [ ] SKETCH
[ ] PHOTO [ ] OTHER
ESTIMATE NO. 8-0415-2

COST ESTIMATE

| | DESCRIPTION | SHOP CODE | LABOR | | | MATERIALS AMOUNT |
			HOURS	RATE	AMOUNT	
SHOP LABOR AND MATERIAL ISSUE	PLUMBING SHOP	51	1064.2	3.33	3544.00	796.00
	METAL SHOP	53	546.8	3.70	2023.00	
	ELECTRIC SHOP	55	290.4	4.32	1255.00	265.00
	PAINT SHOP	58	92.7	3.96	367.00	
	CARPENTER SHOP	59	67.6	3.88	262.00	
DIRECT PURCHASES		98				
		98				
		98				5144.00
	SUB TOTALS		2061.7		7451.00	6205.00

AUTHORIZED AND APPROVED BY: _____ (DIRECTOR, PHYSICAL PLANT) (DATE APPROVED)

TOTAL ESTIMATE 13656.00

REQUESTED BY DR. H. O. LUND

ESTIMATED BY L. W. SCHILB, SR.

WORK CERTIFIED BY:
_____
(SIGNATURE AND TITLE)
DATE

Form 2

is necessary to prepare various kinds of work order reports from information captured through one point of cost flow. If work orders do not flow through a work order clearing account, it would be simple to prepare a report showing work orders charged to each individual account; it would not be so simple to show work order information in other formats usable for other purposes such as by individuals having responsibility for a group of work orders, work order ledger, work order status report, etc. Work order information has to be captured from the various shops prior to the charging to a benefiting activity. Cost summaries of each work order and audit trails are facilitated through the work order clearing mechanism.

COST ESTIMATE

Essential to the establishment of a work order is the preparation of a cost estimate (Form 2). An estimate is prepared, including shop costs and material by cost center and costs of direct material purchases. A total of all cost estimates represents a "budget" for a work order against which shop performance can be evaluated and for which funding can be allocated. Data from the cost estimate may be keypunched into a computerized system to provide information which, along with actual expenditures and charges, provides status and comparative reports, such as a work order status report, work order ledger, work order distribution, work order responsibility report, and pending work order report.

Records and Reports

These reports are further explained as follows:

1. *Work order status report.*

This report includes the following information for each work order:
   a. Work order number and brief description
   b. Physical plant cost account code
   c. Responsibility code—for the individual having overall responsibility for quality, time, and cost performance of the work order
   d. Account to be charged for the work
   e. Estimated total direct labor hours and shop charges by cost center (labor and inventory issues) and total of direct purchases

   "Type of Cost" code is as follows:
   - Type 1—Shop labor
   - Type 2—Inventory issues
   - Type 3—Fuel issues
   - Type 4—Direct purchases (obligations and expenditures)

   f. Actual costs for the current week and month-to-date
   g. Actual work hours expended since the work order was opened
   h. Accumulated actual costs for a specific work order, regardless of the fiscal year in which set up, and for a standing work order since the beginning of the current fiscal year
   i. Unexpended amount representing the difference between the original estimated cost and the actual cumulative costs to date; the percent of difference is also shown, which provides a measure of job status and a measure of cost performance (variances can be indicated on an exception basis)

2. *Work order ledger.*

In addition to the work order status report, a work order ledger is prepared. It is in work order number sequence and lists each detailed transaction posted to a work order in the current month. The ledger provides an audit trail from the status report back to the original source document, such as the daily labor summary and the "Issue/Return of Materials" ticket.

3. *Work order distribution.*

This report presents a list of all work orders charged to an institutional account (benefiting activity). A unique feature of this report is that it accumulates costs over the life of a work order regardless of the fiscal year involved.

4. *Work order responsibility report.*

This report is prepared monthly for each project superintendent or other individual designated as having overall responsibility for a work order. Since many work orders require the services of more than one shop, this report is prepared to show actual versus estimated costs by work order and by individuals responsible for the work. The report shows both open work orders and those that are "pending." (See Item 5 below.)

5. *Pending work order report.*

This report shows those work orders that will be closed at the end of the next month. The purpose of this report is to provide notice so that, if all charges have not been received as of month-end, the work order can be kept open. After a work order is closed, charges will be rejected by an automated system.

Monthly responsibility reports are prepared that compare actual costs against budgeted production (service credits) for the physical plant division. Costs and service credits are displayed in monthly and year-to-date totals for ease of management review.

The three levels of monthly responsibility reporting include the following:

1. Cost center report.
2. Responsibility center report.
3. Physical plant division report.

The system provides quarterly cost reports presented in terms of results, such as cost per square foot of custodial, maintenance, and repair services for a building. The cost reports show the cost account number and description, work code (two high-order positions of work order numbers), costs separated between labor and other, and unit measurements expressed in square feet, miles driven, and other appropriate bases. Cost reports are prepared in sections based on the type of service performed, such as custodial services, grounds, vehicle maintenance, utility operations, and other categories of service identified by an institution.

Each month, a cost summary of each work order is prepared as the physical plant cost ledger. The ledger is in sequence by cost account and work order number. It balances to total costs shown in work order status reports, and provides a link between the work order and cost reports. This trail is useful in performing detailed analyses of cost variances. It enables a user of the cost report to refer to the original source in investigating exceptional performance. In addition, it insures the completeness and accuracy of data shown in the cost report.

A characteristic of any good system is flexibility; the system should provide the capability to refine, expand, and prepare new presentations of information to meet changing demands. Three examples of management reports that can be produced from this physical plant accounting system are (1) shop report within funding group, (2) funding group within shop, and (3) work order within funding group, even though such reports may not have been envisioned when the system was designed. However, they now are provided from data captured by the original system, and are therefore easy to program.

Administrative Service supplements document principles, policies, practices and procedures in the field of college and university management. They provide additional information about subject fields or offer specific guidance in regard to generally accepted principles and policies. Supplements are the result of a comprehensive review process modeled after that used for the basic chapters of the Service.

exhibit 4-b

case study: ohio wesleyan university cost accounting for plant operation and maintenance

A written report of plant operation and maintenance costs was presented at a recent meeting to the finance committee of the board of trustees of Ohio Wesleyan University. The report contained costs per square foot for each building of the university for each of the last five years. These data clearly showed which buildings were comparatively costly and which were becoming significantly more costly over the period. The committee members had an opportunity to study the data, ask questions, and make comments.

The director of physical plant at Ohio Wesleyan had previously furnished copies of this same report to the president and his cabinet (vice presidents and deans), to the planning commission (a committee of faculty and administrators), and to the facilities committee of the board of trustees. These groups share in making decisions about university facilities, including decisions to build, to renovate, and to abandon. Operation and maintenance cost per square foot of existing facilities is one element of information in making such decisions.

The information in the report developed by the director of physical plant was readily available from a computerized cost accounting system. The director compiled the figures from five consecutive, year-end, cost summary reports—routine computer-printed reports—on file in his office.

The physical plant staff and business office personnel make frequent use of this cost-accounting system. They can obtain the latest information by inquiring at a computer terminal and can also refer to a series of reports printed monthly by the data processing department. They find the system to be a valuable tool for operations management as well as for long-range planning.

As an example, by reviewing the cost summary reports referred to above, the director of physical plant can identify buildings or other facilities where the current costs per square foot exceed his expectations. The summaries can also help him begin to identify the reasons for unusual cost increases. They contain for each facility a breakdown of cost by type of work done—maintenance, repairs, alterations, and improvements. They include aggregate costs as well as costs per square foot. If he needs more detail, the director can request from data processing a cost selection report, which is a list of individual jobs or services charged to a specific facility for a given month or for the year to date. With this list, he can usually isolate the cause of the increase and then inquire about the reasons.

Individual jobs or services charged to a facility might include janitorial service, repair work, painting, utilities, grounds care, trash disposal, and work by an outside servicer. In addition to monitoring the costs of facilities, the director of physical plant and his foremen can monitor the costs of these individual jobs. Routine monthly reports list costs for all partially completed jobs and all jobs completed that month. During a month, the up-to-date cost of an individual job in process can be obtained at a computer terminal.

This system is a job order cost accounting system, or, in the words of the *Administrative Service*, a system based on the "Specific Service Method." The Service defines this method as follows (chapter 4:6, formerly numbered 4:5 and dated October 1975):

Specific service method. As the name implies, this cost determination method is used to collect cost incurred for a specific service, which can be identified separately. It is because each unit is unique that cost must be segregated, rather than being identified as part of a continuous process, wherein an average cost can be derived that is representative of each unit of service. In the specific service method, the costs of different units of service are accumulated individually throughout the period during which service is provided. As a result, costs are compiled by each project or job in each organizational unit.

This cost-accounting system complements the university's general accounting procedures. General accounting procedures accumulate expenditures by fund, function, organizational unit, and object. Cost accounting adds figures for facilities, jobs, and type of work. Ohio Wesleyan's computer disk master file of operation and maintenance costs is separate from the general ledger master file. In a broad sense, it is a subsidiary ledger, while operation and maintenance accounts in the general ledger are the control accounts. This structure is roughly parallel to the manufacturing systems described in cost accounting textbooks, where the job-order file is a subsidiary ledger to the work-in-process inventory control account.

Ohio Wesleyan's general ledger chart of accounts follows the recommendations of the Association of Physical Plant Administrators of Universities and Colleges (APPA) (see *Administrative Service* supplement 3:4:2—formerly numbered 3:3:2 and dated June 1975). The ledger has separate accounts for physical plant administration, each individual maintenance shop (carpenters, plumbers, etc.), custodial services, utilities, grounds care, work by outside contractors, motor pool, central receiving, and property insurance. At Ohio Wesleyan, communications, mail, and security are located in other areas; they are not the responsibility of the director of physical plant.

Ohio Wesleyan's general accounting system follows the concepts of responsibility accounting. An account for an organizational unit contains only controllable costs, charges for items under the control of the supervisor. These generally include salaries, wages, employee benefits, supplies, expendable equipment, travel, duplicating, and miscellaneous items. Supervisors receive monthly reports that compare actual expenditures and encumbrances with budgeted expenditures and clearly show the remaining amount of unencumbered budget.

The account number structure facilitates computerized preparation of monthly reports. The account number contains seven digits, arranged as follows:

Position Number

1 and 2	Fund group component
3	Financial statement caption
4 and 5	Organizational unit
6 and 7	Object code

Account numbers for unrestricted current fund educational and general expenditures begin with the fund group component numbers 01. A financial statement caption code of 7 identifies the director of physical plant. The organization unit digits identify the individual shop or activity. For example, the plumber's shop account number is 01711, while custodial services is 01717 and utilities are 01719. The object codes identify the nature of the expenditure. Plumbers' wages are 0171111, plumbers' supplies are 0171113, plumbers' telephone costs are 0171115, etc. Shop foremen receive reports of transactions and of balances arranged by object code. The director receives a summary report of balances for each shop and activity.

The emphasis in the general accounting system, then, is on budget control and general purpose financial statements, while the emphasis in the cost accounting system is on activity (jobs) and results (facilities operated and maintained).

Computer File

The operation and maintenance cost system has a separate computer disk file, which contains one record for each job. Data elements in each record include several code numbers, a description, date started, date completed, estimated hours and dollar cost, and actual hours and dollar cost.

The code numbers make possible the accumulation and reporting of costs in the manner previously described. They are as follows:

Code	Number of Digits or Letters
Document type	1
Document number	5
Work center	2
Work type	1
Facility	5

The system contains four different types of job records, or document types: (1) repair requests, (2) work orders, (3) service orders, and (4) standing orders. A subsequent section of this exhibit contains a complete description of each. The document number is a sequential identification of individual jobs. The work center is the organizational unit. The work center code consists of recognizable letters, such as PL for plumbers and CA for carpenters. Each work center has a corresponding account in the general ledger.

The system uses the following four work-type codes:

Code	Definition
M	Maintenance. Keep plant facilities in designed condition and usefulness and operation.
R	Repair. Return plant facilities to their designed condition and usefulness.
A	Alterations. Change the designed configuration, use, or usefulness of a plant facility without changing its value.
I	Improvement. Add to or improve a facility with an increase in capital value.

Each facility has a four-digit identification number preceded by a letter. The letter is a class or grouping code, as follows:

A	Educational and general buildings
R	Residential buildings
K	Kitchens
U	Utility systems
G	Grounds area
S	Special

The S code covers work not directly related to any of the other facilities. Examples are repair of damage with the cost to be billed to students, setup for campus programs, and equipment testing.

System Development

The development of this cost system took place in 1971. The general idea came from a book by Allen Barber and John Green, *A System of Cost Accounting for Physical Plant Operation in Institutions of Higher Education* (University of Georgia Press, 1968). While this book dealt with a large and complex university, Ohio Wesleyan personnel realized the basic concepts could be applied in a smaller, single-purpose institution.

Ohio Wesleyan had a clear need for such a system. The director of physical plant and the shop foreman were receiving the organizational unit budget reports from the general accounting system, but they had no routine reports focusing on jobs or facilities. Costs of maintaining individual facilities were not known, because the volume of detailed transactions made manual analysis impractical. The office staff did maintain a document file of open work orders and service orders. The director and the foremen could use this file to review jobs in process, but they found this technique slow and ineffective. After he had read the University of Georgia book, the director was anxious to develop a similar system for his own use.

The system design process extended over a period of three months. During that time, a group composed of the director of physical plant, the controller, and the data processing manager met approximately once a week to discuss the Barber/Green book and to relate it to Ohio Wesleyan. Some of these meetings were held in a classroom as part of a managerial accounting course being taught by the controller, and students participated in discussions on those occasions.

By the end of three months, the group had designed the computer record, the source documents, and the reports, and had created flowcharts for the procedures to be followed. They adapted most of the source documents from forms already in use. At this point, they employed one of the managerial accounting students to write the computer programs. He completed the job in approximately six months of part-time work, about 10 hours per week, and programmed the system for batch processing with punched cards.

In 1976, the university purchased a new computer, a PDP 11-70, from Digital Equipment Corporation. The data processing staff have now reprogrammed the system to provide for interactive inquiry and update from a terminal in the office of the director of physical plant. No other significant changes have been made.

The director of physical plant reported an interesting extra benefit obtained from the new system. After it had been in operation for several months, the number of jobs in process dropped dramatically. With clear, concise information available to them, the foremen were able to do a better job of supervising, and individual jobs no longer remained incomplete for extended periods. With the previous open order file system, an incomplete job could escape notice unless someone complained about it.

Source Documents

Source documents include the four document types (repair requests, work orders, service orders, and

62

standing orders), which serve to open and close records on the disk file. Other source documents serve only to add data to existing records. See exhibit 1 for a flowchart of these relationships. Exhibits 2 through 9 are blank forms. The following paragraphs describe each.

Exhibit 1

SOURCE DOCUMENTS

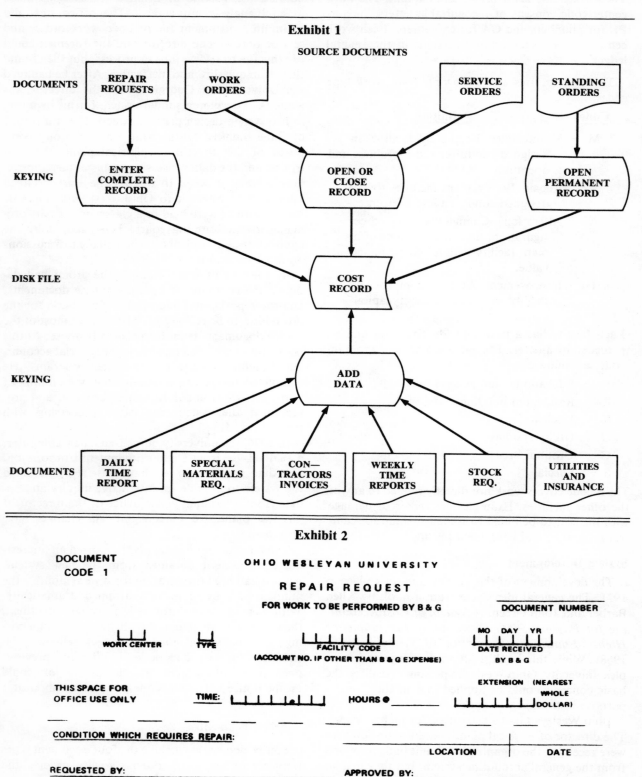

Exhibit 2

DOCUMENT CODE 1

OHIO WESLEYAN UNIVERSITY

REPAIR REQUEST

FOR WORK TO BE PERFORMED BY B & G

DOCUMENT NUMBER

WORK CENTER   TYPE   FACILITY CODE
(ACCOUNT NO. IF OTHER THAN B & G EXPENSE)

MO DAY YR
DATE RECEIVED
BY B & G

THIS SPACE FOR OFFICE USE ONLY   TIME: HOURS @ _____   EXTENSION (NEAREST WHOLE DOLLAR)

CONDITION WHICH REQUIRES REPAIR:

LOCATION   DATE

REQUESTED BY: APPROVED BY:

Repair request (Exhibit 2). The physical plant department uses repair requests for small jobs, which involve only one trade shop and estimated dollar costs under $150. Anyone on campus can initiate a repair request. The physical plant office staff write most of them on the basis of telephone calls or memoranda received. It is a two-part form, with an office copy and a copy for the trade shop foreman. The foreman returns his copy after the job is complete, with the actual work time added. Time is recorded as hours to the nearest one-quarter, in decimal form. For example, one hour and fifteen minutes would be written as 0001.25. The office staff match the foreman's copy to the office copy and insert a standard rate for that trade and the extension amount. They then enter the repair request at the computer terminal. Information below the line of dashes is not entered; it is available only from the form. Both copies are kept on file, one in document-number sequence and one in building sequence.

The standard hourly rate covers direct labor and indirect costs. As a matter of procedure, repair requests cannot contain direct charges for materials. Indirect costs covered by the standard rate include supplies, supervision, physical plant office costs, and employee benefits. Employee benefits include pensions, group insurance, payroll taxes, educational benefits, vacation, holidays, and sick leave. The director calculates and publishes new rates annually, using budgeted expenditures and estimated direct labor hours for calculation.

Note that the computer file contains records only for completed repair requests, not jobs in process. Cost cannot be added to a repair request record after it has been entered. (The staff does have a procedure for correction of errors.) Repair requests cover small jobs that do not merit additional record keeping or formal control beyond that exercised by the shop foremen.

Work order (Exhibit 3). Work orders cover larger jobs, jobs with estimated dollar costs of $150 or more, or jobs involving more than one trade shop. The office staff prepare work orders, and the director or assistant director signs them. The office staff prepare photocopies for each trade foreman involved. The number of trades involved could range from one to eight; a corresponding number of work center lines would be filled in on the form. The office staff keep the original and enter the work order at the computer terminal. The data entered include estimated time and estimated cost by work center. This entry creates a new record; the record does not yet contain actual time or cost.

Exhibit 3

DOCUMENT
CODE 2

OHIO WESLEYAN UNIVERSITY

WORK ORDER

FOR WORK TO BE PERFORMED BY B & G

DOCUMENT NUMBER

DATE | MO DAY YR

FACILITY CODE
(ACCOUNT NO. IF OTHER THAN B & G EXPENSE)

DESCRIPTION

WORK CENTER	WORK TYPE	ESTIMATED TIME (WHOLE HOURS)	RATE	EXTENSION (NEAREST DOLLAR)	SPECIAL MATERIALS	TOTAL ESTIMATE
		.00				
		.00				
		.00				
		.00				
		.00				
		.00				
		.00				
		.00				

DATE RECEIVED: _____ LOCATION: _____

REQUESTED BY: _____ APPROVED BY: _____

WORK TO BE DONE:

Daily time report (Exhibit 4). Actual time and cost data for work orders come from daily time reports. The trade foremen enter everything on these forms except the rate and the extension amount, using a separate line for each employee and work order. For example, if John Smith worked on three work orders in one day, his name would appear on three lines. The office staff add the rate and extensions on the form and then enter the code numbers, the hours, and the dollar extensions at the computer terminal.

Exhibit 4

OWU DAILY TIME REPORT

WORK CENTER NAME: _____   WORK CENTER CODE: _____

PREPARED BY: _____   DATE: _____

	NAME	CODE	DOCUMENT NO.	WORK TYPE	FACILITY CODE	HOURS	RATE	EXTENSION
1								
2								
3								
4								
5								
6								
7								
8								
9								
10								
11								
12								
13								
14								
15								
16								
17								
18								
19								
20								
21								
22								
23								
24								
25								

The entry serves to increase the actual hour and dollar cost fields of work order records already on the disk file. As with repair requests, a standard rate is used that includes direct labor and indirect costs for each department.

The foremen are responsible for making sure that all direct labor time is fully accounted for, either through repair requests or daily time reports, or a combination of the two. The office staff do periodic test checks comparing these source documents to time cards. The computer could have been programmed to do that comparison, but it was decided that that degree of complexity was not necessary in this comparatively small department. The institution relies primarily on the foremen for control.

Special materials requisition (Exhibit 5). Unlike repair requests, work orders can include direct

Exhibit 5

OWU SPECIAL MATERIALS REQUISITION

THIS MATERIAL IS ORDERED SPECIFICALLY FOR:

DOCUMENT CODE · DOCUMENT NO. · WORK CENTER · WORK TYPE · FACILITIES CODE · (ACCOUNT NO. IF OTHER THAN B & G EXPENSE)

BUILDINGS AND GROUNDS: ATTACH THIS FORM TO THE RELATED PURCHASE REQUISITION FORM

PURCHASING: FORWARD THIS FORM TO ACCOUNTING, ALONG WITH REQUISITION, STAPLED TO PURCHASE ORDER COPY

ACCOUNTING: ENTER INVOICE COST _____ (ROUNDED TO WHOLE DOLLARS) AND FORWARD TO DATA PROCESSING

Exhibit 6

DOCUMENT CODE 3

OHIO WESLEYAN UNIVERSITY

SERVICE ORDER

NOT VALID FOR MATERIALS EXCEPT ASSOCIATED WITH REPAIR

WORK CENTER · TYPE · FACILITY CODE (ACCOUNT NO. IF OTHER THAN B & G EXPENSE)

DOCUMENT NUMBER (SHOW THIS NUMBER ON INVOICES)

VENDOR

INVOICE TO: BUILDINGS AND GROUNDS OHIO WESLEYAN UNIVERSITY DELAWARE, OHIO 43015

DATE: _____ MO DAY YR   DESCRIPTION: _____

WHOLE DOLLARS

ESTIMATED AMOUNT _____

INVOICE AMOUNT _____

SIGNED BY

_____
Director of Physical Plant

ALL WORK PERFORMED MUST COMPLY WITH ALL CITY, STATE AND FEDERAL CODES AND SAFETY REGULATIONS. CERTIFICATE OF INSURANCE MUST BE ON FILE IN B&G OFFICE.

materials charges. These come from special materials requisitions, forms that contain processing instructions. One change has occurred in the use of these forms; the office staff now enter the data at their computer terminal. The forms do not go to data processing.

Service order (Exhibit 6). This form covers work done by outside contractors. It is the third document type, serving to open new records on the disk file. It is a three-part form, with one copy for the contractor, one for the physical plant office, and one for the accounting office. Office staff enter the data at their computer terminal.

Contractors' invoices. Actual costs of service orders come from contractors' invoices. The director of physical plant approves such invoices for payment. The office staff enter the amounts on the cost disk file and then forward the invoices to the accounting office for payment.

Standing orders. Repair requests, work orders, and service orders all have completion dates. When the physical plant staff has entered a completion date for one of those records, the computer will no longer process charges to it. Instead, the computer will create an error message stating the job is closed. Standing orders, in contrast, have no completion dates. The fourth document type, they are similar to work orders in other respects. Standing orders exist for custodial care, utilities, property insurance, trash disposal, scheduled preventive maintenance, and other recurring activities.

Weekly time reports (Exhibit 7). Custodial workers whose assignments do not change from day to day use weekly rather than daily time reports. All of these workers are doing maintenance on Standing Order No. 00001, so the document code, document number, and work type are preprinted on the form. Processing of this form is similar to that for the daily time report.

Exhibit 7

OWU WEEKLY TIME REPORT

WORK CENTER NAME _____ WORK CENTER CODE _____

PREPARED BY _____ DATE _____

NAME	DOCUMENT CODE	NUMBER	WORK TYPE	FACILITY CODE	MON	TUES	WED	THUR	FRI	SAT	SUN	TOTAL	RATE	EXTENSION (Whole Dollars)
	4	00001	M											
	4	00001	M											
	4	00001	M											
	4	00001	M											
	4	00001	M											
	4	00001	M											
	4	00001	M											
	4	00001	M											
	4	00001	M											
	4	00001	M											
	4	00001	M											
	4	00001	M											
	4	00001	M											
	4	00001	M											
	4	00001	M											
	4	00001	M											
	4	00001	M											
	4	00001	M											

TOTALS

Stock requisition (Exhibit 8). Custodial workers use this form to draw materials from a central storeroom. It then becomes a source document to charge cost to standing orders, with the data entry being done by the physical plant office staff at their computer terminal. The prices charged include both the unit cost of the item and a markup designed to cover handling and storage costs. This is a three-page form containing a complete list of custodial supplies. Exhibit 8 shows the first page.

Exhibit 8

STOCK REQUISITION

DOCUMENT CODE ☐☐   DOCUMENT NO. ☐☐☐☐☐   WORK CENTER ☐☐   WORK TYPE ☐☐   FACILITY CODE/ACCT # ☐☐☐☐☐☐   TOTAL AMOUNT _____

--OFFICE USE ONLY--

BUILDING _____   FACILITY CODE/ACCT # _____   DATE _____

ORDERED BY _____

INSTRUCTIONS: Procure supplies from B&G Central Receiving, 28 Hayes Street. Order only materials listed. Orders will be delivered on the next delivery date. All empty containers must be cleaned out and placed on the loading dock for pickup when the next order is delivered. Prices effective   subject to change.

QUANTITY	DESCRIPTION	PRICE		QUANTITY	DESCRIPTION	PRICE	
	ASH TRAYS				DUST MOPS		
	Plastic	.60			Handle for green/mop	No/Ch	
	Paper	.30			White Handle & Frame	7.00	
	BATTERIES				A 108-Mop Head	2.50	
	D-Cell	.45			White Head #101	2.10	
	BROOMS				Hand Duster/Complete	4.65	
	5 Tie Household	4.70			Hand Duster Head	2.75	
	18" Push	9.00			MOP HANDLES		
	24" Push	12.00			Wooden - Large	6.59	
	Push Handle	2.50			Wooden - Small	2.80	
	BRUSHES				FLOOR MACHINE PADS (CASES)		
	Radiator	3.15			12" Red Buff	15.00	
	Window 10"	3.15			15" Red Buff	19.90	
	Bowl	1.95			17" Red Buff	24.55	
	Scrub	1.35			20" Red Buff	31.90	
	Counter	2.70			12" Brown Strip	15.00	
	BUCKETS				15" Brown Strip	19.90	
	44 qt. Mop Bucket	34.20			17" Brown Strip	24.55	
	11 qt. Plastic	2.25			20" Brown Strip	29.00	
	Small mop w/cast.	24.00			19" Red Scrubbing	24.30	
	Large mop w/cast.	28.35			20" Blue Scrubbing	31.40	
	FLOOR FINISH				PAPER PRODUCTS (CASE)		
	Soft Buffable (gal)	5.65			Toilet Tissue	27.30	
	Hard Sta-Brite (gal)	5.70			White Roll Towels	20.60	
	Prep-Cote Sealer (gal)	8.95			White Folding Towels	12.76	
	DEODORANT - GEL				SWEEPER BAGS - PAPER		
	Deodorant	1.61			Hoover Upright (pkg)	1.05	
	Dispenser (small)	.95			Hoover Tank (pkg)	1.05	
	Dispenser (large)	3.00			Eureka (pkg)	2.40	
	DISPOSAL BAGS				Carpet King (pkg)	2.85	
	Mosette - small (10/pk)	2.16			World-Widget - large	11.55	
		12.17			World-Widget - small	6.05	
	CLEANERS				SWEEPER BELTS		
	Germicidal (gal)	.75			Small - Eureka	.75	
	Gen. Purpose Dry (sack)	1.50			Large - Hoover	1.35	
	Kling Klean	2.87			Carpet King	.95	
	Cleaning Powder (lb)	.66			WASTE CANS		
	Window Cleaner (gal)	2.50			High Boy	16.20	
	Shower Film Off (gal)	4.50			30 gal. Plastic	10.60	
	Liquid Hand Soap	3.19			Small Waste Basket	6.50	
	Oven Cleaner	2.00			WINDOW SQUEEGEE		
	Bowl Cleaner (qt)	.85			Complete 6"	3.40	
	Spot Lifter/Despot	3.50			Complete 12"	4.15	
	Malco Leather Cleaner	3.75			Complete 16"	4.05	

Exhibit 9

OHIO WESLEYAN UNIVERSITY
Purchased Electricity
Main Campus

(141 S. Sandusky)

Date | | | | | | |

	FACILITY	SQ. FT.	FACTOR	COST
R001	Austin Hall	91,227		
A034	Sanborn Hall	31,880		
A001	University Hall	63,860		
A002	Edgar Hall	36,275		
A003	Merrick Hall	19,684		
A005	Phillips Hall	36,069		
R028	West Selby Stadium	12,740		
A007	East Selby Stadium	9,450		
A008	Bigelow Rice	26,539		
A009	O'Neal Greenhouse	2,770		
A010	Science Building	78,476		
A012	Elliott Hall	13,568		
A013	Slocum Hall	27,400		
A014	Sturges Hall	14,789		
A016	Edwards Gym	42,961		
A017	Natatorium	12,774		
A018	East Boiler House	8,000		
A023	Humphrey Art Hall	12,748		
A024	Bookstore	6,200		
A026	Memorial Union Building	20,295		
K005	MUB Snack Bar	3,150		
K006	MUB PUB	2,415		
A041	Sculpture Annex	2,400		
A042	Service Building	18,000		
A044	Field House	69,934		
A046	Presser Hall	4,470		
U002	Line Rental	–		

KWH _____ Total Sq. Ft. 668,074 Cost _____

Usage dates _____

Exhibit 9 (cont.)

OHIO WESLEYAN UNIVERSITY

Purchased Electricity
Residential

Document Code: 4
Standing Job Order   00003

| P | O | | M | Date:
Work Center   Type

FACILITY CODE	FACILITY	METER READING	K.W. HOURS	COST
A025	16 University Avenue			
	121 S. Franklin St. (Meter Location)			
A027	Beeghly Library			
A043	Chappelear Building			
A028	37 Park Avenue			
A029	255 Park Avenue			
A031	225 W. William Street			
A040	199 S. Henry Street			
A041	45 Spring Street			
R004	235 W. William Street			
R011	65 Oak Hill Ave.			
R012	75 Oak Hill Ave.			
R022	216 N. Franklin Street			
R024	24 University Avenue			
R040	94 University Avenue			
R041	104 University Avenue			
R045	88 Oak Hill Avenue			
R047	127 Elmwood Drive			
R051	62 University Avenue			
R051	62 1/2 University Avenue			
TOTAL				

Utilities and property insurance (Exhibit 9). The university allocates these charges to facilities on the basis of square footage, or separate utilities meters when they are available. The form shown in the exhibit is for electricity. Similar forms are used for steam from the central heating plant, for water and sewage, and for property insurance.

Reports

The Data Processing Department uses the cost disk file to print five routine monthly reports. Copies of one page of each of these reports appear as exhibits 10 through 14.

Cost summary (Exhibit 10). This report was the source of the information provided to the finance

Exhibit 10

B_CC...   COST SUMMARY YEAR TO DATE FEBRUARY , 1970   PAGE 2
FOR DIRECTOR OF PHYSICAL PLANT

FACILITY NUMBER	FACILITY CLASS AND NAME		MAINTENANCE	REPAIR	ALTERATIONS	IMPROVEMENTS	TOTAL
A012	ELLIOTT HALL 13,568 SF	TOTAL COST	9,053 .6672	0	0	0	9,053 .6672
A013	SLOCUM HALL 27,400 SF	TOTAL COST	30,085 1.0980	5,977 .2181	0	0	36,062 1.3161
A014	STURGES HALL 14,789 SF	TOTAL COST	15,453 1.0449	493 .0333	0	0	15,946 1.0782
A016	EDWARDS GYMNASIUM 42,961 SF	TOTAL COST	48,775 1.1353	1,172 .0273	0	0	49,947 1.1626
A017	PFEIFFER NATATORIUM 12,774 SF	TOTAL COST	22,040 1.7254	211 .0165	0	0	22,251 1.7419
A018	EAST BOILER HOUSE 8,000 SF	TOTAL COST	88,957 11.1196	753 .0941	170 .0213	0	89,880 11.2350
A020	PERKINS OBSERVATORY 16,943 SF	TOTAL COST	104 .0061	73 .0043	0	0	177 .0104
A023	HUMPHREY ART HALL 12,748 SF	TOTAL COST	14,978 1.1749	208 .0163	0	0	15,186 1.1912
A024	BOOK STORE 6,200 SF	TOTAL COST	2,855 .4605	0	0	0	2,855 .4605
A025	ALUMNI HOUSE 16-16 1/2 UNIV 3,006 SF	TOTAL COST	7,984 2.6560	0	0	8,918 2.9667	16,902 5.6228
A026	MEMORIAL UNION 70,295 SF	TOTAL COST	37,547 1.8501	546 .0269	0	6,386 .3147	44,479 2.1916

committee and other decision-making groups. The illustrated report contains year-to-date figures. A companion report contains figures for the current month. The reports list all facilities as previously described—educational and general buildings, residential buildings, kitchens, utility systems, grounds areas, and special (work not directly related to any of the other facilities). They contain separate columns for the four work types (maintenance, repair, alterations, and improvements).

The costs by work type can be classified as committed (unavoidable) or discretionary. The first two work types, maintenance and repairs, represent largely committed costs, while the remaining two work types, alterations and improvements, contain discretionary costs. As long as a given facility is in use, the institution cannot avoid doing maintenance and repair work. Maintenance can be deferred, of course, but only at the risk of higher repair costs in the future. Alterations and improvements may have an impact on maintenance and repairs, causing either an increase or a decrease, depending on the nature of the work done.

Several factors influence the magnitude of facility operating costs. These factors include the size of the facility, its complexity, and its age. The cost summary includes the size of each facility expressed in square feet. It provides costs per square foot as well as aggregate costs. Costs per square foot can be expected to vary according to the other two factors, age and complexity. The older and more complicated buildings should have higher unit costs than newer and simpler ones.

Making use of these expectations, the director of physical plant can evaluate facility unit costs by comparing each facility with all the others and by comparing the current year report, line by line, with prior year averages. Any unusual figure would indicate a situation to be investigated.

Exhibit 11

HAGGULS   STANDING ORDER STATUS REPORT   FEBRUARY , 1980
FOR DIRECTOR OF PHYSICAL PLANT

DOCUMENT NUMBER	WORK ORDER DATE	CHARGE NUMBER	DESCRIPTION		THIS MONTH	TO DATE	ESTIMATE	AMOUNT REMAINING	PERCENT REMAINING
00007	10-01-79	PL-U001	DTR	07	DOLLARS	26			
					HOURS	2.00			
00007	07-02-79	PL-U004	DTR	17	DOLLARS	26			
					HOURS	125.00			
					DOLLARS	1,187			
			TOTALS		HOURS	456.50	3,177.00		
					DOLLARS	5,728	37,261		
00008	10-08-79	HO-A005	WTR	42	HOURS	8.25			
					DOLLARS	50			
00008	02-18-80	HO-A008	WTR	83	HOURS	2.00	2.00		
					DOLLARS	12	12		
00008	09-03-79	HO-A026	WTR	23	HOURS	94.50	458.50		
					DOLLARS	567	2,749		
00008	10-08-79	HO-A043	WTR	42	HOURS	2.00			
					DOLLARS	12			
00008	01-01-80	HO-S099	WTR	30	HOURS	1.50			
					DOLLARS	9			
			TOTALS		HOURS	96.50	472.25		
					DOLLARS	579	2,832		
00009	07-24-79	GR-S999	DTR	48	HOURS	24.50			
					DOLLARS	222			
			TOTALS		HOURS	24.50			
					DOLLARS	222			
00010	01-07-80	CA-G009	DTR	33	HOURS	8.00			
					DOLLARS	105			
00010	01-07-80	EL-G001	DTR	33	HOURS	11.00	25.00		
					DOLLARS	143	325		
00010	01-07-80	EL-G009	DTR	33	HOURS	13.00	31.00		
					DOLLARS	171	410		
00010	02-19-80	GR-A036	DTR	72	HOURS	1.50	1.50		
					DOLLARS	14	14		
00010	02-08-80	GR-G001	DTR	36	HOURS	6.00	6.00		
					DOLLARS	54	54		
00010	01-09-80	GR-G002	DTR	41	HOURS	18.00			
					DOLLARS	162			
00010	01-04-80	GR-G007	DTR	26	HOURS	59.50	127.00		
					DOLLARS	537	1,146		
00010	01-07-80	GR-G008	DTR	33	HOURS	103.00	214.50		
					DOLLARS	932	1,936		
00010	02-01-80	HO-G001	WTR	14	HOURS	40.25	40.25		
					DOLLARS	246	246		
00010	12-03-79	HO-G007	WTR	08	HOURS	148.50	234.50		

As a building ages and deteriorates, the institution must eventually decide whether to renovate it or replace it with a new structure. This is usually a complicated decision involving many factors, of which the level of maintenance and repair costs is one. Increases in these costs may be the leading indicator that the time for such a decision is approaching.

With the possibility of declining enrollments, some colleges may face problems of excess capacity. An administration may consider closing a building because of this. In such a case, the cost summary report would provide a basis for estimating savings in maintenance and repair costs. A word of caution is in order, however. These costs cannot be reduced to zero. Some minimal maintenance and repair work is necessary to prevent undue deterioration, and to keep the abandoned facility from becoming a safety hazard.

Standing order status report (Exhibit 11). For the use of the director of physical plant, this report lists all standing orders. He knows from the document number the purpose of the order. In the illustration provided, the four different standing orders are as follows:

00007   Preventive maintenance
00008   Event setup
00009   Vandalism repair
00010   Snow removal

A separate line appears for each work center and each facility (charge number column). Thus, 00010 involves carpenters (CA), electricians (EL), groundsmen (GR), and housekeepers (HO), and several different facilities. Facility numbers beginning with G are grounds areas. On this report, the description column actually contains only a reference to the latest source document. DTR and WTR stand for "daily time report" and "weekly time report." The two-digit number is a batch number. While the system provides for hour and dollar estimates, the staff

Exhibit 12

BFCCEC3   WCRK CRDER STATUS REPORT   FEBRUARY , 1980
FOR DIRECTOR OF PHYSICAL PLANT

DOCUMENT NUMBER	WORK ORDER DATE	CHARGE NUMBER	DESCRIPTION		THIS MONTH	TO DATE	ESTIMATE	AMOUNT REMAINING	PERCENT REMAINING
03869	01-17-80	CA-6004	MAKE NEW SIGNS	70	HOURS 3.00	3.00			
					DOLLARS 39	39			
03869	01-17-80	GR-6004	MAKE NEW SIGNS	70	HOURS 58.50	71.50			
					DOLLARS 530	647			
03869	01-17-80	PL-6004	MAKE NEW SIGNS	70	HOURS				
					DOLLARS				
			TOTALS		HOURS 61.50	74.50			
					DOLLARS 569	686			
03870	01-28-80	GR-R008	MOVE & REFINISH PIANOS	12	HOURS 12.00	12.00			
					DOLLARS 108	108			
03870	01-28-80	PA-R008	MOVE & REFINISH PIANOS	12	HOURS 12.00	12.00			
					DOLLARS 144	144			
			TOTALS		HOURS 24.00	24.00			
					DOLLARS 252	252			
03871	01-29-80	PA-R005	NEW DOOR RM 234	12	HOURS 3.00	3.00			
					DOLLARS 36	36			
			TOTALS		HOURS 3.00	3.00			
					DOLLARS 36	36			
03872	01-29-80	CA-81361	SUPPORT SANBORN HALL	12	HOURS				
					DOLLARS				
03872	01-29-80	EL-81361	SUPPORT SANBORN HALL	12	HOURS				
					DOLLARS				
03872	01-29-80	GR-81361	SUPPORT SANBORN HALL	12	HOURS 108.00	108.00			
					DOLLARS 975	975			
03872	01-29-80	LO-81361	SUPPORT SANBORN HALL	12	HOURS				
					DOLLARS				
03872	01-29-80	PA-81361	SUPPORT SANBORN HALL	12	HOURS				
					DOLLARS				
03872	01-29-80	PL-81361	SUPPORT SANBORN HALL	12	HOURS 12.00	12.00			
					DOLLARS 156	156			
03872	01-29-80	UP-81361	SUPPORT SANBORN HALL	12	HOURS				
					DOLLARS				
			TOTALS		HOURS 120.00	120.00			
					DOLLARS 1,131	1,131			
03873	01-29-80	EL-01668	WOMENS TRACK	31	HOURS				
					DOLLARS				

makes little use of that capability. So the last three columns are blank. The director evaluates the actual costs charged to each order on the basis of past experience. (However, the use of predetermined estimates is recommended for all orders of significant size.)

Work order status report (Exhibit 12). This report, also for the director of physical plant, lists open work orders. Usually a work order covers only one facility, but it may involve several trade shops. For example, 03872, support of contractors renovating Sanborn Hall, includes carpenters, electricians, groundsmen, locksmiths, painters, plumbers, and upholsterers. The director can use this report to evaluate the overall status of the job. Again, the use of predetermined estimates would be desirable for large jobs.

In the Sanborn Hall example, the facility number is an unexpended plant fund account. General ledger account numbers are used in place of facility numbers whenever a job is to be charged in the general accounting system to something other than the director of physical plant's budget accounts. The most common cases are charges to unexpended plant funds for capital projects and to other departmental budget accounts for special work other than regular operation and maintenance.

Outstanding work orders (Exhibit 13). These reports are for the use of individual shop foremen. The illustrated report lists only the painters' jobs, although other trades might be involved in each of these work orders.

Note that the reports illustrated in exhibits 11, 12, and 13 have identified column headings. They are all listings of open orders. They result from the same computer program. Only the selection criteria and sort sequences differ. Exhibit 11 contains document type 3; exhibits 12 and 13 are document type 2. Exhibits 11 and 12 are sorted by document number, ex-

Exhibit 13

HXGCOLG PAINTERS   OUTSTANDING WORK ORDERS   FEBRUARY , 1980

DOCUMENT NUMBER	WORK ORDER DATE	CHARGE NUMBER	DESCRIPTION			THIS MONTH	TO DATE	ESTIMATE	AMOUNT REMAINING	PERCENT REMAINING
03849	12-18-79	PA-6007	CONSTRUCT BENCH	65	HOURS DOLLARS					
03851	01-02-80	PA-S099	MAKE SIGNS	36	HOURS DOLLARS	6.00 72	6.00 72			
03852	01-04-80	PA-S006	REPAIR FURNITURE	36	HOURS DOLLARS					
03862	01-23-80	PA-S016	PAINT ROOMS	70	HOURS DOLLARS	10.00 120	10.00 120			
03864	01-10-80	PA-R006	TERMITE DAMAGE	49	HOURS DOLLARS					
03866	01-16-80	PA-A023	RPR RM 1 HUMPHREY	70	HOURS DOLLARS	28.00 336	28.00 336			
03867	01-15-80	PA-R001	PAINT SMOKER	70	HOURS DOLLARS	112.00 1,344	160.00 1,920			
03870	01-28-80	PA-R008	MOVE & REFINISH PIANOS	12	HOURS DOLLARS	12.00 144	12.00 144			
03871	01-29-80	PA-R005	NEW DOOR RM 234	12	HOURS DOLLARS	3.00 36	3.00 36			
03872	01-29-80	PA-81361	SUPPORT SANBORN HALL	12	HOURS DOLLARS					
03875	01-26-80	PA-R013	PAINT PLYWOOD	12	HOURS DOLLARS					

hibit 13 by work center code and then document number.

These reports list all open orders, regardless of dollar amount. Several reporting variations could be considered. An institution could list only orders with dollar balances over a certain minimum amount, or with estimates over a certain amount, or with dollar balances in excess of the estimates. Such limits would make the lists shorter and would highlight significant data.

Work orders completed (Exhibit 14). For the director of physical plant, this report presents final figures for all jobs finished during the month.

Cost selection (Exhibit 15). To supplement the five routine monthly reports, the director of physical plant can request from data processing a cost selection report for any individual facility. This report lists, and then summarizes, all repair requests, work orders, service orders, and standing orders charged to the facility for a given month or for the year to date. Exhibit 15 shows the final page of such a report, covering Facility S070, a special facility number for nonuniversity functions. The director uses these selections to investigate any facility cost balances that attract his attention when he reviews the cost summary.

Motor Pool and Central Receiving

The director of physical plant oversees both the motor pool and central receiving. However, the cost accounting system for operation and maintenance of plant does not include the costs of these departments. Central receiving expenditures are classified as institutional support in the university's financial statements. The university operates the motor pool as a service department and charges the costs to the using departments.

Exhibit 14

DOCUMENT NUMBER	WORK ORDER DATE	CHARGE NUMBER	DESCRIPTION			ACTUAL	ORIGINAL ESTIMATE	VARIANCE	PER CENT VARIANCE
03522	08-22-79	HO-R018	MISC REPAIRS	06	HOURS	199.00			
					DOLLARS	897			
			TOTAL		HOURS	202.00 **	**	**	**
			TOTAL		DOLLARS	936 **	**	**	**
03523	09-03-79	CA-R015	DTR	33	HOURS	31.00			
					DOLLARS	404			
03523	10-01-79	LO-R015	DOOR & WINDOW REPAIR	08	HOURS	14.00			
					DOLLARS	182			
			TOTAL		HOURS	45.00 **	**	**	**
			TOTAL		DOLLARS	586 **	**	**	**
03524	09-21-79	PA-G007	BARRICADE WALKWAY	08	HOURS	3.00			
					DOLLARS	36			
03524	09-13-79	PL-G007	BARRICADE WALKWAY	08	HOURS	39.75			
					DOLLARS	517			
			TOTAL		HOURS	42.75 **	**	**	**
			TOTAL		DOLLARS	553 **	**	**	**
03525	02-15-80	PA-R001	PAINT ROOMS	08	HOURS	1,113.00			
					DOLLARS	9,380			
			TOTAL		HOURS	1,113.00 **	**	**	**
			TOTAL		DOLLARS	9,380 **	**	**	**
03527	11-15-79	PA-R005	PAINT ROOMS	08	HOURS	1,329.25			
					DOLLARS	9,375			
			TOTAL		HOURS	1,329.25 **	**	**	**
			TOTAL		DOLLARS	9,375 **	**	**	**
03528	11-15-79	PA-R008	PAINT ROOMS	08	HOURS	68.00			
					DOLLARS	652			
			TOTAL		HOURS	68.00 **	**	**	**
			TOTAL		DOLLARS	652 **	**	**	**
03531	11-15-79	PA-R011	PAINT AREAS	08	HOURS	9.00			
					DOLLARS	86			
			TOTAL		HOURS	9.00 **	**	**	**
			TOTAL		DOLLARS	86 **	**	**	**
03533	11-15-79	PA-R024	PAINT AREAS	08	HOURS	31.00			
					DOLLARS	350			
			TOTAL		HOURS	31.00 **	**	**	**
			TOTAL		DOLLARS	350 **	**	**	**
03536	07-13-79	CA-R001	MAINTENANCE INSPECTIONS	36	HOURS	52.00			
					DOLLARS	456			

Depreciation

A matter of continuing controversy is the role of depreciation in college and university accounting. Generally accepted accounting principles do not require depreciation provisions in the financial statements. Educational institutions may, however, record depreciation in the plant funds if they wish to do so, and Office of Management and Budget Circular A-21 does allow depreciation as an indirect cost of government grants and contracts.

Articles calling for mandatory depreciation provisions by colleges and universities appear from time to time. Usually the authors are certified public accountants in public practice rather than college accountants. The influence of public accountants is such, however, that this issue is not going to disappear.

The Financial Accounting Standards Board (FASB) has assumed (from the American Institute of Certified Public Accountants) the jurisdiction for public reporting by what they call "nonbusiness entities." This group includes colleges. Undoubtedly FASB will consider the depreciation question sooner or later.

Ohio Wesleyan does not presently provide for depreciation in its accounting records, either in the general financial statements or in the cost accounting system for operation and maintenance of plant. In one sense, depreciation, the gradual deterioration of buildings and equipment, is clearly a cost of operation. However, the university does not expect its students to bear this cost through their tuition payments. Ohio Wesleyan has consistently raised funds for plant additions and improvements through gifts and grants. This is the practice followed by the

Exhibit 15

```
DATE  04/29/80                          BUILDINGS AND GROUNDS                        REPORT BG302.8
TIME  01:39                             COST SELECTION REPORT                           PAGE  110
                                  MONTH-TO-DATE           APRIL    1980
```

DOCUMENT: CODE/NUMBER	WORK: CENTER/TYPE		ACCOUNT NUMBER	DATES: DOCUMENT/ COMPLETION	DESCRIPTION	ESTIMATED DOLLARS	MONTHLY: HOURS/ DOLLARS	YEARLY: HOURS/ DOLLARS	BATCH: MONTH, YEAR/ NUMBER
2 03963	EL	M	S070	04/01/80	SCIENCE FAIR 1980	0	84.00 1,092	84.00 1,092	APR, 80 93
2 03963	GR	M	S070	04/01/80	SCIENCE FAIR 1980	0	0.00 0	0.00 0	APR, 80 18
2 03963	HO	M	S070	04/01/80	SCIENCE FAIR 1980	0	0.00 0	0.00 0	APR, 80 18
2 03963	SE	M	S070	04/01/80	SCIENCE FAIR 1980	0	0.00 0	0.00 0	APR, 80 18
3 03059	OS	M	S070	11/26/79 10/31/79	CHAIR RENTAL	650	0.00 0	0.00 530	NOV, 79 02
3 03228	OS	M	S070	04/23/80 04/21/80	MOVE PIANO	80	0.00 92	0.00 92	APR, 80 02
4 00012	HO	M	S070	02/04/80	WTR	0	0.00 0	5.00 30	FEB, 80 28

```
                              *** SUBTOTALS:   HOURS            89.00         239.50
                                               DOLLARS    730   1,214         2,762
```

```
                        *** BREAKDOWN BY DOCUMENT CODE

                        REPAIR REQUEST:   HOURS            0.00          0.00
                                          DOLLARS     0      0             0

                        WORK ORDER:       HOURS            89.00         234.50
                                          DOLLARS     0    1,122         2,110

                        SERVICE ORDER:    HOURS            0.00          0.00
                                          DOLLARS   730     92            622

                        STANDING ORDER:   HOURS            0.00          5.00
                                          DOLLARS     0      0            30
```

majority of colleges and universities, and it is the reason depreciation is not required by generally accepted accounting principles.

If it should be decided to add depreciation to the physical plant cost accounting system, it could easily be done. In the plant funds section of the general ledger is a separate account for each building and for the equipment in each building. There are also separate accounts for such high cost equipment items as computers, organs, etc. The book values of these assets are cost for assets purchased and fair market value at date of gift for donated assets. Using these records, the institution could calculate and record depreciation individually for each facility.

Regardless of what may happen in the area of generally accepted accounting principles, it is expected that the university will give further consideration to depreciation as a factor in the physical plant cost accounting system.

Internal Control

The university uses various internal control features to insure the reliability of cost figures. The director of physical plant, his assistant, and the shop foremen review and sign the various source documents. Office staff batch source documents together for data entry and run tapes to obtain dollar batch totals. They subsequently balance those dollar batch totals to computer-printed batch lists. Prior to the month-end reporting, they and the data processing staff balance all dollar transactions on the disk file to cumulative batch totals. The computer updating program guides the terminal operator with a sequence of questions and responses, and allows for a visual review of data on the terminal screen. All employees involved with the system are carefully trained and supervised, and the work follows a well-established routine.

As part of the month-end balancing, the computer prints out year-to-date dollar totals for each work center. Accounting office personnel reconcile these totals to the corresponding account balances in the general ledger. They prepare a report showing the differences for the director of physical plant. Significant differences could be caused by wage rate or price changes not yet reflected in the standard rates used in the cost system. They could also be caused by a failure of workers to account for all of their time on repair requests or work orders, or simply by errors not detected through other means. The director investigates any significant differences and takes corrective action.

Use of the calendar month as the time interval for internal reports is fairly common. Of course, the time interval could be shorter (a week) or longer (a quarter or semester). Extending the period might make balancing and investigating problems more difficult, however, as more transactions would be involved and people's memories of specific events would be less clear. Shortening the period would result in more timely data, but it might produce too many reports and discourage careful study of any of them.

Accounting Office

Personnel in the university's accounting office use the cost summary reports as a source of data for certain entries made in the general ledger. They prepare a monthly journal entry to charge auxiliary enterprise operations with the cost of operation and maintenance of auxiliary enterprise-related facilities. The credit goes to an account in the 01700 group entitled "Physical Plant Charges Redistributed." They make similar entries for costs to be charged to unexpended plant funds or to individual departments. As previously described, these latter costs appear in the cost summaries by account number rather than by facility number. A separate study deals more fully with auxiliary enterprise costs.

Conclusion

The director of physical plant says the system is valuable to him and well worth the cost. The cost includes a small amount of time devoted by each of the foremen to source documents, and the equivalent of one office employee. In return, the director, his assistant, and the foremen receive information for controlling the operation. Each month, they review the routine cost reports to determine the status and cost of jobs in process, and the cost of completed jobs. They confer on these matters, often rearranging priorities and investigating the reasons for cost overruns.

Accounting office personnel make use of the cost summary reports monthly to write certain journal entries. These journal entries transfer appropriate facilities costs from educational and general expenditures to auxiliary enterprise expenditures and to other departmental or capital accounts. The cost summary reports also provide data for long-range planning and top-level management decision making. This is probably the most significant benefit of the system.

support and services

This chapter describes cost accounting procedures for three specific areas identified by the *CUBA* chart of accounts—academic support, institutional support, and student services. The academic support area encompasses several activities necessary to the instructional program. Foremost among these activities are libraries, without which the instructional program could hardly function. Institutional support includes the central administration and the range of services required for effective operation of the educational enterprise. The student services area embraces a diverse set of activities ranging from cultural programs to athletics and recreation, from counseling to health services, from housing to admissions and financial aid. A detailed description of support activities is given in exhibit 1-A, which follows chapter 1.

Need for and Uses of Cost Data

Academic support, institutional support, and student services contribute significantly to the instruction, public service, and research missions of colleges and universities. A determination of the full costs of these final cost objectives, therefore, relies on cost data for the support and service areas. The costs in the support and service areas can also affect the costs of providing auxiliary services. The institutional support area, for example, contributes to the management and operation of the bookstore, food service, and housing functions.

Several of the academic support activities contribute to the institution's public service mission. Libraries, museums, galleries, and clinics may all be available to the general public. The costs of operating these activities may be supported by user charges. In such cases, a cost accounting system can enable administrators to determine the full costs of each activity and to develop unit costs by user groups.

This information can assist policy makers in setting appropriate user charges for both the academic community and the community at large.

Cost data on institutional support and student services can assist managers and policy makers in the often difficult retrenchment or expansion decisions necessary to preserve institutional vitality. Cost information also provides administrators with the data necessary to evaluate alternative levels of service.

Cost data for institutional support may be useful in decisions regarding how an institution should organize its services. To what extent should duplicating services, for example, be a central administration function, and how much of this function should be done by individual organizational units?

Cost Centers in the Support and Service Areas

The major headings in the *CUBA* chart of accounts (exhibit 1-A) define academic support, institutional support, and student services activities as follows:

Academic Support
  Libraries
  Museums and Galleries
  Audiovisual Services
  Ancillary Support
  Academic Administration/Personnel Development
  Computing Support
  Course and Curriculum Development
Student Services
  Student Services Administration
  Social and Cultural Activities
  Counseling and Career Guidance
  Financial Aid Administration
  Student Admissions and Records
  Health and Infirmary Services

Institutional Support
  Executive Management
  Fiscal Operations
  General Administrative Services
  Logistical Services
  Community Relations

For the purposes of this handbook each of these activities has been designated as a cost center. Each of the *CUBA* subcategories outlined in exhibit 1-A, such as purchasing, motor pool, and print shop, may also be identified as a specific cost center in a cost accounting system designed to determine costs at lower organizational levels. Where the *CUBA* structure does not agree with the institutional chart of accounts, the institution should determine the definition and organization of cost centers. At some institutions, for example, audiovisual services may be a part of the library system. The cost centers suggested here may be merged, or additional centers may be established according to institutional needs and ability to support the system.

The allocation of costs should follow a set of cost categories including—at a minimum—personnel compensation, supplies and operating expenses, and other objects of expenditure contained in cost center budgets. The direct costs for each cost center include personnel and supplies along with other objects of expenditure identified in the unit's financial records and budget. These direct costs comprise the tier one costs outlined in chapter 1.

Allocation of Indirect Costs

A tier two analysis requires information on not only the tier one or direct costs, but also on the indirect costs that should be allocated to the benefiting cost centers. This section considers the potential sources of indirect costs for cost centers within the support and service cost objectives.

Many of the sources of indirect costs affect virtually all of the cost centers in the institution. Fiscal operations, general administrative services, logistical services, and plant operation and maintenance contribute indirect costs to all of the support and service area cost centers. These sources of indirect costs include a host of institutionwide services, such as accounting, data processing, employee personnel and records, purchasing, security, custodial services, buildings and equipment maintenance, and utilities.

Executive management also contributes indirect costs to the entire institution, but the procedure used for allocating executive management costs in the student services area differs from the procedure used for

the sources of indirect costs mentioned above. The student services area has its own administrative cost center, so all executive management indirect costs that should be allocated to the student services cost objective are first allocated to the student services administration cost center. The costs of the student services administration cost center—including executive management indirect costs—are then allocated as indirect costs to the other student services cost centers.

Two Illustrations

The following illustrations demonstrate how cost accounting can be used in the support and service areas discussed in this chapter. The first is a counseling and career guidance center in the student services area; the second is a gallery in the academic support area. For an illustration of cost accounting in the institutional support area, refer to the motor pool example in chapter 1.

Illustration 1: Counseling and Career Guidance

The counseling and career guidance cost center—according to the *CUBA* chart of accounts—includes counseling, placement, and foreign students' programs. The illustration here, however, does not consider the individual components, but rather the cost center as a whole. Some institutions may need further disaggregation to achieve their purposes.

Figure 5.1 outlines the tier one (direct) costs for counseling and career guidance. The tier one costs are the familiar items identifiable in the unit's budget and financial records. The total tier one costs in this illustration are $66,950.

Figure 5.1
Counseling and Career Guidance Costs
(Tier One)

Tier one costs

Personnel compensation	
Salaries or wages	$48,400
Employee benefits	8,550
Supplies	6,000
Other items in unit budget, such as travel and postage	4,000
Total tier one costs	$66,950

Indirect costs for counseling and career guidance have several sources and are allocated on different bases. Figure 5.2 highlights the sources of indirect costs and the allocation bases selected for this illustration.

Figure 5.2
Indirect Cost Allocation Bases for Counseling and Career Guidance

Indirect Costs	Allocation Bases
Plant operation and maintenance, e.g., custodial services, utilities, and building and equipment	Assignable square feet
Fiscal operations, e.g., accounting and cashier's office	Actual usage data such as number of accounting transactions, or total direct costs
General administrative services, e.g., administrative data processing personnel	Actual usage data such as job orders, computer time, or total direct costs
Logistical services, e.g., business management, material management, and service departments (motor pool, duplicating, etc.)	Actual usage data such as vouchers or purchase orders, or total direct costs

Chapter 2 provides a set of allocation bases for these as well as other indirect costs. The methods chosen depend on the data systems of the institution and on the specific objectives of the cost accounting system.

The allocation of student services administration costs to the counseling and career guidance cost center can illustrate the total compensation proration technique. The total compensation of each of the student services cost centers is divided by the total compensation for the student services cost objective (not including the student services administration cost center), as shown in figure 5.3.

Figure 5.3
Allocation of Student Services Administration Costs to Benefiting Cost Center

Cost Centers	Total Compensation	Percentage
Social and cultural activities	$ 16,750	5%
Counseling and career guidance	56,950	17
Financial aid administration	60,300	18
Student admissions and records	167,500	50
Health and infirmary services	33,500	10
Total	$335,000	100%

The percentage column represents the proration factors to be applied to the cost of student services administration in order to allocate all the administrative costs to benefiting cost centers. In this illustration the cost of student services administration is $90,000; the amount prorated as indirect costs to counseling and career guidance is $15,300 (17 percent of $90,000). Included in the student services administration costs are those executive management costs allocated to the student services cost objective.

Other indirect costs attributable to the counseling and career guidance cost center include the cost associated with fiscal operations, plant operation and maintenance, general administration, and logistical services. Figure 5.4 provides the details. Note that only those indirect costs that are material to the operation of the cost center have been included in figure 5.4. The total indirect costs attributable to the cost center are $19,800, and the total tier two costs are $86,750.

A facilities usage charge of $2,000 is attributable to the cost center. When this cost is combined with the tier two costs of $86,750, the total tier three or *full* costs for the counseling and career guidance cost center are $88,750.

Figure 5.4
Counseling and Career Guidance Costs (Tiers Two and Three)

Tier two costs

Indirect costs	
Student services administration (see figure 5.3 and narrative following)	$15,300
Plant operation and maintenance	
Buildings and equipment maintenance	500
Utilities	700
Custodial services	900
Institutional support	
Fiscal operations (accounting, cashier's office)	500
General administrative services	
Administrative data processing	650
Other general administrative services	300
Logistical services (purchasing, motor pool, duplicating costs)	950
Attributable indirect costs	$19,800
Total tier one costs (see figure 5.1)	66,950
Total tier two costs	$86,750

Tier three costs

Facilities usage charge	$ 2,000
Total tier two costs (see above)	$86,750
Total tier three costs	$88,750

The cost data developed in this illustration may be used to derive unit costs and to examine historical trends in the costs of providing counseling and career guidance. Further disaggregation of the data would allow analysts to compare the full costs of different types of counseling services, e.g., foreign student programs and placement.

Illustration 2: The Gallery

The following illustration uses the gallery cost center to demonstrate cost accounting procedures in the academic support area. Figures 5.5 and 5.6 present the tiers one, two, and three costs for a small,

---

Figure 5.5
Costs for the Gallery Cost Center
(Tiers One and Two)

Tier one costs

Personnel compensation

Salaries or wages	$30,000
Employee benefits	5,300
Supplies	1,000
Refurbishing	5,000
Membership (National Society of Museum Directors)	100
Other	1,000
Total tier one costs	$42,400

Tier two costs

Indirect costs

Executive management	$ 400
Plant operation and maintenance	
Building and equipment maintenance	3,000
Utilities	2,400
Custodial services	5,000
Institutional support	
Fiscal operations (accounting and cashier's office)	900
General administrative services (administrative data processing and personnel)	600
Logistical services (purchasing, duplicating, and motor pool)	1,500
Attributable indirect costs	13,800
Total tier one costs (see above)	42,400
Total tier two costs	$56,200

---

college-operated gallery. The tier one, or direct, costs are the gallery budget items—personnel, supplies, refurbishing, membership, and others. In this illustration, the total tier one costs are $42,400.

The membership costs are included in tier one because they appear in the gallery budget. According to the *CUBA* chart of accounts, membership is listed in the "general" category under institutional support. This illustration assumes that the institution does not have a centralized membership function and that each organizational unit is responsible for its own membership fees.

The indirect costs in tier two come from several areas of institutional support and plant operation and maintenance. The cost accounting system may allocate these indirect costs in a variety of ways (see chapter 2). In this illustration, the allocation bases are as follows:

Indirect Costs	Allocation Bases
Executive management	Total direct costs
Plant operation and maintenance, e.g., custodial services, utilities, and building and equipment maintenance	Assignable square feet
Fiscal operations, e.g., accounting and cashier's office	Total direct costs
General administrative services, e.g., administrative data processing and personnel	Actual usage data or total direct costs
Logistical services, e.g., purchasing, duplicating, and motor pool	Actual usage data, such as purchase orders

These bases for allocation—as the example itself—are illustrative and are not intended as prescribed methods. The objectives of the cost accounting system and the availability of data should guide analysts in the selection of reasonable allocation methods for their institutions.

The attributable indirect costs for the gallery in this illustration are $13,800. The tier two costs of operating the gallery are $56,200.

Figure 5.6 shows the tier three costs—tier two plus depreciation or use charge on facilities and capital equipment. The depreciation costs in this illustration include a $3,000 facilities usage charge and $1,000 for depreciation of equipment. The total tier three or *full* costs of operating the gallery are $60,200.

Figure 5.6
Costs for the Gallery Cost Center
(Tier Three)

<u>Tier three costs</u>

Buildings use charge and depreciation on capital
equipment

Facilities usage charge	$ 3,000
Equipment depreciation	1,000
Subtotal depreciation costs	4,000
Total tier two costs (see figure 5.5)	56,200
Total tier three costs	$60,200

Policy makers at the institution can use the full cost data in any decisions regarding user charges. The college may choose to operate the gallery as a part of its commitment to public service. As with public services provided by governmental units, the gallery can be subsidized—in this case by the college—or it can charge its users. In a period of financial retrenchment, the aim may be to establish a user charge that covers all or part of the cost of providing the service.

Cost Accounting for Libraries

The importance and usefulness of cost accounting for libraries are reflected in the literature on the subject. This section offers a brief review of relevant documents (see References for full citations).

Leimkuhler and Cooper (1971) offer a general approach to library planning based on cost accounting models developed and tested with data from the University of California, Berkeley. The Office of Management Studies of the Association of Research Libraries produces a user series, entitled "Systems and Procedures Exchange Center (SPEC)." The SPEC publication, "Library Materials Cost Studies" (January 1980), is a set of documents designed to assist library analysts in the tasks of data collection and economic trend analysis. *Costing for Policy Analysis* includes a study of fixed and variable costs of library services for four academic libraries within the University of Wisconsin System.

Three studies consider the unit cost and fee-setting issues. Densmore and Bourne (1965) analyze the Stanford University library system to determine the proper allocation of charges to four user groups—undergraduate students, graduate students, faculty and staff, and non-Stanford users. Nachlas and Pierce (1979) illustrate a microcosting methodology by determining the unit costs of tracking overdue materials. SPEC's "Fees for Services" (1981)

discusses the policy issues of which services should have fees and which users should be charged.

Unit Costs for Support Activities

Unit cost data in the support and service areas may help administrators in several ways. Among these is the determination of user charges and fees for specific services.

As in other areas of the institution, unit costs for academic support services are useful in analyzing historical trends. The costs of particular library services—periodicals, for example—may be especially important to track: unit cost data can support requests for external funding or can justify user fees.

The illustration of the motor pool cost center in chapter 1 demonstrates the use of unit cost data in the institutional support area. In that illustration the data generated by the cost accounting system are combined with related data in the motor pool function to produce certain output measures, such as the cost per vehicle per mile by type of vehicle. Institutional analysts can compare these output measures with the cost of leasing vehicles from outside vendors.

In the student services area, cost data can be combined with a wide range of student data to produce unit cost measures. The student data may be available in institutional records and may include such distinctions as the following:

Enrollment by program	Degree, nondegree; liberal arts, occupational
Enrollment status	Full-time, part-time; credit, noncredit
Residence	Student housing, commuter
Financial aid	Recipients by source of aid

In the financial aid administration cost center, for example, unit cost data could include administrative costs per student receiving aid or the administrative costs per total student aid awarded. The costs per aid awarded by source of aid would enable analysts to compare the administrative efficiency of external and internal student aid programs. These data can supplement other institutional planning and evaluation techniques, such as the planning and data system module on student financial aid of the Council of Independent Colleges (CIC, formerly CASC).

Unit cost data collected over a period of years can help administrators determine cost trends in different functions. These trends may guide internal management decisions regarding the type and level of services to provide and may assist administrators in projecting future costs.

The literature on cost analysis in the student services area is limited. One particularly good source is *Costing for Policy Analysis* (NACUBO/NCHEMS), which includes a student services case study for Santa Fe Community College in Gainesville, Florida. The case study emphasizes the variable and fixed costs aspect of cost analysis as well as the usefulness of marginal costing in the student services area.

Costing for Computer Services Case Study

Computer services is a support area in which the need for cost information is particularly important. Exhibit 5-A, which follows, explains the use of cost data in that area.

exhibit 5-a

case study:
maricopa county community college
computer services

Background

The Maricopa County Community College District is located in Arizona, and its center of population is Phoenix. Computer services are supplied centrally for both instruction and administrative purposes. A separate system is dedicated to each group of users.

Although this district is not considered to be "small," the principles in this case study are basically the same for any institution, regardless of size. For example, a small college with one computer will provide service to both instructional (academic) and administrative users. The costs involved for the single computer can easily be prorated to the two (or more) categories of users. Additional user groups, such as researchers, may be evident and significant in an institution.

The System

For approximately 15 years, the cost of computer services was budgeted centrally and no chargeback system was involved. The basis for the centralized budgeting system was the promotion of greater computer usage, both in scope and in volume. There was no "hindrance to the instructional program" in that the district was experiencing rapid growth and adequate resources were available. However, no control or discipline was exercised, and student game-playing (not necessarily a negative phenomenon) became widespread. During those years, a highly centralized organizational mode existed.

The centralized mode was changed in 1979-80 to one of decentralization of authority and responsibility, with each college president being given much greater authority over expenditures. This was a major factor in establishing computer services as a support department. A distinction can be drawn between "service" and "support" departments: a "ser-vice department" provides predetermined services and/or work on the basis of individual or project-type requests for or within a specified period of time; a "support department" performs activities, services, or work that is recharged or charged back to the users in instruction, research, and public services areas. Within the technical definitions, this system is a mixture of both "service" and "support." A centrally funded department, regardless of the nature of the service and/or support functions, may be a "free" or a "paid for" service. The college's experience has shown that "paid for" services lead to more efficient use of resources because users must analyze future (one-year and long-range) needs realistically, justify the requested appropriation through budget hearings, and pay for services rendered.

Each cost center* is a potential user of computer services. Therefore, each cost center budgets annually for such services. Rates are established annually for services and this enables cost centers to establish amounts needed. Computer center personnel aid budget units, particularly in the area of requested new services. (Figure 5-A-1 contains a computer services price schedule.) For example, the unit price for CPU time is based on actual costs for the system. Actual costs include the lease or rental of equipment and the amortization of purchased software packages or the lease-purchase payments. If the hardware has been purchased, its amortized cost becomes a cost factor. Neither the amortization of the cost of the building nor the cost of maintaining and operating the space is considered a cost in this process. Such costs may be considered in the future, but they are presently absorbed within the central budget. Peripheral equipment usage is priced in ac-

---

*A department/division or other organizational unit.

Figure 5-A-1
1981-82 Price Schedule for Computer Services

Equipment	Internal Users	Outside* Users
**Univac Computer		
Cards read/card (600 cards/minute)	$ .0010	$ .0010
Printed lines/thousand (600 lines/minute)	1.00	2.00
Punched cards/card (400 cards/minute)	.0015	.0030
Mass storage/track/day (10,752 character/track)	.01	.02
SUP/hour (demand) or block time	55.00	110.00
Connect time/hour (demand)	.50	.50
SUP/hour (batch)	45.00	75.00
Tape storage/day	.16	.25
Tape usage/hour	1.00	1.00
Tape mount	1.00	1.00
**Itel Computer		
Cards read/card (600 cards/minute)	$ .0010	$ .0010
Printed lines/thousand (600 lines/minute)	1.00	2.00
Mass storage/track/day (10,752 character/track)	.01	.02
Block time/hour	55.00	110.00
Tape storage/day	.16	.25
Tape usage/hour	1.00	1.00
Tape mount	1.00	1.00
Connect time/hour (demand)	.50	.50
Staff		
Analyst/hour ($120/day)	$15.00	$ 20.00
Programmer/hour ($96/day)	12.00	17.00
Unit record operator/hour	9.00	13.00
Control clerk/hour	8.00	13.00
Computer operator/hour	9.00	13.00
Keypunch/verify/hour	8.00	9.00
$\frac{(12,000/\text{strokes/hour})}{60} = 200$ cards/hour keypunch		
Supplies		
Cards (5081/1000 cards)	$ 2.20	$ 2.75
Paper (one-part wide/2400 sheets)	16.50	16.50
Microfiche/frame (copies @$.06/copy)	.0061	.0061
Microfilm/frame (copies @$.02/¼ ft.)	.01	.01

---

*Nonprofit organizations only.

** Does not include labor charges, which are calculated on the basis of staff time costs.

---

cordance with usage. Special computer services are priced individually, based on the level of personnel and time devoted to the project (the development of a new program or the enhancement of a present program for one user are examples of factors to consider in pricing). Costing for computer services encompasses the following:

1. Calculation of CPU time charges (see figure 5-A-1).

2. Calculation of peripheral equipment charges (see figure 5-A-1).

3. Calculation of rates for personnel and equipment devoted to special or developmental projects (see figure 5-A-1 and examples of computer charges displayed at the end of the case study).

Another question that should be addressed in costing for computer services is whether *all* costs of the computer services department should be borne by the users. The college's conclusion is that computer services should not operate entirely on this basis because many of the costs are fixed. However, this *can* be done if desired by adjusting the rate at the end of the year and charging back all costs to the users. It was found that users strongly prefer to have definite costs prior to budget adoption. This system, of course, causes the computer services department to budget for and absorb the difference between total costs and "revenue" generated from or paid for by

the users. This system, however, does encourage the computer services department to market its products more efficiently so that its costs are reduced and the basis for requesting funds for central development of applications is expanded.

The costing process for computer services outlined above works well in this district, and it is believed that the principles underlying the system can be effectively applied to any computer system, regardless of size.

RUN DATE 4/29/81 (ITLACT-01)   DETAIL LISTING BY ACCOUNT/INSTRUCTOR/JOB   REPORTING SYSTEM   PAGE 1

REPORTING FROM 4/01/1981 THRU 4/30/1981 SELECTED FROM : THRU : DAILY   ITEL VSI

ACCOUNT	JOB NAME	CPU TIME MIN:SEC	CONNECT TIME HRS:MIN	DEMAND/ BATCH	TERMINAL LINE ID	DATE	START TIME	CPU $	I-O $	CONNECT $	TOTAL $
D1000	SYO01	0:09	0:00	BATCH	000	27 APR 81	7:09	1.80	0.00	0.00	1.80
D1000	SYO01	0:09	0:00	BATCH	000	27 APR 81	8:08	0.20	0.00	0.00	0.20
D1000	SYO01	0:09	0:00	BATCH	000	27 APR 81	8:52	1.80	0.00	0.00	1.80
D1000	DAPTPLBL	0:00	0:00	BATCH	000	27 APR 81	9:37	0.00	0.00	0.00	0.00
D1000	SYO01	0:07	0:00	BATCH	000	27 APR 81	10:20	1.60	0.00	0.00	1.60
D1000	SHART	0:09	0:00	BATCH	000	27 APR 81	10:26	2.00	0.00	0.00	2.00
D1000	SYO01	0:00	0:00	BATCH	000	27 APR 81	10:43	0.00	0.00	0.00	0.00
D1000	DAPTPLBL	0:00	0:00	BATCH	000	27 APR 81	10:51	0.00	0.00	0.00	0.00
D1000	SDBRESLR	0:12	0:00	BATCH	000	27 APR 81	11:12	2.60	0.00	0.00	2.60
D1000	SDBRESLR	0:12	0:00	BATCH	000	27 APR 81	11:21	2.60	0.00	0.00	2.60
D1000	SYO01	0:00	0:00	BATCH	000	27 APR 81	16:32	0.20	0.00	0.00	0.20
D1000	SHART	0:07	0:00	BATCH	000	27 APR 81	17:25	1.60	0.00	0.00	1.60
D1000	SHART	0:07	0:00	BATCH	000	27 APR 81	19:39	1.60	0.00	0.00	1.60
D1000	SHART	0:07	0:00	BATCH	000	27 APR 81	20:24	1.60	0.00	0.00	1.60
D1000	SDPROB3	0:09	0:00	BATCH	000	27 APR 81	21:43	2.00	0.00	0.00	2.00
D1000	SDPROB3	0:09	0:00	BATCH	000	27 APR 81	21:43	2.00	0.00	0.00	2.00
D1000	SYO01	0:09	0:00	DEMAND	000	28 APR 81	12:46	2.00	0.00	0.00	2.00

TOTALS FOR ACCOUNT   2:00   0:00   25.40   0.00   0.00   25.40
TOTALS FOR ACCOUNT   2:02   0:00

GROUP TOTALS   0:00   0:00   0.00   0.00   0.00   0.00
GROUP TOTALS   2:02   0:00   25.40   0.00   0.00   25.40

UNIVAC

[LG6-01] RUN DATE 04/01/80   DISTRICT DP (TEST)   T CALDWELL   PAGE 1

ACCOUNTING AND BILLING SYSTEM FROM 3/01/80 THRU 3/31/80
D E T A I L   L I S T I N G BY ACCOUNT/JOB/PROJECT/RUN-ID

ACCOUNT SECTION	JOB OR PROJECT OR NAME	RUN IDENT	RUN TYPE	CARDS IN	CARDS OUT	PAGES	TOTAL TIME HRS:MM:SS.DEC	DATE	TIME ON	TIME OFF	CONNECT TIME
DDPTST	-SDPS-	AHFM1	BATCH	156	0	107	2:56:28.071	3/24	9:06:15	10:26:56	1:20:41
DDPTST	-SDPS-	AHFM1	BATCH	1,161	0	617	2:44:28.042	3/25	15:42:40	19:43:59	4:01:19
DDPTST	-SDPS-	AHFM1	BATCH	17	0	67	55.979	3/25	6:10:18	6:13:29	0:03:11
RUN TOTALS FOR AHFM1				*1,334	0	*791	3:42:12.093			********	5:25:11
DDPTST	-SDPS-	AHFM2	BATCH	16	0	351	4:18.709	3/24	19:44:31	19:54:47	0:10:16
RUN TOTALS FOR AHFM2				*16	0	*351	4:18.709			********	0:10:16
DDPTST	-SDPS-	COFA	BATCH	4	0	1	2.049	3/31	14:59:21	14:59:23	0:00:02
RUN TOTALS FOR COFA				*4	0	*1	2.049			********	0:00:02
DDPTST	-SDPS-	COFAA	BATCH	2,557	0	127	1:29.617	3/31	14:59:24	15:35:24	0:36:00
RUN TOTALS FOR COFAA				*2,557	0	*127	1:29.617			********	0:36:00
DDPTST	-SDPS-	SSIS9	BATCH	20	0	31	4:3.934	3/31	10:47:34	10:52:37	0:05:03
RUN TOTALS FOR SSIS9				*20	0	*31	4:3.934			********	0:05:03
PROJECT TOTALS FOR -SDPS-				*3,931	0	*1,301	3:52:6.403				
JOB TOTALS FOR				*3,931	0	*1,301	3:52:6.403				

BATCH
7 JOBS:
ACCOUNT TOTALS: DDPTST   *3,931 CARDS IN.   3:52:6.403 TOTAL TIME.
3,931 CARDS IN.   6:16:32 WALL CLOCK TIME.
0 CARDS OUT.
1,301 PAGES.

DEMAND
D-DDO JOBS:
D-DDO TOTAL TIME.
0:00:00 WALL CLOCK TIME.

TOTAL
7 JOBS:
3:52:6.403 TOTAL TIME.
6:16:32 WALL CLOCK TIME.

Attachments/Example of Computer Charges

RUN DATE 5/01/80 (ITLACT-01) ITEL MUSIC REPORTING SYSTEM PAGE 2

DETAIL LISTING BY ACCOUNT/INSTRUCTOR/JOB

REPORTING FROM 4/01/1980 THRU 4/30/1980 SELECTED FROM 0:00 THRU 24:00 DAILY

ACCOUNT	CPU TIME MIN:SEC	CONNECT TIME HRS:MIN	DEMAND/ BATCH	TERMINAL ID	LINE ID	DATE	START TIME	CPU $	I-O $	CONNECT $	TOTAL $
DH12 3 06	0:04	1:14	DEMAND	53	3	01 APR 80	7:32	.61	.100	3.05	3.76
DH12 3 06	0:04	1:14	DEMAND	53	3	01 APR 80	7:32	.61	.100	3.02	3.70
DH12 3 06	0:01	0:06	DEMAND	83	3	05 APR 80	20:35	.07	.05	.11	.23
DH12 3 06	0:00	0:00	DEMAND	83	3	05 APR 80	20:35	.01	.05	.10	.21
DH12 3 06	0:09	0:00	DEMAND	50	0	16 APR 80	8:04	.01	.05	.00	.01
DH12 3 06	2:36	0:09	DEMAND	50	0	16 APR 80	8:04	1.25	.20	6.23	7.01
TOTALS FOR ACCOUNT	0:00	2:36	BATCH					1.30		6.00	7.80
TOTALS FOR ACCOUNT		0:00	BATCH					1.00			0.00
DH13 3 06	0:01	0:33	DEMAND	54	4	10 APR 80	15:03	.22	.007	2.22	2.44
DH13 3 06	0:01	0:01	BATCH	20	25	10 APR 80	15:03	.06	.07	.607	0.73
DH13 3 06	0:18	0:58	DEMAND	6	56	11 APR 80	10:21	.28	1.15	3.90	8.65
DH13 3 06	0:20	1:33	BATCH	20	25	11 APR 80	10:28	4.06	1.06	6.19	11.44
TOTALS FOR ACCOUNT	0:01	1:00	DEMAND					4.14	1.13	1.20	11.47
TOTALS FOR ACCOUNT											
DH15 3 06	0:20	0:45	DEMAND	76	26	03 APR 80	11:21	3.67	.55	2.68	6.90
DH15 3 06	0:20	0:45	DEMAND	76	26	03 APR 80	11:21	3.67	.55	2.68	6.90
DH15 3 06	0:00	0:04	DEMAND	15	65	17 APR 80	14:21	3.04	.55	.24	6.26
DH15 3 06	1:21	3:01	BATCH	82	32	23 APR 80	8:16	.73	2.40	10.24	28.13
TOTALS FOR ACCOUNT	0:00	1:21	BATCH					14.78		10.95	0.00
TOTALS FOR ACCOUNT								14.00		10.00	
DH25 3 06	0:03	0:01	DEMAND	89	39	01 APR 80	7:21	.44	.000	.03	.47
DH25 3 06	0:07	0:01	DEMAND	89	39	01 APR 80	7:21	.88	.000	.06	.94
TOTALS FOR ACCOUNT	0:00	0:03	BATCH					.00		.00	0.00
TOTALS FOR ACCOUNT											
DH39 3 06	0:10	0:16	DEMAND	86	36	01 APR 80	10:06	1.94	.15	1.09	3.18
DH39 3 06	0:43	1:50	DEMAND	86	36	01 APR 80	10:06	1.26	.70	5.55	13.51
DH39 3 06	0:07	0:12	DEMAND	72	22	04 APR 80	12:06	7.26	.70	5.55	13.51
DH39 3 06	0:04	0:12	DEMAND	46	98	07 APR 80	8:09	1.80	.52	.62	1.87
DH39 3 06	2:28	1:07	DEMAND	85	51	24 APR 80	9:06	5.07	2.15	4.21	9.56
TOTALS FOR ACCOUNT	2:00	5:43	BATCH					25.07	2.15	18.61	46.30
TOTALS FOR ACCOUNT								25.00		0.00	40.00
DH41 3 06	0:08	0:16	DEMAND	83	33	03 APR 80	8:05	1.29	.30	.67	2.26
DH41 3 06	0:08	0:16	DEMAND	83	33	03 APR 80	8:05	1.29	.30	.67	2.26
DH41 3 06	0:12	0:45	DEMAND	83	34	05 APR 80	17:31	1.63	1.15	.76	3.84
DH41 3 06	0:06	1:33	DEMAND	83	35	09 APR 80	19:10	.87	1.00	.73	2.85
DH41 3 06	0:43	0:43	DEMAND	16	66	09 APR 80	13:01	4.34	.505	2.16	6.74
DH41 3 06	1:04	1:02	DEMAND	26	36	11 APR 80	13:35	.47	.005	.00	6.50
DH41 3 06	0:14	0:14	DEMAND	52	2	11 APR 80	11:32	2.33	.25	.82	3.40

6

instruction

This chapter provides background information on cost accounting for instruction. The need for and uses of instructional cost data are reviewed, and some general procedures for collecting data on instructional costs are described. These procedures are illustrated through the use of a costing example. In addition, case studies at the end of this chapter describe two approaches to instructional costing. Exhibit 6-A, a case study from Fairleigh Dickinson University, describes the full cost and revenue approach to instructional costing, while exhibit 6-B, a case study from Ohio Wesleyan University, illustrates a direct cost approach.

The Literature on Instructional Costs

In recent years, higher education researchers have expressed a growing interest in applying cost accounting procedures to colleges and universities. Perhaps the most widely known studies in the area of cost analysis are *A Study of Cost Analysis in Higher Education,* by Adams, Hankins, and Schroeder (1977); *Procedures for Determining Historical Full Costs,* a joint NACUBO/NCHEMS publication (1977); and *The Costs of Higher Education,* by Howard R. Bowen (1980). (Other material is cited in the References section at the end of the book.) These studies address the issues surrounding instructional costs but do not advocate use of one particular cost accounting procedure for all institutions.

In addition to studies on instructional costs, a number of instructional costing manuals have also been produced. *An Approach to Cost Studies in Small Colleges* (1978) provides a set of guidelines for developing unit-cost data in academic disciplines, such as average cost per credit hour. The Council of Independent Colleges (CIC, formerly CASC) produced *User Manual for the Instructional Program Analysis Module* (1978). This manual highlighted the use of department and program unit costs, class size analyses, and other income and expenditure summaries.

Need for and Uses of Cost Data

Instructional cost data can be used to enhance the planning and budgeting process. In planning, cost data can be useful in assessing the implications of pursuing alternative courses of action. For example, historical cost data, in limited ranges of enrollment and in the context of fixed and variable cost components, can be used to project the probable future costs of existing instructional programs at different enrollment levels. Historical cost data can also be used to examine trends in program costs over time. Cost and revenue data can also be used to identify the point at which total revenue equals total cost. This point is referred to as the "break-even point" and is a useful indicator of the fiscal feasibility of new programs. In addition, historical cost data can be used to review trends in tuition and fee levels and together with projections of future costs can be used to establish future tuition and fee levels. For example, a number of state higher education coordinating agencies currently conduct cost studies in order to develop tuition and fee schedules. Cost data have also been used in developing funding formulas and in making adjustments to formulas over time. In budgeting, cost data can identify high cost areas and alert administrators to potential problems. (For a more detailed discussion on the uses of cost data, refer to chapter 1.)

Instructional Cost Considerations

Instruction is one of the most complex areas in which to implement cost accounting procedures. Instructional costs can vary depending on the mode of instruction, such as laboratories, seminars, and lectures, and can also vary by class size, course level, and academic discipline. At institutions in which research is an important part of the institution's role and mission, the question of joint service costs adds to the complexity of instructional costing. The research function, for example, is often an integral part of the instruction function, particularly when students and faculty are involved in research projects. Under these circumstances, the most frequently used method of separating the compensation costs associated with research from those associated with instruction is to allocate compensation costs to each activity on the basis of a *faculty activity reporting system*. Such a system is a method of determining the percentage of a faculty member's effort devoted to a number of specified activities, such as teaching a lower-division physics course, conducting sponsored research in physics, or engaging in course and curriculum development. This effort-distribution pattern is then related to the compensation accounts from which the faculty member is paid. This information, combined with effort patterns for other faculty members paid from the same account, is used to determine the amount of compensation attributable to each instructional cost center. *Procedures for Determining Historical Full Costs* (1977) provides some useful guidelines for using a faculty survey as a means of distributing faculty compensation to specific cost centers.

An Illustration of Instructional Costing

Instructional costs can be determined by using the five-step general cost accounting procedure outlined in chapter 1. The following illustration describes the use of this procedure to determine instructional costs at Institution A.

Step 1. *Designate specific cost objectives and/or cost centers.* The first step in conducting instructional costing involves the designation of specific cost centers. Figure 6.1 shows designated cost centers for Institution A. The designation as cost centers of instructional divisions, such as arts and humanities and natural sciences, and instructional departments, such as economics and history, is advocated since it is easier to reconcile direct instructional costs to the financial records of individual divisions and departments. If there is an interest in a more detailed breakdown of costs, academic disciplines within departments can also be designated as cost centers. In addition, other instructional cost studies, including one of the case studies (exhibit 6-B) following this chapter, identify costs by academic discipline, course level, and course section.

Figure 6.1
Instructional Costs
(Tier One)

Step 1. *Designate specific cost objectives and/or cost centers*

Step 2. *Select consistent cost categories*

Step 3. *Assign all tier one costs*

A. By Division	a) Personnel Compensation	b) Supplies	c) Other Expenditures	Total Tier One Costs
Division of Arts and Humanities	$1,286,960	$191,763	$ 39,277	= $1,518,000
Division of Natural Sciences	1,053,088	175,797	13,115	= 1,242,000
Division of Business Administration	389,988	58,110	11,902	= 460,000
Division of Education	272,992	40,677	8,331	= 322,000
Division of Social Sciences	896,972	133,653	27,375	= 1,058,000
Total	$3,900,000	$600,000	$100,000	$4,600,000

B. By Departments for the Division of Social Sciences				
Economics Department	$150,727	$ 22,424	$ 4,592	$ 177,743
History Department	163,287	24,293	4,976	192,556
Political Science Department	73,570	10,945	2,242	86,757
Other Departments	509,388	75,991	15,565	600,944
Total	$896,972	$133,653	$27,375	$1,058,000

Step 2. *Select consistent cost categories.* Once cost centers have been designated, it is necessary to select a consistent set of cost categories. Cost categories outlined in figure 6.1 are based on the major object-of-expenditure categories found in most colleges and universities and are consistent with the categories outlined in NACUBO's *A Management Reporting Manual for Colleges* (1980) and *College & University Business Administration* (1982). Breakdowns within these major categories depend on the level of detail in the institution's financial records and the usefulness of the detail to decision makers.

Step 3. *Assign all tier one costs to designated cost centers.* The tier one or direct costs associated with specific instructional cost centers are obtained directly from the institution's accounting system and are arrayed in a format similar to that outlined in figure 6.1. Depending on the purpose of the cost study, each category of tier one costs can be broken into its component parts, such as personnel compensation and specific supply and expense items. Figure 6.1 shows tier one costs for both instructional divisions and departmental cost centers. Figure 6.1 is based on data contained in figures 3.1 through 3.9 in chapter 3.

Step 4. *Assign all tiers two and three costs to designated cost centers.* After all tier one costs have been assigned, the next step in the costing process is to allocate all tiers two and three costs to all benefiting cost centers in the instructional area. The assignment of these costs to instructional cost centers is best accomplished by using the following sequence: (a) annual use charge on facilities and capital equipment; (b) plant operation and maintenance costs; (c) institutional support costs; (d) academic support costs; and (e) student service costs. Figure 6.2a shows the assignment of tiers two and three costs to instructional divisions; figure 6.2b shows the assignment of these costs to departments within the division of social sciences. Figures 6.2a and 6.2b are based on data contained in figure 3.2 in chapter 3. Specific details of the assignment process are as follows:

Step 4a. *Allocate annual use charge on all buildings, land improvements, and capital equipment to all benefiting cost centers.* The annual use charge on facilities and capital equipment is calculated using the procedures outlined in chapters 1 and 3. Figure 6.3 shows the allocation of the annual use charge on buildings and land improvements to benefiting in-

structional division and departmental cost centers. Figure 6.4 illustrates the allocation of equipment usage charges to benefiting cost centers. In both instances facilities and equipment usage charges are allocated on the basis of the assignable square feet of benefiting cost centers.

Step 4b. *Allocate all plant operation and maintenance costs to all benefiting cost centers.* The costs of plant operation and maintenance are allocated to instructional cost centers on the basis of assignable square feet. The allocation process is outlined in figure 6.5.

Step 4c. *Allocate all institutional support costs to all benefiting cost centers.* Institutional support costs are allocated to benefiting instructional cost centers on the basis of direct costs. The procedure is shown in figure 6.6.

Step 4d. *Allocate all academic support costs to all benefiting cost centers.* It is preferable to allocate academic support costs on the basis of actual use studies. In the case of libraries or museums and galleries, this could involve studies of the number of users of each service by type of user, e.g., student, faculty member, or visiting scholar. Frequently, however, studies of actual use are not available and the costs of academic support must be allocated on a basis that best approximates actual use. For the purpose of this illustration, academic support costs have been allocated to instructional cost centers on the basis of student credit hours. The allocation of academic support costs is shown in figure 6.7.

Step 4e. *Allocate all student service costs to all benefiting cost centers.* The costs of student services are allocated to instructional cost centers on the basis of student credit hours. Figure 6.8 illustrates the allocation process.

Step 4f. *Calculate tier three costs for all final cost objectives.* After the costs associated with all support activities and facilities and equipment usage charges have been allocated to benefiting cost centers, the tier three costs for all instructional division and departmental cost centers can be determined. Figure 6.2a shows the tier three costs for all instructional divisions; figure 6.2b shows tier three costs for departments within the division of social sciences. Figure 6.9 shows the tier three costs for the division of social sciences.

Figure 6.2a
Instructional Costs
Tiers Two and Three

	Benefiting Cost Objective	Benefiting Cost Centers					
	Instruction	Division of Arts and Humanities	Division of Natural Sciences	Division of Business Administration	Division of Education	Division of Social Sciences	Total

Step 4. *Assign all tiers two and three costs to designated cost objectives and cost centers.*

Step 4a. *Allocate annual use charge on buildings, land improvements, and capital equipment to all cost objectives and centers.*

(i) Tier one costs of instructional cost objective (see figure 6.1): Instruction $4,600,000; Total $4,600,000

(ii) Tier one costs of instructional cost centers: Instruction (4,600,000); Arts and Humanities $1,518,000; Natural Sciences $1,242,000; Business Administration $460,000; Education $322,000; Social Sciences $1,058,000

(iii) Use charge on buildings and land improvements allocated on the basis of assignable square feet of cost objective (from figures 3.3 and 3.5, chapter 3): Instruction 90,000; Total 90,000

(iv) Use charge on buildings and land improvements allocated on the basis of assignable square feet of cost centers (from figure 6.3): Instruction (90,000); Arts and Humanities 29,700; Natural Sciences 24,300; Business Administration 9,000; Education 6,300; Social Sciences 20,700

(v) Use charge on capital equipment allocated on the basis of assignable square feet of cost objective (from figures 3.3 and 3.6): Instruction 6,794; Total 6,794

(vi) Use charge on capital equipment allocated on the basis of assignable square feet of cost centers (from figure 6.4): Instruction (6,794); Arts and Humanities 2,242; Natural Sciences 1,834; Business Administration 679; Education 476; Social Sciences 1,563

(vii) Total tier one costs plus buildings, land improvements, and equipment usage cost of cost centers: Arts and Humanities $1,549,942; Natural Sciences $1,268,134; Business Administration $469,679; Education $328,776; Social Sciences $1,080,263; Total $4,696,794

Step 4b. *Allocate all plant operation and maintenance costs to all benefiting cost objectives and centers.*

(i) Allocate all plant operation and maintenance costs on the basis of assignable square feet of cost objective (from figure 3.7, chapter 3): Instruction 574,103; Total 574,103

(ii) Allocate all plant operation and maintenance costs on the basis of assignable square feet of benefiting cost centers (from figure 6.5): Instruction (574,103); Arts and Humanities 189,454; Natural Sciences 155,008; Business Administration 57,410; Education 40,187; Social Sciences 132,044

Step 4c. *Allocate all institutional support costs to all benefiting cost objectives and centers.*

(i) Allocate all institutional support costs on the basis of total direct costs of cost objective (from figure 3.8): Instruction 669,015; Total 669,015

(ii) Allocate all institutional support costs on the basis of total direct costs of benefiting cost centers (from figure 6.6): Instruction (669,015); Arts and Humanities 220,775; Natural Sciences 180,634; Business Administration 66,902; Education 46,831; Social Sciences 153,873

Step 4d. *Allocate all academic support costs to all benefiting cost objectives and centers.*

(i) Allocate all academic support costs to benefiting cost objectives on the basis of total direct costs of cost objective (from figure 3.9): Instruction 626,526; Total 626,526

(ii) Allocate all academic support costs on the basis of student credit hours (SCH) of benefiting cost centers (from figure 6.7): Instruction (626,526); Arts and Humanities 206,754; Natural Sciences 125,305; Business Administration 81,448; Education 62,653; Social Sciences 150,366

Step 4e. *Allocate all student service costs to all benefiting cost objectives and centers.*

(i) Allocate all student service costs to the instructional cost objective (from figure 3.2): Instruction 776,658; Total 776,658

(ii) Allocate all student service costs on the basis of student credit hours (SCH) of benefiting cost centers (from figure 6.8): Instruction (776,658); Arts and Humanities 256,297; Natural Sciences 155,332; Business Administration 100,965; Education 77,666; Social Sciences 186,398

Step 4f. *Calculate tier three costs for all final cost objectives and centers.* Arts and Humanities $2,423,222; Natural Sciences $1,884,413; Business Administration $776,404; Education $556,113; Social Sciences $1,702,944; Total $7,343,096

Step 5. *Develop unit costs or output measures.*

(i) Cost per student credit hour (from figure 6.9): Arts and Humanities $163/SCH; Natural Sciences $215/SCH; Business Administration $132/SCH; Education $127/SCH; Social Sciences $155/SCH; Total $164/SCH

Figure 6.2b

Tiers Two and Three Instructional Costs for Departments in the Division of Social Sciences

	Benefiting Cost Centers					
	Division of Social Sciences	Economics Department	History Department	Political Science Department	Other Departments	Total
Step 4. *Assign all tiers two and three costs to designated cost centers.*						
Step 4a. *Allocate annual use charge on buildings, land improvements, and capital equipment to all cost centers.*						
(i) Tier one costs of Division of Social Sciences (from figure 6.1)	$1,058,000					$1,058,000
(ii) Tier one costs of departmental cost centers in the Division of Social Sciences (from figure 6.1)	(1,058,000)	$177,743	$192,556	$ 86,757	$600,944	
(iii) Use charge on buildings and land improvements allocated on the basis of assignable square feet of Division of Social Sciences (from figure 6.3)	20,700					20,700
(iv) Use charge on buildings and land improvements allocated on the basis of assignable square feet of departmental cost centers (from figure 6.3)	(20,700)	3,312	3,519	2,277	11,592	
(v) Use charge on capital equipment allocated on the basis of assignable square feet of Division of Social Sciences (from figure 6.4)	1,563					1,563
(vi) Use charge on capital equipment allocated on the basis of assignable square feet of departmental cost centers (from figure 6.4)	(1,563)	250	266	172	875	
(vii) Total tier one costs plus buildings, land improvements, and capital equipment usage costs of departmental cost centers		$181,305	$196,341	$ 89,206	$613,411	$1,080,263
Step 4b. *Allocate all plant operation and maintenance costs to all benefiting cost centers.*						
(i) Allocate all plant operation and maintenance costs on the basis of assignable square feet of Division of Social Sciences (from figure 6.5)	132,044					132,044
(ii) Allocate all plant operation and maintenance costs on the basis of assignable square feet of benefiting departmental cost centers (from figure 6.5)	(132,044)	21,127	22,447	14,525	73,945	
Step 4c. *Allocate all institutional support costs to all benefiting cost centers.*						
(i) Allocate all institutional support costs on the basis of total direct costs of Division of Social Sciences (from figure 6.6)	153,873					153,873
(ii) Allocate all institutional support costs on the basis of total direct costs of benefiting departmental cost centers (from figure 6.6)	(153,873)	26,158	27,697	12,310	87,708	
Step 4d. *Allocate all academic support costs to all benefiting cost centers.*						
(i) Allocate all academic support costs on the basis of student credit hours of Division of Social Sciences (from figure 6.7)	150,366					150,366
(ii) Allocate all academic support costs on the basis of student credit hours of benefiting departmental cost centers (from figure 6.7)	(150,366)	25,562	27,066	12,029	85,709	
Step 4e. *Allocate all student service costs to all benefiting cost centers.*						
(i) Allocate all student service costs on the basis of student credit hours of Division of Social Sciences (from figure 6.8)	186,398					186,398
(ii) Allocate all student service costs on the basis of student credit hours of benefiting departmental cost centers (from figure 6.8)	(186,398)	31,688	33,551	14,912	106,247	
Step 4f. *Calculate tier three costs for all departmental cost centers in Division of Social Sciences.*		$285,840	$307,102	$142,982	$967,020	$1,702,944
Step 5. *Develop unit costs or output measures.*						
(i) Cost per student credit hour (from figure 6.9)		$153/SCH	$155/SCH	$162/SCH	$154/SCH	$155/SCH

Figure 6.3
Allocation of Annual Use Charge on Buildings and Land Improvements to Benefiting Cost Centers

Cost Center	Assignable Square Feet (ASF)	Percentage of Total ASF	×	Annual Use Charge on Buildings and Land Improvements (see figure 3.5)	=	Annual Use Charge on Buildings and Land Improvements Allocated to Benefiting Cost Centers
A. By Division						
Division of Arts and Humanities	59,400	33%	×	$90,000	=	$29,700
Division of Natural Sciences	48,600	27		90,000		24,300
Division of Business Administration	18,000	10		90,000		9,000
Division of Education	12,600	7		90,000		6,300
Division of Social Sciences	41,400	23		90,000		20,700
Total	180,000	100%		$90,000		$90,000
B. By Department for Division of Social Sciences				(see above)		
Economics Department	6,615	16%	×	$20,700	=	$ 3,312
History Department	7,146	17		20,700		3,519
Political Science Department	4,345	11		20,700		2,277
Other Departments	23,294	56		20,700		11,592
Total	41,400	100%		$20,700		$20,700

Figure 6.4
Allocation of Equipment Usage Charges to Benefiting Cost Centers

Cost Center	Assignable Square Feet (ASF)	Percentage of Total ASF	×	Annual Equipment Use Charge (see figure 3.6)	=	Equipment Use Charge Allocated to Cost Center
A. By Division						
Division of Arts and Humanities	59,400	33%	×	$6,794	=	$2,242
Division of Natural Sciences	48,600	27		6,794		1,834
Division of Business Administration	18,000	10		6,794		679
Division of Education	12,600	7		6,794		476
Division of Social Sciences	41,400	23		6,794		1,563
Total	180,000	100%		$6,794		$6,794
B. By Department for Division of Social Sciences				(see above)		
Economics Department	6,615	16%	×	$1,563	=	$ 250
History Department	7,146	17		1,563		266
Political Science Department	4,345	11		1,563		172
Other Departments	23,294	56		1,563		875
Total	41,400	100%		$1,563		$1,563

Figure 6.5

Allocation of Plant Operation and Maintenance Costs to Benefiting Cost Centers

Cost Center	Assignable Square Feet (ASF)	Percentage of Total ASF	×	Plant Operation and Maintenance Costs (see figure 3.7)	=	Plant Operation and Maintenance Costs Allocated to Benefiting Cost Centers
A. By Division						
Division of Arts and Humanities	59,400	33%	×	$574,103	=	$189,454
Division of Natural Sciences	48,600	27		574,103		155,008
Division of Business Administration	18,000	10		574,103		57,410
Division of Education	12,600	7		574,103		40,187
Division of Social Sciences	41,400	23		574,103		132,044
Total	180,000	100%		$574,103		$574,103
B. By Department for Division of Social Sciences		(see above)				
Economics Department	6,615	16%	×	$132,044	=	$ 21,127
History Department	7,146	17		132,044		22,447
Political Science Department	4,345	11		132,044		14,525
Other Departments	23,294	56		132,044		73,945
Total	41,400	100%		$132,044		$132,044

Figure 6.6

Allocation of Institutional Support Costs to Benefiting Cost Objectives

Cost Center	Direct Costs of Cost Centers (see figure 6.1)	Percentage of Total Direct Costs	×	Institutional Support Costs (see figure 3.8)	=	Institutional Support Costs Allocated to Benefiting Cost Centers
A. By Division						
Division of Arts and Humanities	$1,518,000	33%	×	$669,015	=	$220,775
Division of Natural Sciences	1,242,000	27		669,015		180,634
Division of Business Administration	460,000	10		669,015		66,902
Division of Education	322,000	7		669,015		46,831
Division of Social Sciences	1,058,000	23		669,015		153,873
Total	$4,600,000	100%		$669,015		$669,015
B. By Department for Division of Social Sciences		(see above)				
Economics Department	$ 177,743	17%	×	$153,873	=	$ 26,158
History Department	192,556	18		153,873		27,697
Political Science Department	86,757	8		153,873		12,310
Other Departments	600,944	57		153,873		87,708
Total	$1,058,000	100%		$153,873		$153,873

Figure 6.7
Allocation of Academic Support Costs to Benefiting Cost Centers

Cost Center	Student Credit Hours (SCH) of Benefiting Cost Centers	Percentage of Total SCH	×	Academic Support Costs (see figure 3.9)	=	Academic Support Costs Allocated to Benefiting Cost Centers
A. By Division						
Division of Arts and Humanities	14,841	33%	×	$626,526	=	$206,754
Division of Natural Sciences	8,780	20		626,526		125,305
Division of Business Administration	5,859	13		626,526		81,448
Division of Education	4,382	10		626,526		62,653
Division of Social Sciences	11,015	24		626,526		150,366
Total	44,877	100%		$626,526		$626,526
B. By Department for Division of Social Sciences				(see above)		
Economics Department	1,872	17%	×	$150,366	=	$ 25,562
History Department	1,983	18		150,366		27,066
Political Science Department	881	8		150,366		12,029
Other Departments	6,279	57		150,366		85,709
Total	11,015	100%		$150,366		$150,366

Figure 6.8
Allocation of Student Service Costs to Benefiting Cost Centers

Cost Center	Student Credit Hours (SCH) of Benefiting Cost Centers	Percentage of Total SCH	×	Student Service Costs (see figure 3.2)	=	Student Service Costs Allocated to Benefiting Cost Centers
A. By Division						
Division of Arts and Humanities	14,841	33%	×	$776,658	=	$256,297
Division of Natural Sciences	8,780	20		776,658		155,332
Division of Business Administration	5,859	13		776,658		100,965
Division of Education	4,382	10		776,658		77,666
Division of Social Sciences	11,015	24		776,658		186,398
Total	44,877	100%		$776,658		$776,658
B. By Department for Division of Social Sciences				(see above)		
Economics Department	1,872	17%	×	$186,398	=	$ 31,688
History Department	1,983	18		186,398		33,551
Political Science Department	881	8		186,398		14,912
Other Departments	6,279	57		186,398		106,247
Total	11,015	100%		$186,398		$186,398

Figure 6.9
Costs for the Division of Social Sciences
(Tier Three)

1. Tier one costs (see figure 6.1)	$1,058,000
2. Annual use charge on buildings and land improvements (see figure 6.3)	20,700
3. Equipment usage (see figure 6.4)	1,563
4. Support costs (see figure 6.2a)	
Plant operation and maintenance	132,044
Institutional support	153,873
Academic support	150,366
Student services	186,398
5. Tier three costs of Division of Social Sciences (see figure 6.2a)	$1,702,944

Step 5. *Develop unit costs or output measures.* The cost information developed in steps 1 through 4 can be combined with data from other information systems, such as student records, to produce a number of output measures. Figure 6.9a, for example, shows the cost per student credit hour for each of the divisional cost centers and for departmental cost centers within the division of social sciences. In addition, a number of other output measures are discussed in the case studies (exhibits 6-A and 6-B) that follow this chapter. Unit costs can be useful in examining trends in costs over time and in evaluating the cost implications of changes in enrollment levels.

Case Studies of Instructional Costing At Two Institutions

The institutional case studies (exhibits 6-A and 6-B) highlight two approaches to cost accounting for instructional activities. While these institutions differ in size and types of program offerings, they provide excellent illustrations of how to develop and implement instructional cost accounting procedures to meet the needs of institutional decision makers. The Fairleigh Dickinson University case study (exhibit 6-A) describes a full cost and revenue approach to cost accounting for instruction. The system uses data from the accounting, budgeting, and registration systems. The purpose of the system is to aid all levels of managers in their decision making by focusing their attention on specific data items and trends. The goals of the system are to provide governing board members with an overview of financial operations and to help institutional administrators improve management decision making in the areas of planning, budgeting, control, and evaluation.

Figure 6.9a
Cost per Student Credit Hour (SCH) by Benefiting Cost Centers

Cost Center	Full Cost of Cost Center (from figures 6.2a & b)	÷	Student Credit Hours (SCH) of Cost Centers	=	Cost per SCH by Cost Center
A. By Division					
Division of Arts and Humanities	$2,423,222	÷	14,841	=	$163/SCH
Division of Natural Sciences	1,884,413		8,780		215/SCH
Division of Business Administration	776,404		5,859		132/SCH
Division of Education	556,113		4,382		127/SCH
Division of Social Sciences	1,702,944		11,015		155/SCH
Total	$7,343,096		44,877		164/SCH
B. By Department for Division of Social Sciences					
Economics Department	$ 285,840	÷	1,872	=	$153/SCH
History Department	307,102		1,983		155/SCH
Political Science Department	142,982		881		162/SCH
Other Departments	967,020		6,279		154/SCH
Total	$1,702,944		11,015		155/SCH

The Ohio Wesleyan University case study (exhibit 6-B) describes a computer-based system for determining the direct costs of instruction. This system calculates and reports unit costs for: (1) each academic department; (2) each academic discipline; (3) each of two course levels, freshman-sophmore and junior-senior; and (4) each course section. The primary purpose of the system is to evaluate financial resource utilization. To assist administrators in this evaluation, the system generates four reports: (1) a faculty compensation analysis; (2) instruction depart-ment cost groupings; (3) a course cost report; and (4) an academic discipline cost report.

Both case studies describe the use of cost accounting procedures to meet specific needs of administrators at different institutions. They also highlight the importance of implementing cost accounting procedures that reflect the organizational structure and information needs of these institutions. Readers interested in a further discussion of instructional costing should refer to appendix A and to the References.

exhibit 6-a

case study: fairleigh dickinson university cost accounting for instruction— the full cost and revenue method

Introduction

Fairleigh Dickinson University (FDU) is an independent, nonsectarian, coeducational institution offering programs in business administration, education, liberal arts, science and engineering, and dentistry on the undergraduate, graduate, and professional levels.

Incorporated as a nonprofit institution in 1942, the university has grown to three major campuses in northern New Jersey; a campus in Wroxton, England; and another in St. Croix, U.S. Virgin Islands. FDU is fully accredited by the Middle States Association of Colleges and Schools.

Overview and Scope of Cost Analysis at FDU

In 1974, FDU adopted its cost accounting system—the Cost Analysis of Budgeted Results. The system is user-oriented and has improved over the years on the strength of user suggestions. The purpose of the cost analysis is to aid all levels of management in decision-making processes by focusing attention on certain trends and data. The analysis is not intended to serve as a value judgment of the quality of instruction.

FDU subscribes and conforms to all of the NACUBO Costing Standards, with the exception of Standard No. 11; however, expenditures for capital items are recorded by FDU for normal replacement of equipment and library books.

Goals

FDU developed its Cost Analysis of Budgeted Results to achieve the following specific goals:

- To provide the Board of Trustees an overview of financial operations;

- To improve management decisions in the areas of planning, budgeting, control, and evaluation;

- To provide a basis for outside funding of specific programs, such as the School of Dentistry;

- To permit different constituencies to focus attention on financial and enrollment data through a common viewing lens; and

- To enhance the credibility of all financial data by providing the entire University community with linkage and reconciliation to the Audited Financial Statements, departmental budgets, and student enrollment.

Users

The Cost Analysis users include the following constituencies:

University Community

- Board of Trustees
- Senior Administrators
- Academic Deans and Chairpersons
- Faculty Bargaining Unit
- Students

Outside Agencies
- New Jersey Department of Higher Education
- Middle States Accreditation Team

In addition, the Cost Analysis of Budgeted Results is placed in the University's libraries for the use of all members of the University community.

Description of Financial and Statistical Records at FDU

Exhibit 1 presents an overview of the relationships of the various records and reports at FDU. All financial and enrollment data are reconciled and linked to the University's Audited Financial Statements. The cost accounting report is the Cost Analysis of Budgeted Results (box 7).

Source Documents Needed for Cost Analysis

There are two primary source documents required for the preparation of the Cost Analysis report—the Budgeted Results report and the Registration report.

The Budgeted Results report (see Exhibit 2) accumulates income and expenses by function and by organizational unit (see box 6, Exhibit 1). The Registration report (see Exhibit 3) displays student enrollment and student credit hours taught for all courses within each organizational unit (see box 3, Exhibit 1).

Description of Cost Analysis System at FDU

Definition of Cost Centers. Cost Centers have been defined at FDU as academic (instructional) units.

These units or cost centers are organized into organizational tiers (see Exhibit 4), with each tier composed of components of the tier below. This configuration can be viewed as a pyramid with total University as the vertex and the Campuses at the next lower tier. Each Campus is composed of its Colleges, and each College of its Departments.

Calculated Accumulated Surplus (Deficit) figures have been inserted in Exhibit 4 for illustrative purposes. The Surplus (Deficit) figures for each organizational tier will equal the Surplus of $464,045 for the Total University (see Exhibit 5).

The illustrations in this case study focus on the Rutherford Campus, the College of Business (at Rutherford), and the Departments within the College of Business (at Rutherford).

Exhibit 1
Fairleigh Dickinson University
Flow Chart of Financial & Statistical Data

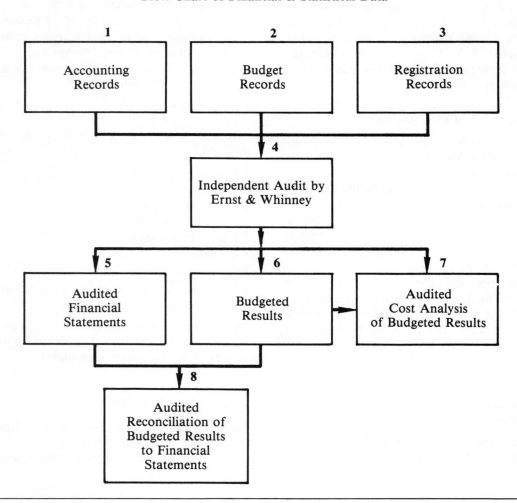

Exhibit 2
Fairleigh Dickinson University
Budgeted Results Summary
Fiscal Year 1979-80

	Income	Exhibit Reference	Expenses
Rutherford Campus			
Instructional:			
College of Business:			
Dean's Office	—	9	$ 191,101
Accounting Department	$ 1,362,576	3, 9	356,746
Management Department	996,037	9	159,847
Marketing Department	1,314,353	9	263,616
Other Departments	1,951,926	9	548,160
Total College of Business	5,624,892	8, 9	1,519,470
College of Education	886,993		551,604
College of Arts & Sciences	4,530,947		2,699,772
Wayne Special Program	179,097		81,052
Total Instructional	11,221,929	8	4,851,898
Noninstructional (Campus Administration)	1,700,026	8	5,676,665
Total Rutherford Campus	12,921,955	7, 8	10,528,563
Teaneck Campus	25,643,558		24,224,008
Madison Campus	12,351,941		10,157,589
Other Campuses	2,358,210		2,295,729
Total Campuses	53,275,664	5, 7	47,205,889
University Administration	7,356,858	5, 7	12,962,588
Total	60,632,522 (60,168,477)	5, 7	$60,168,477
Total University Surplus	$ 464,045	5, 7	

Exhibit 3
Fairleigh Dickinson University
Registration Report
Academic Year 1979-80

Account Number Campus	College	Dept.	Course Catalog Code	Course Title	Level of Instruction	Registered Seats ×	Number of Student Cr. Hrs. per Course =	Total Student Cr. Hrs. ×	Tuition Rate per Student Credit Hour	Total Tuition = Revenue
Ruth.	Bus.	Acctg.								
01	41	02	AC 101	Accounting 1	Undergrad.	38	3	114	111	$ 12,654
01	41	02	AC 102	Accounting 2	Undergrad.	21	3	63	111	6,993
01	41	02	AC 103	Inter. Acctg.	Undergrad.	19	3	57	111	6,327
01	41	02	AC 501	Adv. Acctg.	Graduate	24	3	72	133	9,576
01	41	02	All Other Courses							1,327,026
01	41	02	Total (agrees with Budgeted Results—see Exhibit 2)							$1,362,576

Exhibit 4
Components of the University Surplus (Deficit)
by Cost Center

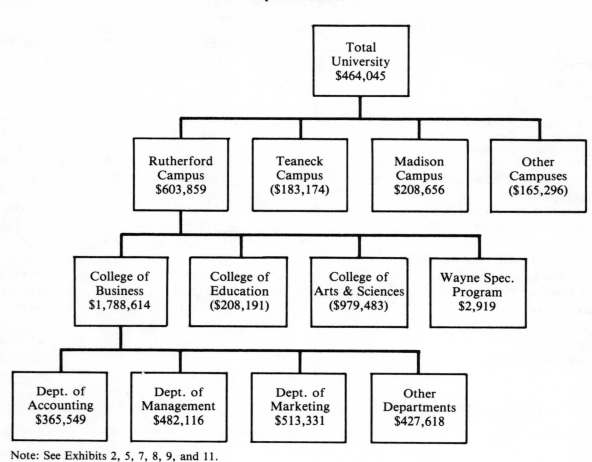

Note: See Exhibits 2, 5, 7, 8, 9, and 11.

Definition of Direct and Indirect Income and Expenses and Description of Flow into Cost Centers

The Cost Analysis of Budgeted Results is an annual historical full cost and revenue analysis. It represents a complete distribution of all University Unrestricted Current Fund income and expenses to the campuses, colleges, and departments, as illustrated in Exhibit 5. Revenues for each cost center are calculated on the basis of Student Credit Hours taught (on a Production as opposed to a Major basis). Corresponding expenditures are accumulated on the basis of effort expended by each academic unit.

On completion of the independent audit of FDU's financial records, a Budgeted Results report is prepared and reconciled to the University's audited financial statements. This report reflects actual income and expenditures recorded during the fiscal year for each department (academic as well as nonacademic).

The Audited Budgeted Results report is used as the starting point for the Cost Analysis of Budgeted Results. Income and Expenses falling within budget control of campuses are considered "direct income and expenses" of campuses. Income and Expenses falling within budget control of General University or "Central Administration" must be allocated to campuses and therefore are considered to be "indirect" from the perspective of the campuses. These "University" indirect items are allocated first to campuses, then to colleges within each campus, and finally to departments within each college.

Exhibit 5
Fairleigh Dickinson University
Cost Analysis of Budgeted Results
Components of Surplus/Deficit by Cost Center
Fiscal Year 19xx-xx

Line Ref.		Col. 1 Total University	Col. 2 Indirect Inc. & Exp.	Col. 3 Campus Cost Centers	Col. 4 Indirect Inc. & Exp.	Col. 5 College Cost Centers	Col. 6 Indirect Inc. & Exp.	Col. 7 Department Cost Centers
1	Direct Income	$60,632,522[a]	($ 7,356,858)[a]	$53,275,664[a]	($ 5,603,027)	$47,672,637	$ -	$47,672,637
2	Direct Expenses	60,168,477[a]	(12,962,588)[a]	47,205,889[a]	(23,074,329)	24,131,560	(2,492,399)	21,639,161
3	Net University Indirect Expenses		5,605,730 ⟶	5,605,730 ⟶		5,605,730 ⟶		5,605,730
4	Net Campus Indirect Expenses				17,471,302 ⟶	17,471,302 ⟶		17,471,302
5	Net College Indirect Expenses						2,492,399 ⟶	2,492,399
6	Surplus (Deficit) (see Exhibit 4)	$ 464,045[a]	$ -	$ 464,045	$ -	$ 464,045	$ -	$ 464,045

[a]See Exhibits 2 & 7.

Income and expenses falling within budget control of colleges are considered to be "direct income and expenses" of colleges. Income and expenses falling within budget control of Campus Administration (but not colleges) must be allocated to colleges and therefore are considered to be "indirect" from the perspective of the colleges. These "Campus" indirect items are allocated first to colleges within each campus and then to departments within each college.

Income and expenses falling within budget control of (academic) departments are considered to be "direct income and expenses" of departments. Income and expenses falling within budget control of College Administration (but not departments) must be allocated to departments and therefore are considered to be "indirect" from the perspective of the departments. These "College" indirect items are allocated to each department.

To summarize, the effect of the cost analysis techniques used at FDU is to allocate *University* indirect income and expenses to each campus; *University* and *Campus* indirect income and expenses to each college; and *University, Campus,* and *College* indirect income and expenses to each department.

Format of Cost Analysis Report

The Cost Analysis of Budgeted Results Report is organized into four sections. Section I displays the current year's distribution of income and expenses to Campuses, Colleges, and Departments.

Section II expresses the income, expense, and resulting surplus (deficit) figures for each cost center on a unit basis. This calculation is made by dividing cost center dollar amounts by student credit hours taught. Unit surplus (deficit) figures for the current year are compared to corresponding figures from the preceding year.

Section III displays the current year's surplus (deficit) figures for each cost center alongside various statistical data in order to highlight correlations. Examples of statistical data included are average class size, percentage of tuition income generated, ratio of full-time faculty salary dollars to total faculty salary dollars, ratio of direct expenses to tuition and fee income, and ratio of indirect expenses to direct expenses.

Section IV contains tables and graphs of financial and statistical data plotted over a seven-year period. This format reveals trends and patterns not readily discernible by examination of separate annual reports.

Cost Analysis Allocation Methodology

The first step in the allocation of income and expenses from one organizational tier (University, Campuses, Colleges) to the tiers below is to identify those items that can be clearly and precisely identified with Campus, College, or Departmental cost centers. Examples of such items are State Aid to the Dental School on the Teaneck Campus and Debt Service charges for buildings on the Madison Campus. This allocation procedure is referred to as *attribution*.

Income and expense items that cannot be *attributed* (for example, the President's Office) must then be *prorated* to cost centers using the most appropriate method available, such as direct expenses, salaries, and/or full-time equivalent (FTE) students. The proration basis chosen is applied uniformly and consistently among all cost centers and from year to year.

FDU uses practical methods (direct costs, salaries, and full-time equivalent (FTE) students) of proration that result in an equitable allocation of indirect income and expense items to the cost centers.

A description of each proration method follows:

1. Proration on the Basis of FTE Students. Income and expense items that vary with enrollments are identified, such as expenses of the Registrar's and Bursar's Offices and Library and State Aid based on enrollment. These items are accumulated and the totals prorated to cost centers based on the percentage of FTE students taught by each cost center, as shown in Exhibit 6 below:

Exhibit 6
Expenses to be Prorated

Registrar's Office	$ 259,080
Bursar's Office	65,172
Library	504,989
Other	1,746,877
Total Expenses to be Prorated	$2,576,118

Rutherford Campus	Proration Basis		Expenses to be Prorated
	FTE Students	%	
College of Business	1,703	49.46	$1,274,044a
Other Colleges	1,740	50.54	1,302,074a
Total Colleges	3,443	100.00	$2,576,118a

aSee Exhibit 8.

2. Proration on the Basis of Salaries. Only the expenses for Employee (Fringe) Benefits are prorated on the basis of Salaries. Employee Benefits are recorded centrally as a General University expense and must, therefore, be allocated to each Cost Center. (A more precise, but less practical method of prorating Employee Benefits would be to develop separate proration bases for each component of Employee Benefits—Health Insurance, Life Insurance, Pension, FICA taxes, etc.) Employee Benefit expenses are prorated to cost centers based on the percentage of total salaries paid by each cost center.

3. Proration on the Basis of Direct Expenses. Income and expense items that do not vary with enrollments are identified, such as Endowment Income and Physical Plant Expenses. These items are accumulated and the totals prorated to cost centers based on the percentage of Total Direct Expenses incurred by each cost center. Total Direct Expenses are defined as the total of Direct and Attributed Expenses of each cost center.

The choice of Total Direct Expenses as a proration basis has provided each cost center with the desired incentive to minimize costs. The lower the Direct Expenses, the lower will be the prorated Net Indirect Expenses.

Cost Analysis Allocation Report Format

The format for the allocation of Indirect Income and Expenses is shown in Exhibits 7, 8, and 9.

Exhibit 7 displays the income and expenses of the Total University and the distribution of University income and expenses to the Campuses. The Surplus (Deficit) of all Campuses equals the Surplus of the Total University.

Exhibit 7
Fairleigh Dickinson University
Costs & Revenues Distribution
Total University—By Campus
1979-80 Budgeted Results

		Col. 1	Col. 2	Col. 3	Col. 4	Col. 5
			University Indirect		Campuses	
Line Ref.		Total University[a]	Income & Expenses[a]	Total[a]	Rutherford[b]	All Other
1	**Direct Income** (see Exhibit 2)	$60,632,522	($ 7,356,858)	$53,275,664	$12,921,955	$40,353,709
2	**Direct Expenses** (see Exhibit 2)	60,168,477	(12,962,588)	47,205,889	10,528,563	36,677,326
3	**Balance**	$ 464,045	$ 5,605,730	6,069,775	2,393,392	3,676,383
	Allocation of Univ. Indirect Income					
4	Attributed			5,468,709	724,592	4,744,117
	Prorated on the Basis of:					
5	Direct Campus Expenses			1,888,149	421,624	1,466,525
	Total Univ. Indirect Income			7,356,858	1,146,216	6,210,642
	Allocation of Univ. Indirect Expenses					
7	Attributed			1,156,499	247,836	908,663
	Prorated on the Basis of:					
8	Direct Campus Expenses			5,475,053	1,222,579	4,252,474
9	Salaries			6,331,036	1,465,334	4,865,702
	Total Univ. Indirect Expenses			12,962,588	2,935,749	10,026,839
11	Net Univ. Indirect Expense Allocation			5,605,730	1,789,533	3,816,197
12	**Surplus (Deficit)** (see Exhibits 4 & 11)			$ 464,045	$ 603,859	($ 139,814)

[a]See Exhibit 5.
[b]See Exhibit 8.

Exhibit 8 displays the income and expenses of the Rutherford Campus (see Column 4 of Exhibit 7) and the distribution of University and Rutherford Campus income and expenses to the Rutherford Colleges. The Surplus (Deficit) of all Rutherford Colleges equals the Surplus of the Rutherford Campus.

Exhibit 9 displays the income and expenses of the Rutherford College of Business (see Column 4 of Exhibit 8) and the distribution of University, Rutherford Campus, and Rutherford College of Business income and expenses to the Rutherford College of Business Departments. The Surplus (Deficit) of all Rutherford College of Business Departments equals the Surplus of the Rutherford College of Business.

Exhibit 8
Fairleigh Dickinson University
Costs & Revenues Distribution
Rutherford Campus—By Colleges
1979-80 Budgeted Results

Line Ref.		Col. 1 Rutherford Campus[a]	Col. 2 University & Campus Indirect Income & Expenses	Col. 3 Total	Col. 4 Colleges Business[b]	Col. 5 All Other
1	**Direct Income** (see Exhibit 2)	$12,921,955	($1,700,026)	$11,221,929	$5,624,892	$5,597,037
2	**Direct Expenses** (see Exhibit 2)	10,528,563	(5,676,665)	4,851,898	1,519,470	3,332,428
	Allocated University Indirect:					
3	Income	(1,146,216)	1,146,216	-		
4	Expenses	2,935,749	(2,935,749)	-		
5	Net Allocation	1,789,533	(1,789,533)	-		
6	**Balance**	$ 603,859	5,766,172	6,370,031	4,105,422	2,264,609
	Allocation of Univ. & Campus Indirect Income					
7	Attributed			157,365	808	156,557
	Prorated on the Basis of:					
8	Direct College Expenses			2,115,150	670,291	1,444,859
9	FTE Students			573,727	198,167	375,560
10	Total Univ. & Campus Indirect Income			2,846,242	869,266	1,976,976
	Allocation of Univ. & Campus Indirect Expenses					
11	Attributed			(56,919)	-	(56,919)
	Prorated on the Basis of:					
12	Direct College Expenses			5,163,314	1,636,254	3,527,060
13	Salaries			929,901	275,776	654,125
14	FTE Students			2,576,118	1,274,044	1,302,074
15	Total Univ. & Campus Indirect Expenses			8,612,414	3,186,074	5,426,340
16	Net Univ. & Campus Indirect Income & Expenses Allocation			5,766,172	2,316,808	3,449,364
17	**Surplus (Deficit)** (see Exhibits 4 & 11)			$ 603,859	$1,788,614	($1,184,755)

[a]See Exhibit 7.

[b]See Exhibit 9.

Exhibit 9
Fairleigh Dickinson University
Costs & Revenues Distribution
Rutherford Campus—College of Business by Departments
1979-80 Budgeted Results

Line Ref.		Col. 1 College of Business[a]	Col. 2 University, Campus, & College Indirect Income & Expenses	Col. 3 Total	Col. 4 Accounting	Col. 5 Management	Col. 6 Marketing	Col. 7 All Other
					Departments			
1	**Direct Income** (see Exhibit 2)	$5,624,892		$5,624,892	$1,362,576	$996,037	$1,314,353	$1,951,926
2	**Direct Expenses** (see Exhibit 2)	1,519,470	($ 191,101)	1,328,369	356,746	159,847	263,616	548,160
	Allocated Univ. & Campus Indirect							
3	Income	(869,266)	869,266	-				
4	Expenses	3,186,074	(3,186,074)	-				
5	Net Allocation	2,316,808	(2,316,808)	-				
6	**Balance**	$1,788,614	2,507,909	4,296,523	1,005,830	836,190	1,050,737	1,403,766
	Allocation of Univ., Campus, & College Indirect Income							
7	Attributed			808		808		
	Prorated on the Basis of:							
8	Direct Dept. Expenses			670,291	180,040	80,636	133,053	276,562
9	FTE Students			198,167	71,297	46,944	57,817	22,109
10	Total Univ., Campus, & College Indirect Income			869,266	251,337	128,388	190,870	298,671
	Allocation of Univ., Campus, & College Indirect Expenses							
11	Attributed							
	Prorated on the Basis of:							
12	Direct Dept. Expenses			1,858,656	499,235	223,596	368,943	766,882
13	Salaries			244,475	72,888	32,100	53,639	85,848
14	FTE Students			1,274,044	319,495	226,766	305,694	422,089
15	Total Univ., Campus, & College Indirect Expenses			3,377,175	891,618	482,462	728,276	1,274,819
16	**Net Univ., Campus, & College Indirect Expense Allocation**			2,507,909	640,281	354,074	537,406	976,148
17	Surplus (Deficit) (see Exhibits 4 & 11)			$1,788,614	$ 365,549	$482,116	$ 513,331	$ 427,618

[a]See Exhibit 8.

Examples of Cost Analysis Summary Reports

Upon completion of the current year's cost analysis distribution of income and expenses, the calculated Surplus (Deficit) for each cost center is summarized together with relevant statistical data. Examples of Summary schedules are shown in Exhibits 10, 11, 12, and 13. The purpose of such information is to highlight trends and to identify correlations and significant relationships.

Exhibit 10 displays unit Income-Cost data. Income, Direct Expenses, Net Indirect Expenses, and Surplus (Deficit) figures are divided by Student Credit Hours taught to calculate per credit hour data.

Exhibit 11 displays various statistical data next to the calculated Surplus (Deficit) in order to show relationships.

Exhibit 12 displays calculated Surplus (Deficit) figures over a two-year period plotted on a graph. This format, which can be extended over many years, is especially useful in highlighting trends.

Exhibit 10
Rutherford College of Business

	Per Credit Hour			
	Income	Direct Expenses	Net Indirect Expenses	Surplus (Deficit)
Accounting Department	$110.75	$29.00	$52.04	$29.71
Management Department	114.70	18.41	40.77	55.52
Marketing Department	112.91	22.65	45.16	44.10
Other Departments	128.15	32.04	58.75	37.36
Total Rutherford College of Business	$124.39	$29.38	$55.46	$39.55

Exhibit 11
Rutherford Campus

	Surplus (Deficit)[a]	Average Class Size	Full-time Salaries as Percentage of Total Salaries	College Salaries as Percentage of Tuition Income	Net Indirect Expenses as Percentage of Total College Expenses
College of Business	$1,788,614	26.1	58.6	22.9	152.5
Other Colleges	(1,184,755)	19.2	84.1	52.8	112.0
Total Rutherford Campus	$ 603,859	22.0	76.0	39.7	123.5

[a]See Exhibits 4, 7, 8, and 9.

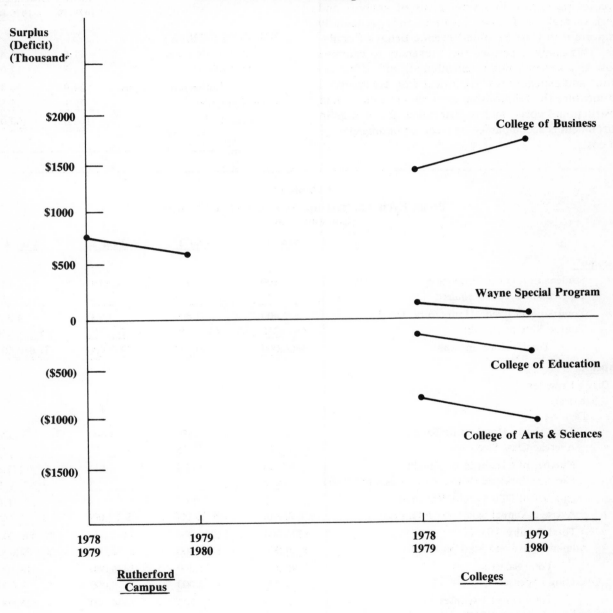

Exhibit 12
Fairleigh Dickinson University
Rutherford Campus & Colleges
Surplus (Deficit)
Fiscal Years 1978-79 through 1979-80

Surplus
(Deficit)
(Thousands)

$2000

College of Business

$1500

$1000

$500

Wayne Special Program

0

($500)

College of Education

($1000)

College of Arts & Sciences

($1500)

1978   1979
1979   1980

Rutherford
Campus

1978   1979
1979   1980

Colleges

Exhibit 13 displays the percentage of tuition income generated by the Colleges on the Rutherford Campus over a two-year period. Such information reveals enrollment trends over time.

Other Uses of the Cost Information

FDU uses the data generated by its instruction cost accounting system in several areas of analysis and decision making. The cost information is particularly important in Cost-Volume-Revenue Behavior analysis. This analysis permits the University to examine how changes in volume (enrollment) will affect income and expenditures. Historical data are analyzed to measure the relationship between enrollment and instructional costs, and to determine if a change in enrollment is accompanied by a corresponding change in costs.

Exhibit 13
Percentage of Tuition Income
Generated by Rutherford Campus Colleges
Over a Two-Year Period

	% of Total Tuition Income Generated	
	1978-79	1979-80
Rutherford Campus		
College of Business	11.6	12.4
Other Colleges	13.3	12.0
Total Rutherford Campus	24.9	24.4
Other Campuses	75.1	75.6
Total University	100.0	100.0

Exhibit 14
Break-Even Analysis for New Academic Program
(Constant Dollars)

	Year 1	Year 2	Year 3	Year 4
Income				
Student Enrollment Projection	100	120	150	180
Curriculum Credits Required	× 24	× 24	× 24	× 24
Total Student Credit Hours to be Taught	2,400	2,880	3,600	4,320
Tuition Rate per Credit	× $ 250	× $ 250	× $ 250	× $ 250
Total Tuition Income	$600,000	$720,000	$900,000	$1,080,000
Expenses				
Direct Expenses:				
Salaries:				
Faculty:				
Total Credit Hours to be Taught	2,400	2,880	3,600	4,320
Average Class Size	÷ 25	÷ 25	÷ 25	÷ 25
Number of Classes to be Taught	96	115.2	144	172.8
Faculty Workload (Number of Classes per Year)	÷ 8	÷ 8	÷ 8	÷ 8
Number of FTE Faculty Required	12	14.4	18	21.6
Average Annual Salary per FTE Faculty	× $ 23,000	× $ 23,000	× $ 23,000	× $ 23,000
Total Faculty Salaries	$276,000	$331,200	$414,000	$ 496,800
Administrative and Staff Salaries	$ 20,000	$ 20,000	$ 22,000	$ 22,000
Total Salaries	$296,000	$351,200	$436,000	$ 518,800
Operating Expenses	$ 6,000	$ 6,000	$ 8,000	$ 8,000
Total Direct Expenses	$302,000	$357,200	$444,000	$ 526,800
Net Indirect Expenses (105% x Direct Expenses)[1]	$317,100	$375,060	$466,200	$ 553,140
Total Expenses	$619,100	$732,260	$910,200	$1,079,940
Surplus (Deficit)	($ 19,100)	($ 12,260)	($ 10,200)	$ 60

[1]Net indirect expense percentage of 105% represents the net indirect expenses percentage of the existing program that most closely resembles the new program being analyzed.

To the extent that historical trends reveal future implications, the University can examine the potential impact of a range of policy decisions. FDU analysts can, for example, estimate the effects of changing the average class size, the faculty workload level, or the tuition and fee charge. In addition, the cost information can be used to create models to measure the impact of changes in the configuration of campuses, colleges, and departments, as well as the addition or deletion of programs.

In evaluating potential new academic programs, FDU uses its cost data to determine a break-even point. The technique is similar to the Cost-Volume-Revenue Behavior analysis. Exhibit 14 summarizes the calculations for a hypothetical new program.

The analysis includes the establishment of tuition and fee levels and a determination of enrollment requirements. The preliminary calculations are based on faculty salary and workload, operating expenses, and a projection of indirect expenses based on the historical data of the closest existing academic program. The break-even point for the proposed program is Year 4 (see Exhibit 14). At FDU this type of analysis is used internally to determine the financial feasibility of new programs, and externally to obtain State Department of Higher Education approval and to obtain outside funding.

Conclusion

The Cost Analysis system at FDU has earned wide acceptance within the University community. It has provided management with an effective tool for dealing with rapidly changing conditions.

exhibit 6-b

case study:
ohio wesleyan university—a direct
cost approach to instructional costing

Ohio Wesleyan University has a computer-based system for calculating and reporting unit costs of instruction. The system has been in operation since the 1969-70 fiscal year. At this writing, comparative information for 11 years is available. The university's administrators have thus had a substantial amount of experience in this area of costing.

The system calculates two types of unit cost: cost per student enrolled and cost per student credit unit earned. It provides unit costs and aggregate costs for each instruction department, each academic discipline within an instruction department, each of two course levels within each discipline (freshman-sophomore, junior-senior), and each individual course section.

The term "academic discipline" refers to course offerings grouped according to classifications of the Higher Education General Information Survey (HEGIS). Generally, the groupings correspond to the university's department structure. Because some departments contain multiple disciplines for organizational convenience and efficiency, focusing in those cases on the disciplines as well as on the department provides a clearer picture of the academic program and its costs.

Reporting instructional costs is an annual job at Ohio Wesleyan. Shortly after the end of the fiscal year (June 30), the controller and the data processing staff work together to create an instructional cost disk file. Most of the data for this file are obtained from three other computer disk files—the class file, the payroll-personnel file, and the accounting file. Some additional information generated by use of computer terminals is added. The data processing staff use the instructional cost disk file to prepare four computer reports: (1) Faculty Compensation Analysis, (2) Instruction Department Cost Grouping, (3) Course Cost Report, and (4) Academic Discipline

Cost Report. The controller then manually prepares multiyear comparisons and analyses of unit costs.

The reports and analyses are sent to the president and to other administrators with academic or financial responsibilities. Certain of those persons prepare additional analyses. The full set of analyses is forwarded to the members of one or more faculty committees.

Ohio Wesleyan, a private liberal arts college with an enrollment of 2,200, has a strong tradition of academic freedom and shared governance. The 170 faculty members have primary responsibility for the curriculum, academic standards, and faculty employment policies. Faculty committees make recommendations on various budget matters and, in particular, on the allocation of resources among instruction departments. Therefore, it is important for faculty as well as administrators to be informed about cost and workload matters.

The instructional cost system serves a limited purpose—evaluation of financial resource utilization in the various academic disciplines. Its characteristics include relative simplicity and ease of use. Calculated instructional costs include all faculty compensation (salary and benefits) and other expenditures of instruction departments. Administrators and faculty committee members consider these costs, along with other relevant data, when making decisions about the academic program.

The university's decision makers operate within a relatively stable environment. They have seldom had to deal with large enrollment changes, new degree programs, or major research efforts, and they do not have to work with any state agency, coordinating board, or legislature. For example, Ohio Wesleyan's instructional cost system does not significantly address the joint cost problem associated with faculty activity; the system does not go beyond discipline course offerings to calculate the unit cost of student majors; and finally, there is no allocation of support costs to academic disciplines.

Development and Implementation

Three different factors combined to influence the development of the instructional cost system. The first influence was external. In the latter part of the 1960s, costing for colleges and universities began to receive an increased amount of attention in periodicals and at professional meetings. The other influences were internal. Ohio Wesleyan was actively developing an integrated computer system and data base for administrative use. Cost information seemed to be a logical extension of that system. Finally, the university community was turning its attention to long-range planning, and administrators were developing data that would be useful for both planning and program evaluation.

The controller's interest in the subject of costing was first aroused by William T. Jerome's presentation at the 1965 annual meeting of the Ohio Association of College and University Business Officers. Jerome complained at some length about the general lack of cost accounting data in educational institutions. The controller carefully studied subsequent journal articles on the subject and followed with interest the work being done by WICHE's Planning and Management Systems Division, which later changed its name to the National Center for Higher Education Management Systems (NCHEMS). In 1970 the controller had an opportunity to meet and work briefly with several staff on what at that time was called the Cost Finding Principles Project.

Development of Ohio Wesleyan's administrative computer system began in 1967 with the installation of a small, business-oriented machine dedicated exclusively to administrative applications. (There was a separate computer installation for instruction and research.) The staff followed a team approach for systems development. Data processing personnel worked with the primary users, such as the admissions director, registrar, or director of physical plant, to develop the input-output specifications, master file contents, and systems flow charts, making use of material from periodicals and other published sources whenever possible. Systems designs were reviewed widely throughout the campus community before the data processing staff began programming.

In the late 1960s, data processing experts were already writing about data bases and integrated systems. Influenced by these concepts, the Ohio Wesleyan staff tried to create a data base with little redundancy, composed of disk files that could be used in various combinations. In doing so, they also created, incidentally, a readily accessible computerized source for most of the data elements used to calculate instruction costs.

By the 1969-70 fiscal year, the administrative data processing system included integrated subsystems for student and class records, accounting, billing, accounts payable, payroll, applicants for admission, alumni (plus parents and "friends"), gifts, and pledges. The addition of an instructional cost subsystem was a logical extension of this work, since the subsystem draws on data in the class, accounting, and payroll disk files. (Subsequently, student financial aid and plant operation and maintenance costing subsystems were added to complete the administrative data processing system. The physical plant costing subsystem is the subject of exhibit 4-B, which appears at the end of chapter 4.)

The final impetus for instructional costing came from two ad hoc, long-range planning committees, the first of which was appointed in 1968. The university then faced a number of decisions about the academic program, new construction, and finances. The first long-range planning committee made a thorough study of the goals of the institution and the related implications for resources. The committee membership included faculty, administrators, and students, with a majority being faculty members.

The university controller was a member of the committee. He supplied and interpreted needed financial data, including some manually prepared unit cost studies. Those early cost studies, largely experimental, drew on the articles and speeches referred to above. The resulting committee discussions clarified many procedural points and computational matters.

Because of the resignation of the university president, this first long-range planning committee never issued a formal report. It continued its work into 1969, however, and accumulated a significant file of working papers, which eventually were made available to a second long-range planning committee.

The university's new president appointed the second long-range planning committee in December 1970. It included the controller and many other members of the previous committee, and its charge was as follows:

"To develop and articulate a set of objectives for Ohio Wesleyan for the 1970s and to prepare a consistent and integrated program for obtaining those objectives."

The committee divided itself into three subcommittees. One subcommittee examined financial and space priorities. The controller, a member of this subcommittee, again supplied and interpreted financial data.

To provide additional information for the subcommittee, the controller began to work with the data processing staff to design the instruction cost system described here. In doing this work, he made use of information gained from reading and from professional meetings, as well as from his experience with the first long-range planning committee and the experimental costing studies. The system design was completed in spring 1971. A student employee, one of the controller's accounting students, wrote the computer programs during the summer. The priorities subcommittee received the first two sets of reports at an early fall meeting. Those reports contained data for the 1969-70 and 1970-71 academic years.

The influence of these data was such that the committee's final report contained several references to unit costs and several recommendations concerning high cost areas. Of course, not all the recommendations were followed. Instructional costing, however, had become a permanent part of the administrative data processing system.

The move from manually prepared, experimental cost analysis to a computer-based system was a significant step. The controller and the data processing staff could now produce unit cost data efficiently and routinely each year and, in fact, have done so for each fiscal year since 1969-70.

Computer-Generated Reports

Following are descriptions and illustrations of the four computer-generated reports. The illustrations show the actual formats of these reports but contain fictitious names and amounts.

Faculty Compensation Analysis. The Faculty Compensation Analysis is a workload study with cost figures added. It presents the full load of all individual faculty members, full-time and part-time. The faculty appear in departmental sequence, alphabetically within department. The report lists each course section taught by each faculty member, showing number (including abbreviated department name)

and title. Also shown for each course section are the time and days of class meetings, the building and room, the enrollment, the amount of student credit earned, the term, and the amount of faculty workload credit given. The report contains each faculty member's compensation, with an amount of compensation apportioned to each course on the basis of load credit.

The compensation figures include both salary and allocated benefits. The benefits are pension and group insurance premiums, payroll taxes, and tuition remission for dependents. The benefit allocation is a certain percentage of salary, revised annually. There are separate percentages for salary and hourly wage employees, as the benefit levels differ.

Some faculty members have assignments other than the teaching of course sections. These assignments count as part of their total workload. Examples include giving private music lessons, coaching athletic teams, performing academic computing, coordinating off-campus studies, and serving as departmental chairperson. The university has a formal leave program, and a leave taken counts toward a faculty member's total workload. The Faculty Compensation Analysis lists all these assignments in a manner similar to the listing of course sections, with compensation apportioned according to the amount of faculty credit given.

Ohio Wesleyan has one special session, in the summer. Summer teaching is in addition to the regular workload and carries extra pay. The instructional cost reports do not include summer session costs. They also do not include sponsored research done in the summer or as an overload during the regular year. The Faculty Compensation Analysis does include sponsored research, however, if a faculty member has a reduced teaching load because of it.

The apportionment of an individual's compensation is based on official credits given rather than on time and effort reports. For course sections, the university has a formula for awarding teaching credit. For other assignments, the academic administrators have established an amount of credit in consultation with the individuals involved and their department chairpersons. The university develops faculty assignments and assesses staffing needs on the basis of these official credit figures. There is widespread agreement that the figures are fair and properly used. For this reason, they seem to be the appropriate basis for apportioning cost.

116

Figure 6-B-1									1980

Faculty Compensation Analysis

Course Number	Course Name	Time	Days	Bldg.	Room	Enrollment	Student Credit	Term	Faculty Credit	Faculty Compensation
1949	Smith, R.W.									
EC 11A	Principles of Economics	9:00	MTWTF	ED	211	37	1	FA	1	$ 4,307
EC 11A	Principles of Economics	9:00	MTWTF	ED	211	41	1	WI	1	4,307
EC 51	Managerial Economics	11:00	MTWTF	ED	214	32	1	FA	1	4,307
EC 59	Monetary & Fiscal Policy	11:00	MTWTF	ED	212	40	1	WI	1	4,307
EC CH	Chairperson								1	4,307
EC LV	Leave								2	8,615
								Totals	7	$30,150
1312	Jones, W.J.									
PE 1007A	Racquetball	11:00	MW	BR	13	16	1/3	WI	1/3	$ 1,295
PE 1007B	Racquetball	11:00	TH	BR	13	12	1/3	WI	1/3	1,295
PE 1007C	Racquetball	9:00	MW	BR	13	18	1/3	WI	1/3	1,295
PE 61	History of Sport	10:00	MTTF	BR	119	24	1	WI	1	3,884
PE 61	History of Sport	10:00	MTTF	BR	119	27	1	SP	1	3,884
PE FB3	Asst. Football Coach							FA	2	7,769
PE IM	Intramural Director							YR	2	7,769
								Totals	7	$27,191

In examining the Faculty Compensation Analysis (see figure 6-B-1), the reader will note that Ohio Wesleyan does not use a conventional credit-hour system. The university has a limited course plan, and most courses carry one unit of credit for both students and faculty. Faculty are supposed to perform seven units of work. Certain items are omitted from the Faculty Compensation Analysis on the grounds of materiality. Faculty members are expected to do nonsponsored research, advise students, and serve on university committees. The official assignment policy assumes that each faculty member will spend an equal amount of time on these three activities combined. Therefore, listing them in the Faculty Compensation Analysis would not particularly add to that report's usefulness, and assigning costs to them would not ultimately affect the relative costs of academic disciplines.

As an alternative to assignment credit, the university could use faculty time and effort reporting to apportion faculty compensation. Institutions with federal grants and contracts must use time and effort reporting procedures specified in Office of Management and Budget Circular A-21, "Cost Principles for Educational Institutions." Since Ohio Wesleyan uses the A-21 "Simplified Method" (Section H) for federal indirect cost rate determination, the time and effort reporting required is limited to faculty with federal grants and contracts and to individuals with joint assignments spanning both direct and indirect cost activities. The number of individuals covered is relatively small. Still, the university's administration could extend the requirement to others for internal costing purposes.

However, there are several objections to faculty time and effort reporting. One is that in academic pursuits time spent does not necessarily measure work accomplished, certainly not as directly as it does on a factory assembly line. Universities do not pay faculty for putting in time. Another objection concerns the joint cost problem. A faculty member may well have difficulty separating the time spent on course preparation from the time spent on research. These objections have been and are being discussed in the higher education literature. Ohio Wesleyan's administrators do not pretend to have solved these problems. They have, instead, chosen to avoid time and effort reporting because the existing assignment structure is well understood and accepted, and is simple to use. That structure places primary emphasis on instruction and instruction-related activities, with research and public service considered as supplements to the instruction function.

Instruction Department Cost Grouping. This report shows the combination of expenditures that are directly attributable to individual instruction and instruction-related departments but indirectly attributable to academic disciplines or courses. The instruction-related departments included are academic computing, off-campus study, debate, and athletics. Teaching faculty are involved with these activities as directors and coaches. Also included are interdepartmental instruction programs that have separate account numbers (urban studies, women's studies).

The items grouped for each department are faculty compensation apportioned to chairperson assignments and to leaves in the Faculty Compensation Analysis, plus other departmental expenditures from current funds. Other departmental expenditures consist of clerical wages, student wages, teaching supplies and equipment, office supplies and equipment, travel, duplicating, and miscellaneous. Expenditures from both unrestricted and restricted current funds are included if they benefit the entire department. Although charged to separate accounts in the fund accounting system, they are combined here for costing purposes. Special projects are excluded, however.

In figure 6-B-2, the reader can trace the hypothetical Professor Smith's chairperson assignment and leave from the Faculty Compensation Analysis (figure 6-B-1) to the economics, management, and accounting figures in the Instruction Department Cost Grouping.

Figure 6-B-2
1980 Instruction Department Cost Grouping

Department	Acct. No.	Description	Amount
Economics,	00116	Chairperson	$ 4,307
Management,	00116	Leave	8,615
and	00116	Leave	6,021
Accounting	00116	Unrestricted expenditures	12,742
	31116	Endowed expenditures	1,520
	32116	Gift expenditures	2,019
	00116	Total	$35,224

Capital expenditures by instruction departments present a procedural question. OMB Circular A-21 specifies that cost figures may include depreciation or use allowances, but may not include capital expenditures. Ohio Wesleyan has chosen a more expedient course of action, again on grounds of materiality. The Instruction Department Cost Grouping includes capital expenditures charged to departmental accounts (such expenditures tend to be relatively small and are consistent from year to year). It does not include major additions financed with restricted plant funds, nor does it include depreciation or use allowances.

Course Cost Report. The Course Cost Report (see figure 6-B-3) lists individual course sections, showing number and title. The course sections are grouped first by department, then by academic disciplines and by course level (of which there are two). The university numbers freshman-sophomore courses below 50, and junior-senior courses 50 and above. Ohio Wesleyan offers no graduate work. Dollar figures supplied for each course section include faculty cost and departmental cost. The faculty cost is the same as that shown in the Faculty Compensation Analysis (figure 6-B-1). By comparing figure 6-B-1 to figure 6-B-3, the reader can cross-reference the figures for EC 11A (fall), EC 11A (winter), EC 51, and PE IM. The departmental cost is an allocated portion of the total amount accumulated in the Instruction Department Cost Grouping. That total is spread equally over all the courses offered in the department.

Figure 6-B-3 presents additional data for each course section. These include the enrollment, the amount of student credit given, the total cost (the sum of the faculty cost and the department cost), and, for reference, the time and the term the course was offered. Two unit cost figures appear—the credit unit cost and the student cost. The credit unit cost is the total cost divided by the product of the enrollment and the amount of student credit, while the student cost represents the total cost divided by the enrollment. These two unit cost figures differ only when the amount of student credit is other than one.

The instruction-related departments referred to earlier (academic computing, off-campus study, debate, and athletics) do not have course sections or enrollments. For those departments the Course Cost Report lists individual work assignments with aggregate dollar costs only.

Figure 6-B-3
Course Cost Report
Fiscal Year 1980

Course Number	Course Name	No. Sec.	Std. Enroll.	Credit Unit Cost	Std. Cost	Total Cost	Faculty Cost	Dept. Cost	Student Credit	Time	Term
	2204 Economics										
	Lower Level										
EC 11A	Principles of Economics		37	$134	$134	$4,959	$4,307	$652	1	9:00	FA
EC 11A	Principles of Economics		41	121	121	4,959	4,307	652	1	9:00	WI
EC 11A	Principles of Economics		44	61	61	2,671	2,019	652	1	9:00	SP
EC 11B	Principles of Economics		35	89	89	3,114	2,462	652	1	10:00	FA
EC 11B	Principles of Economics		40	112	112	4,472	3,820	652	1	10:00	WI
	etc.										
	Totals and Averages	14	564	97	97	54,792	45,660	9,132			
	Upper Level										
EC 51	Managerial Economics		32	155	155	4,959	4,307	652	1	11:00	FA
EC 95	Senior Seminar		12	111	222	2,671	2,019	652	1/2	3:00	SP
	9920 Intramurals										
PE IM	Intramural Director					12,561	7,769	4,792			
	Totals and Averages					$12,561	$7,769	$4,792			

Figure 6-B-4
Academic Discipline Cost Report
Fiscal Year 1980

		No. Sec.	Std. Enroll.	Credit Unit Cost	Std. Cost	Total Cost	Faculty Cost	Dept. Cost
0016	Economics, Management, and Accounting							
0502	Accounting							
	Lower level	8	318	$ 98	$ 98	$ 31,308	$ 26,090	$ 5,218
	Upper level	6	194	101	101	19,570	15,656	3,914
	Discipline totals	14	512	99	99	50,878	41,746	9,132
0506	Management							
	Lower level	3	115	85	85	9,785	7,828	1,957
	Upper level	5	131	149	149	19,572	16,310	3,262
	Discipline totals	8	246	119	119	29,357	24,138	5,219
2204	Economics							
	Lower level	14	564	97	97	54,792	45,660	9,132
	Upper level	18	523	129	129	67,721	55,980	11,741
	Discipline totals	32	1,087	113	113	122,513	101,640	20,873
	Department totals	54	1,845	$110	$110	$202,748	$167,524	$35,224

The Course Cost Report contains cost totals and unit cost averages for each department, each academic discipline within a department, and each of the two course levels for each discipline. Some departments contain only one academic discipline, while others have two or more.

Academic Discipline Cost Report. This is a summary report (see figure 6-B-4) containing the total and average cost lines from the Course Cost Report (figure 6-B-3). In the two figures, the reader can cross-reference the numbers for lower-level economics courses.

Computer Processing

The instructional cost subsystem is an extension of other administrative computing subsystems. Most of the needed data exist in other disk files. The costing reports are run shortly after the end of the fiscal year. A brief description of the process follows:

Step 1. The subsystem pertaining to students and courses includes a disk file that provides most of the needed information about individual course sections. Data elements transferred from this file to a new instructional cost disk file are the course number (including abbreviated department name), course name, student enrollment, student credit, time, days, building, room, term (fall, winter, spring), and instructor's name. The instruction cost disk file is built in department and course number sequence.

Step 2. The staff use terminals to enter additional information for each course section. These additional data elements are a departmental account number (corresponding to the accounting system chart of accounts), the HEGIS discipline number, the instructor's payroll system number, and the faculty workload credit.

Step 3. The staff use terminals to enter other faculty assignments. The format is the same as that for course sections and includes a dummy course number, a descriptive title, account number, payroll number, and workload credit. The other data elements are blank.

Step 4. The payroll-personnel disk file provides each faculty member's total compensation (salary and benefits). The instructional cost file is sorted into faculty payroll number sequence. A computer program apportions each individual's compensation to his or her course sections and other assignments on the basis of the workload credits. The computer then prints the Faculty Compensation Analysis.

Step 5. The accounting disk file provides the records of instruction department expenditures other than compensation. Those records are listed in the Instruction Department Cost Grouping, along with dummy course records created in Step 3 for chairperson assignments and faculty leaves. The department identification digits in the account number are the selection and sort key. The computer accumulates and prints a total for each department.

Step 6. The computer then apportions each department's expenditures total equally among all cost records containing that department number, with the cost file first having been resorted into department and course number sequence.

Step 7. From tape, the data processing staff load two name-number tables, one for departments and one for academic disciplines.

Step 8. With the disk files now complete, the computer prints the Course Cost Report and the Instruction Discipline Cost Report.

Step 9. The controller and staff review the reports for omissions, inconsistencies, and other apparent errors. They balance department totals to predetermined control figures for student enrollment, student credit units, faculty cost, and department cost. The staff enter necessary corrections, and the computer prints a new set of reports for review. Usually, the second set of reports is satisfactory for distribution.

Use and Analysis

The instruction cost system is an evaluation tool. Copies of the four computer-printed reports go to five administrative officials: the president, the provost, the academic dean, the chief business officer, and the controller. These persons use the reports primarily to compare the financial performance of the various academic disciplines.

By themselves, the reports usually raise questions rather than provide answers, and that is their real purpose. For this and other reasons, the instructional cost system is only indirectly a planning tool. It looks back at historical costs, rather than forward to projected or budgeted costs. It does not distinguish between variable and fixed costs (such a distinction is necessary for projections). For budgeting and projecting, university administrators make use of a separate computer software package, a modeling language that solves equations expressing relationships among applicant, student, staff, and financial data.

Neither is the costing system a budget control device. The university's accounting system produces an extensive series of budget control reports, based on the concepts of responsibility accounting. These reports segregate expenditures according to individuals' budget responsibilities and include comparisons of actual and budget amounts.

To aid in the use of the cost data for evaluation purposes, the controller manually prepares multiyear comparisons of the discipline and course-level unit cost figures. Those comparisons are arranged in a number of different sequences—low to high campuswide, low to high in four broad groups (sciences, social sciences, arts, humanities), and in narrower groups of similar disciplines (biological sciences, physical sciences). The comparisons clearly reveal trends as well as identify any discipline with a cost figure that is out of line within its own grouping.

Administrators and faculty have certain expectations about costs. Physical sciences and the arts are supposed to be more expensive than the social sciences and the humanities. This is partly because of teaching methods (laboratory and studio instruction versus classroom lectures) and partly because of equipment and materials costs. Unit cost comparisons, however, may reveal disciplines that do not fit these expectations, such as high-cost social science or humanities disciplines, or low-cost physical science or arts disciplines.

Other administrators use the Faculty Compensation Analysis to develop statistical measures of individual teaching loads and departmental ratios of student enrollments to full-time equivalent faculty members.

The administration annually furnishes many of these analyses to one or more faculty committees. One key committee has the responsibility for reviewing vacant faculty positions. That committee makes recommendations to the president as to whether each position should be filled and studies the various

analyses resulting from the instructional cost system, along with other information about the departments involved. The departments themselves supply written reports describing their academic programs and plans for the future. After reviewing all the written information, the committee meets with department members for a thorough discussion of the situation. Thus, the instructional cost system is one of several sources of the information considered in making these important recommendations.

The faculty have formally approved guidelines used by the committee. Those guidelines, including "cost of program per graduation unit," are reproduced in figure 6-B-5.

Figure 6-B-5
Ohio Wesleyan University
Guidelines for Allocation and Review
of Faculty Positions

Decisions as to whether to authorize new positions or reauthorize vacant ones require considering several more or less independent kinds of data and circumstances, and are always affected by the overall distribution of positions among teaching areas and the ratio of students to faculty that the institution has decided it can support. Because of the unique and varied conditions of each department, it is not possible to attach fixed weights to the factors that will be considered. For initial authorization and reauthorization decisions, the following factors will be weighed:

- Extent to which the curriculum of the department and the position under consideration fit into the statement of aims and the liberal arts traditions of Ohio Wesleyan.
- Relation of the position to the curriculum of the department.
- Need for a viable curriculum for the major.
- Departmental method of determining faculty teaching load and consistency of that method with university teaching load policy.
- Number of graduation units generated by each faculty member.
- Cost of program per graduation unit.
- Versatility of other faculty in department (i.e., their ability to teach courses associated with the position under review).
- Grade distribution.
- Number of majors.
- Service functions of the department.
- Nonteaching responsibilities unique to the department.
- Course proliferation and overlap.
- Impact of new courses and/or new programs on curriculum and total enrollment.
- Distribution of course offerings (upper and lower levels).

The various reports and analyses do not include costs of student majors. The liberal arts curriculum at Ohio Wesleyan does not contain rigid patterns of courses for each major. Major requirements constitute only about one-third of a student's total course load. Students are encouraged to take a wide variety of courses, and do not declare a major until the end of their sophomore year. Under these circumstances, the university's administrators and faculty have simply shown no interest in the costs of student majors.

There has been a similar lack of interest in the full costs of academic disciplines. Because Ohio Wesleyan has had a history of relatively stable enrollment for many years, decisions about support activities are generally separate and distinct from decisions about academic disciplines. The instructional cost system accordingly does not include allocations of support costs—academic support, student services, institutional support, and plant operation and maintenance.

Conclusion

Decisions are made at an educational institution such as Ohio Wesleyan through a complex political process. The administrative officers are not managers in the business sense. The code of regulations specifies that the faculty have primary responsibility for the academic program. They also have a great deal of influence in staffing and budget matters.

All the administrators who receive the instructional cost reports indicate that the data are useful, though they cannot point to specific accomplishments attributable solely to costing. University governance is not that simple. Certainly the entire administrative information system has contributed to positive results, and instructional cost reports and analyses are one part of that system.

The instructional cost subsystem provides information not available in the fund accounting subsystem. That information consists of cost data for instruction and instruction-related departments, academic disciplines, course levels, and course sections.

7

auxiliary enterprises

Auxiliary enterprises furnish nonacademic services directly or indirectly to students, faculty, or staff, and charge a fee related to, but not necessarily equal to, the cost of the services. Traditionally, auxiliary enterprises have encompassed food services, student housing, and college stores. In recent years, however, they have expanded to include faculty dining, confectionery shops, ice cream parlors, vending machines, guest houses, athletic concessions, ski lodges, and bicycle shops. At a number of institutions, intercollegiate athletics and student health services are considered to be auxiliary enterprises, especially if they are essentially self-supporting. This handbook, however, excludes the costs associated with intercollegiate athletics and health services. For a more complete description of the auxiliary enterprises area, refer to *CUBA*, chapter 3:2.

Cost accounting procedures can be particularly useful in the auxiliary enterprises area in part because of the similarity between auxiliaries and service operations in private industry. Some auxiliaries—food service and student housing, for example—provide services during specific time intervals. Others, such as college bookstores, provide consumer goods ranging from textbooks and supplies to trade books and apparel. Auxiliaries, however, do differ from service industries in that they are an integral part of the student services provided by colleges and universities.

Most auxiliary enterprises are managed basically as self-supporting activities, although sometimes a portion of student fees or other support is allocated to assist these activities. In order to be fully self-supporting, an auxiliary enterprise must generate sufficient revenue to cover both its direct and indirect costs. Indirect costs can include a share of central administrative expenses, debt service, and provisions for renewal and replacement of facilities and equipment.

Certain auxiliaries, such as housing and food service, are sometimes subsidized by an institution. In order to determine the amount of the subsidy, it is necessary to be aware of the full cost of providing these services. This cost information is also valuable in institutional planning and budgeting and in setting rates and fees for auxiliary services. During periods of inflation, the collection and analysis of cost data can be particularly useful in insuring that revenues keep pace with costs.

Need for and Uses of Cost Data

Accurate and timely cost data are essential to the efficient management of auxiliary enterprises. As noted in chapter 1, cost accounting information is useful in the planning, budgeting, control, and evaluation of institutional operations.

Cost data enable managers to make informed decisions concerning the prices or fees to be charged for auxiliary services and to identify high cost areas and evaluate the cost of providing alternative levels of service. Cost data are also useful in comparing the costs of in-house services with the cost of contracting with external vendors.

Cost Centers for Auxiliary Enterprises

The organization and structure of the auxiliary enterprises area can vary from institution to institution. Designation of specific auxiliary enterprise cost centers, however, should be according to the institution's organizational structure and chart of accounts. The auxiliary enterprise cost centers used in this handbook are given in figure 7.1 and are based on the chart of accounts in *CUBA*, chapter 5:6 (see exhibit 1-A). Each cost center listed in figure 7.1 can be further disaggregated into specific enterprises, such as snack bars, student cafeterias, and vending machines.

Figure 7.1
Auxiliary Enterprise Cost Centers

Auxiliary enterprise administration[1]
Bookstore
Food service
Housing
Other[2]

Notes

[1] Auxiliary enterprise administration can be under a director of auxiliary enterprises or under the control of the business office or office of student affairs. For a more complete description of auxiliary enterprise organization, refer to *CUBA*, chapter 3:2.

[2] Other auxiliary enterprises could include student unions, student health centers, and rental property. For a description of other types of auxiliary enterprises, refer to *CUBA*, chapter 3:2.

Once cost centers have been designated, a set of cost categories should be selected. At minimum, these categories should include the three major object-of-expenditure classifications: personnel compensation, supplies and expenses, and capital expenditures. These cost categories serve as the basis for assigning costs to the designated cost centers.

Tier one, or direct, costs are the first type of cost to be assigned to the cost centers. Normally reflected in the financial records and budgets of the cost center, tier one costs include personnel compensation, supplies, and other expenses. Some auxiliaries, such as bookstores and food service operations, employ a significant number of part-time staff. A further breakdown of personnel compensation by part-time and full-time staff and by student and nonstudent workers may provide useful information in evaluating the tier one costs of these operations.

In college bookstores and in other auxiliaries such as food service operations, some system of inventory valuation should be implemented. Information from inventory valuation is used in determining tier one costs and in calculating the cost of goods sold. College stores generally use one of two widely accepted inventory valuation systems: the retail method or the cost method. Stores using the retail method take physical inventories at retail price while stores using the cost method establish inventory values directly, by taking physical inventories at cost. For a more detailed description of these two methods, refer to *Administrative Service*, supplement 3:2:1.

Tier one cost data can provide a general idea of the cost of operating auxiliary enterprises. Tier one data alone, however, do not provide sufficient informa-tion to allow assessment of the degree to which auxiliary enterprises are self-supporting, nor can tier one data be used to set prices for auxiliary services since they do not reflect the full costs of providing those services. Functions such as those above require not only an understanding of tier one costs but also of indirect costs and of the costs associated with the depreciation of facilities and capital equipment.

The primary sources of indirect costs for the auxiliary enterprises area are plant operation and maintenance and institutional support services. These two functions include activities such as custodial services, building and equipment maintenance, accounting, and purchasing. Chapter 2 describes methods of allocating those costs to the benefiting cost centers.

At some institutions student services are included as a source of indirect costs for the housing cost center because dormitory resident counselors may be part of the student services staff. The organization of housing services varies among intitutions, however, and, as in figure 7.3, the dormitory resident counselors may be part of the housing function itself. In such cases compensation for the dormitory resident counselors would be included in the direct costs of the housing cost center.

The costs associated with the depreciation of facilities and capital equipment should also be allocated to the auxiliary enterprise cost centers. These costs can have a significant impact on auxiliary operations. Dormitories, including furnishings and equipment, for example, can represent substantial capital investments. In addition, institutions may incur long-term debt obligations in the construction or renovation of auxiliary enterprise facilities. The cost of both debt service and depreciation must be considered in assessing the full costs of operations. The combination of direct, indirect, and depreciation costs represents tier three, or full, costs.

The evaluation of alternative courses of action in the auxiliary enterprises area can also include an assessment of imputed costs. Imputed costs relate to the value of potential resources that would have been available to an institution but that have been foregone because one alternative was chosen over another. In the auxiliary enterprises area, the costs of building a new bookstore could be compared to the alternatives of leasing space off campus or of housing the bookstore in an existing campus facility.

Determining how much cost data to collect depends on the purposes for which the data will be used. Program evaluation and pricing should at least include data from tier two and, where feasible, from tier three.

An Illustration of Costing for Student Housing

The following cost analysis of a residence hall illustrates how cost accounting procedures can be used in student housing. *It describes cost accounting procedures at one institution only and, as a result, reflects that institution's policies concerning debt service and depreciation.* At other institutions, different policies may be in effect. Cost analysis should reflect an institution's own policies in regard to debt service and depreciation.

Figure 7.2 presents general information on the residence hall.

Figure 7.2
General Information on Residence Hall A

Capacity	405
Year completed	1965
Costs, as of June 30, 1981	
Building	$2,300,000
Furnishings	
Current balance after additions and replacements	210,000
Fully depreciated portion	60,000
Debt, U.S. Government revenue bonds	
(Interest rate 3%)	
Original amount	1,940,000
Current balance, June 30, 1981	1,575,000
Required debt service reserve	$ 88,000
Year of final payment	2007

Figure 7.3 shows the tier one, or direct, costs associated with the residence hall. Under the direct expenditures for residence hall counselors, the item "social program" reflects expenditures for social activities of the residence hall. Figure 7.4 shows the tier two costs associated with the residence hall. Plant operation and maintenance costs are allocated to the residence hall on the basis of assignable square feet. Institutional support costs, including activities such as purchasing, motor pool, duplicating, administrative data processing, and executive management, are allocated to the residence hall on the basis of direct costs. The costs associated with the residence hall management office are allocated to the residence hall on the basis of occupancy. Figure 7.5 highlights the procedure for allocating the costs associated with that office.

The costs associated with the depreciation of the residence hall building (based on a 50-year life) and its furnishings (based on a 15-year life) are illustrated in figure 7.4. Those costs are calculated using straight-line depreciation. The useful life of both the building and its furnishings is based on the experience of administrators at this particular institution.

Based on the data in figure 7.3, the total tier one costs associated with the residence hall are $99,000. The tier three, or *full*, costs of operating the residence hall, as highlighted in figure 7.4, are $399,870. The gross revenues for the residence hall as of June 30, 1981, were $415,125. When tier three costs are taken into consideration, a net revenue of $15,255 is generated.

Figure 7.3
Residence Hall A
(Tier One Costs)

Tier one costs (for fiscal year ending June 30, 1981)[1]

Direct expenditures	
Residence counselors	
Salaries	$31,000
Benefits	3,000
CW-S wages	5,000
Social program	4,000
Office supplies and other	2,000
	45,000
Debt service mandatory transfer	
Interest	47,000
Principal	30,000
Repair and replacement reserve	21,000
	98,000
Adjustments for costing purposes	
Delete debt service principal, to be replaced in tier three by depreciation (see figure 7.5).	(30,000)
Delete repair and replacement deposit (asset available for future use), less authorized expenditures made from reserve last year.[2]	(14,000)
	(44,000)
Total adjusted tier one costs	$99,000

Notes

[1] This building contains a dining hall. Dining hall revenues and expenditures are accounted for separately.

[2] The repair and replacement reserve required by the bond indenture is a funded reserve available for expenditures authorized by the government. To the extent that such expenditures are capitalized, the costs are recognized through depreciation. To the extent that they are expensed, they are included in tier one in the year they are expended.

The cost information in figures 7.3 and 7.4 can be used to determine the degree to which the residence hall operation is self-sufficient. In addition, cost figures combined with occupancy data (see figure 7.2) can be used as factors in setting room fees. For example, room fees for the residence hall are currently $1,107 per academic year, and the residence hall generates a net revenue of $15,255 per year. If costs, however, increase by 12 percent and occupancy remains constant at 375 residents, the residence hall would incur a deficit of $32,729. To reduce this deficit, the institution may decide either to increase the occupancy of the residence hall or raise room fees. If the latter step is chosen, the fees would have

---

Figure 7.4

Residence Hall A

(Tiers Two and Three Costs)

Tier two costs

Indirect costs

Residence hall management office, allocated on the basis of occupancy (see figure 7.5)	$ 9,870
Plant operation and maintenance, allocated on the basis of assignable square feet	227,000
Institutional support, including executive management fiscal operations, general administrative services, and logistical services allocated on the basis of direct costs	8,000
Subtotal indirect costs	244,870
Tier one costs (see figure 7.3)	99,000
Total tier two costs	$343,870

Tier three costs

Depreciation (straight line)[1]

Building depreciation (50 years)	$ 46,000
Furnishings depreciation (15 years)	10,000
Subtotal depreciation	56,000
Tier two costs	343,870
Total tier three costs	$399,870

Note

[1] Building depreciation cost is greater than the debt service principal payment because the original amount financed was less than the total building cost. Also, principal payments vary from year to year based on a schedule in the bond indenture. Depreciation is calculated on a straight-line basis.

Figure 7.5

Procedures for Allocating Costs of Residence Hall Management Office

1. Occupancy of residence halls (number of residents for fiscal year ending June 30, 1981)

Residence hall A	375
Residence hall B	425
Residence hall C	500
Residence hall D	500
Total occupancy	1,800

2. Occupancy of residence hall A as a percentage of total occupancy $\frac{375}{1,800} = 21\%$

3. Direct costs of residence hall management office $47,000

4. Direct costs of residence hall management office allocated to residence hall A

$$\begin{array}{r} 47,000 \\ \times\ \ 21\% \\ \hline \$\ 9,870 \end{array}$$

---

to be increased by approximately 8 percent to $1,195 per academic year in order to cover the increased cost. It should be noted that any decision to raise room fees should include an analysis of a number of other factors, such as demand for dormitory space, other sources of revenue (summer sessions and residential seminars), and the room fees charged by similar institutions.

Unit Costs

In auxiliary enterprises, pricing and subsidization decisions present the most important opportunity to use unit cost data. Such decisions are necessary in every area—bookstore, food service, and housing—where fees or prices are charged. Cost analysis, however, becomes more complex at lower levels of disaggregation. In setting prices in the bookstore, for example, the analyst must consider the costs of specific product lines, such as textbooks, trade books, supplies, clothing, and others. Unit cost data may also help in the examination of historical trends and projection of future costs. For a more complete description of quantitative and nonquantitative data that are useful for unit cost measures in the auxiliary enterprises area, refer to *Administrative Service*, supplement 3:2:2, and to NACUBO's *Contracting for Services* (1982).

*fundamental considerations for determining cost information in higher education**

FOR MANY YEARS cost information and cost analysis have been recognized by administrators in higher education as useful tools in managing the internal affairs of their institutions. More recently, federal, state, and other funding and policy-setting bodies have indicated additional needs for cost information, especially in the process of appropriating and granting funds to higher education.

For cost information to be useful, it is essential that the fundamentals for determining and using costs be understood. Heretofore, these fundamentals have not been compiled as a basis for developing cost information in higher education.

In formulating fundamental considerations for the development and use of costs, higher education has available the existing body of knowledge already developed, tested, and proven in areas other than higher education. After appropriate modifications, such cost fundamentals are helpful in identifying how cost can be determined and applied by institutions of higher education. However, in applying such fundamentals, consideration should be given to the particular characteristics and objectives of these institutions.

The determination of cost information is a process of approximation, and requires the individual performing cost determinations to exercise judgment based on circumstances relevant to the purposes for which cost information is collected. Different cost results occur even when equally valid alternative approaches are used. Determination of the approach is often based on practicability, as long as the results are valid and meaningful for the purposes intended.

There have been attempts to use a single methodology for determining cost to satisfy a wide variety of purposes for which cost information is used. This chapter indicates the need for different cost determination methods and approaches to satisfy the variety of purposes for determining cost rather than using a single method for all purposes. It describes the available methods, approaches, and related considerations for determining costs.

In order to place in perspective the various aspects of costing described in the sections that follow, it is well to visualize the complete costing process. The term "costing" is used here to denote the cost determination process. The essential factors involved in determining costs in higher education and their interrelationships are shown in the exhibit on the following page.

Foremost among these factors are costing standards to be applied in determining cost; they serve as the foundation on which costing is performed. Before costing can begin, however, it is necessary that the purposes of cost information be clearly identified. Once the purposes are defined, then the definitions of cost, the cost objectives and costing units, the types and classifications of cost, and the financial accounting and statistical data to be used to provide the desired cost information can be specified.

At this stage the appropriate cost determination methodology should be formulated. The methodology can be either the specific service method (job order method), the continuous service method (process method), or a combination of the two methods. These methods are described in detail in the section "Cost Determina-

---

*From *Administrative Service.*

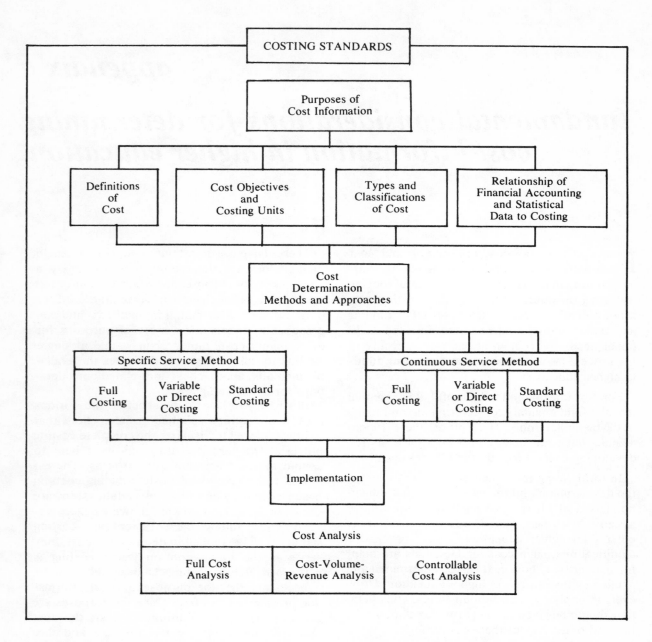

tion Methods and Approaches." Within these methods full costing, variable or direct costing, or standard costing approaches can be employed. Based on the methodology selected, costing procedures are implemented. The resultant cost information serves as the subject of cost analysis, which is the process of examining cost and statistical information and deriving meaning to satisfy the needs of users. The three basic cost analysis categories are full cost analysis, cost-volume-revenue analysis, and controllable cost analysis.

PURPOSES OF COST INFORMATION

There are many purposes for determining cost information to satisfy both internal and external requirements. It is essential that the purpose of obtaining cost information be identified at the outset in order that appropriate definitions and methods of costing can be selected.

For a college or university, cost information is used for purposes of assisting in planning and budgeting, in controlling, and in evaluating performance. The process of planning and budgeting is designed to formulate the approach to be followed by an institution in achieving its long-term mission and shorter-term goals and objectives. In the planning and budgeting process, cost information is one factor used in examining alternatives, determining the cost requirements of each alternative, and selecting those alternatives consistent with the most effective utilization of available resources. Cost information may be used in modifying the budget plan during the operating period by indicating the cost consequences of proposed actions in view of changes in priorities, economic conditions, and other circumstances that could not have been foreseen during the planning and budget process.

In controlling current operations, cost information is a valuable indicator for identifying areas in which current budgetary adjustments may be required or corrective actions needed. The control process involves the comparison of incurred cost to budgeted cost. Variances identified in the control process are examined to determine the appropriate action to be taken.

Cost information is one among many important aspects in the evaluation of performance. Evaluation involves an after-the-fact examination of results and assists in determining whether the educational and related activities conducted were as effective as anticipated and whether institutional resources were appropriate to support these activities. By comparing the results of operations to the original plan, areas can be identified in which adjustments may be needed in future planning and budgeting. Cost information also is used in determining interdepartmental charges in the financial accounting system.

Cost information is used by federal, state, and local bodies responsible for appropriating public funds. Foundations and other granting bodies also are interested in cost information. Through the years, these granting bodies have been interested in cost information (and other information) to assist them in determining whether they will use their funds to support a need. This information also has been used by granting bodies to reimburse direct and indirect costs related to grants and contracts for specific programs. Certain governmental and private funding agencies have established required costing procedures for reimbursement purposes.

COSTING TERMS

For the purpose of determining cost information, it is necessary to establish definitions of cost and their relationship to cost objectives and costing units.

Definitions of Cost

The term "cost" is defined in different ways, depending on the objectives for which costs are determined. Three commonly used definitions of cost are derived from financial accounting, cost accounting, and economics.

Financial accounting is concerned with recording, classifying, summarizing, and analyzing financial data. The financial accounting definition treats cost as the amount or equivalent paid or charged for something of value. In this sense, cost represents the total value sacrificed to obtain assets and to receive goods and services. Another term very much a part of the cost concept is "expense." For financial accounting purposes, expense is the expired portion of cost applicable to a specific period. Therefore, the cost of acquired assets that benefit future periods, such as inventories and capital assets, is not considered an expense at the time of acquisition, but is deferred until the assets are used. The term "expense" should not be confused with the term "expenditure." Expenditures include all expenses except depreciation and also include the acquisition cost of capital assets.

Cost accounting is concerned with accumulating, classifying, summarizing, interpreting, and reporting the cost of personnel, goods and services, and other expenses incurred to determine unit costs. Expenses incurred during a specified period, as defined by financial accounting, are the prime ingredient of cost accounting for cost determination purposes. The costing process is designed to assign or allocate costs to particular units of service provided. The costs derived may be actual costs or may be other costs such as replacement, projected, or imputed costs. The primary difference between cost accounting and financial accounting is that the former involves obtaining unit cost information and the latter involves obtaining costs primarily by organizational unit and function.

In economics, cost can be viewed from the "macro" or "micro" point of view. The macro definition of cost typically considers society as a whole rather than focusing attention on a particular institution. For example, the economist considers opportunities sacrificed by the community at large as societal costs external to the institution. On the other hand, the micro definition of cost used in economics focuses on the activities of an organization. This definition, in addition to considering expired cost (expense), may include other costs such as replacement, projected, or imputed costs. This latter definition is similar to that often used in cost accounting.

The definition of cost depends on the purposes for which cost information is to be used. There is no single definition of cost that will satisfy the variety of needs for cost information. Accordingly, significant differences in cost information will be derived, depending on the selection of cost definitions used for different purposes.

Cost Objectives and Costing Units

A cost objective is a defined entity to which cost is related, and can be an organizational unit, a project, responsibility center, function, program, or some other identifiable entity. Cost is accumulated and assigned to cost objectives for purposes of measuring the cost of processes or specific services. The cost objectives used in the costing process are based on the purposes for which cost information will be used and the level of cost aggregation desired. Different costs, and therefore different cost objectives, are required for different purposes.

Costing units are measures reflecting the activities or outputs of cost objectives, and bear a relationship to the incurrence of cost.

In commercial organizations, cost generally can be assigned to well-defined and measurable products or services. In higher education, however, the services of instruction, research, and public service may not be measurable or separable in terms of units of output. For example, the instructional process produces an output sometimes referred to as an acquired body of knowl-

edge; however, there is no consensus on how to measure the acquired knowledge as an output. Full-time-equivalent students, student credit-hours, student contact-hours, student head-count, student major by level, and degrees awarded are examples of costing units of service used to measure the instructional process in lieu of output measures. These units are not measures of quality or efficiency.

Measurable units of output are available for certain support activities such as meals served in food service facilities, jobs run by computer centers, and pounds of steam produced by heating plants.

Types and Classifications of Cost

Depending on the intended use of cost information, one type of cost or a combination of types of cost may be employed. Five basic types of cost are:

1. Historical cost.
2. Projected cost.
3. Standard cost.
4. Replacement cost.
5. Imputed cost.

For certain cost determination purposes, components of the above types of cost may be classified as either direct or indirect. For other cost determination purposes, components may be classified as fixed, variable, or semivariable.

Historical Cost. Historical cost usually is expressed in terms of the monetary value of economic resources released to pay faculty and staff salaries, to acquire materials and services, and to utilize facilities. Historical cost results from an expenditure involving the disbursement of cash or incurrence of a liability.

The two methods of determining historical cost are referred to as the cash basis and the accrual basis. The cash basis of accounting recognizes revenues when cash is received and expenditures when cash is paid, whereas accrual accounting recognizes revenues when earned and expenditures when materials are used and services are performed. To provide valid and consistent historical cost information, college and university accounting standards, as promulgated by authoritative bodies, require that accounting records and resulting financial statements be based on the accrual method of accounting. For cost determination purposes, the accrual basis should be used. In this regard, an important concept inherent in accounting and costing is materiality, which provides that it is not necessary to recognize certain items of expense and revenue if their omission does not have a significant effect on the final results.

Projected Cost. Projected cost for an educational institution is an estimate of the cost to be incurred in a future period. Changes anticipated in programs, student demand, faculty mix, faculty workload, support required, salary rates, and economic conditions all affect cost expectations. Projected cost is based on available knowledge about past activities, along with expectations of new and planned activities and the effect of changing conditions on cost.

Standard Cost. Standard cost is a predetermined cost, used as a target or basis of comparison with actual cost when units of service are provided. Establishment of standard cost involves a detailed examination of past occurrences and an evaluation of expectations to establish meaningful standards of performance. Standard costs may be developed by estimating costs based on historical experience or based on special studies.

Replacement Cost. Replacement cost refers to that cost which would be incurred at present or in the future to construct or acquire physical facilities or to purchase comparable services and materials to replace those obtained in the past. Replacement cost is not recorded as part of the financial accounting system. It may be used to measure the effects of inflation or deflation against the original cost incurred.

Cost viewed in terms of replacement highlights the fact that an institution is utilizing assets purchased in the past, which may be replaced at a cost different from historical cost. Because of changing price levels, recognition of historical cost alone may misrepresent the cost if replacement is considered. Therefore, since certain assets presumably will be replaced by an institution, replacement cost is measured at the current or future market level.

Imputed Cost. Imputed cost relates to potential resources that would have been available to an institution, but that were forgone because one alternative was chosen over another. Imputed cost does not consider the past, present, or eventual disbursement of cash or its equivalent, but rather is concerned with measuring the cost of alternative opportunities. By considering forgone resources as a cost, management is able to evaluate the imputed cost of one alternative versus another.

An example of imputed cost is the interest income forgone by an institution, which could have been earned if the funds utilized for a particular activity had been invested. This imputed cost represents economic resources forgone by an institution in selecting one alternative over another.

Direct Costs and Indirect Costs. For cost determination purposes, components of cost may be classified into direct costs and indirect costs. Direct costs are those expenses that are readily identifiable with a cost objective. For example, where the chemistry department is the cost objective, identifiable faculty compensation and supplies associated with teaching chemistry courses are direct costs of the department.

Indirect costs are those costs not readily identifiable with a cost objective. Indirect costs of a chemistry department include an allocated portion of the expenses of the president's office, libraries, and operation and maintenance of plant. These costs are incurred for more than one cost objective and are not readily related in a direct fashion to each cost objective.

The distinction between direct and indirect cost has to be judgmental in many cases. A major factor in distinguishing between direct and indirect cost is the level of aggregation of the cost objective. For instance, a portion of the compensation paid to a chemistry department chairman may be considered an indirect cost of a chemistry course. However, if the cost objective is the chemistry department as a whole, instead of the individual courses conducted by the department, the cost of the department chairman is direct.

The determination of whether cost is direct or indirect also is affected by the practicality of assigning costs directly to the cost objective to achieve greater precision. In many situations, much effort is required to relate cost directly to the cost objective, with the results not being materially different from the identification of cost as indirect. Therefore, an important factor for consideration in the assignment of costs is the added expense of identifying costs as direct rather than indirect. The expense of making a precise assignment of costs as direct must be weighed against the precision required in satisfying the purpose for which cost information is used.

Other factors affecting the distinction between direct and indirect cost include the individual judgments that must be exercised in classifying costs and the differences among institutions, such as organizational structure and operating policies.

Fixed, Variable, and Semivariable Costs. Components of cost also may be identified as being fixed, variable, or semivariable (also referred to as mixed or step-variable) costs. Total variable costs fluctuate in direct proportion to the volume of units of service provided. Total fixed costs, on the other hand, remain constant over a period regardless of the number of units of service provided. Semivariable costs include both fixed and variable elements, the fixed portion relating to capacity and the variable portion depending on usage. These semivariable costs typically react to volume changes in an irregular fashion; thus, cost that is fixed for a certain range of units of service becomes variable as that range is exceeded.

Certain costs are classified as fixed because of policy decisions of an institution, and may be further referred to as committed or discretionary. Committed fixed costs are those that must be expended because of existing contractual arrangements, plant facilities, and other activities that are necessary to maintain a viable program within the institution. For example, faculty compensation may be a committed cost because of employment contracts. Discretionary fixed costs (also referred to as managed costs) result directly from policy decisions of management. An example of discretionary cost is preventive maintenance. The incurrence of such costs has no relationship to volume of service, but because of their nature, may be adjusted within a particular costing period.

Costing and Financial Accounting

In the determination of cost information, there are important relationships between financial accounting and cost accounting that need to be recognized. A financial accounting system is used by all colleges and universities to provide information to administrators, governing boards, and others. The information obtained from this system, however, often cannot completely satisfy the needs for unit cost information. For specific purposes, cost information may be developed by conducting special cost studies, which typically utilize data contained in established financial accounting systems as well as financial and statistical data available from other sources. To meet the repetitive requirements for certain cost information, an institution may expand its financial accounting system or develop supplemental costing procedures. The distinguishing characteristic of cost accounting is the introduction of statistical data to determine unit costs.

A financial accounting system in higher education is based on generally accepted accounting principles and is designed to satisfy the institution's need for recording, collecting, classifying, and reporting financial information. This involves maintaining separate accounts in the financial accounting system for (1) the unrestricted and restricted funds received and expended by the institution; (2) the organizational entities within the institution responsible for expending funds according to budgets; and (3) the objects of expenditures incurred, such as salaries and wages, supplies, and equipment. The classification of different accounts is in accordance with the institution's chart of accounts. Except for the broad classifications of financial accounting information promulgated by authoritative bodies for external financial reporting purposes, the chart of accounts usually varies among institutions. The variations are due in part to differences in institutional characteristics and information requests.

Because a chart of accounts is designed to serve specific purposes, the information obtained from the financial accounting system usually does not satisfy the variety of needs for cost information. Expenditures such as interest on plant indebtedness recorded in certain fund groups for financial accounting purposes may have to be·combined with expenditures of other fund groups for cost determination purposes. Furthermore, there are instances where the financial accounting system does not include certain costs such as retirement plan expense recorded by a state agency and depreciation expense, which is not required to be recognized by institutions of higher education.

Accounts in the financial accounting system may or may not coincide with cost objectives. In determining cost information, certain accounts in the financial accounting system may require analysis to identify their direct or indirect relationship to a cost objective or to identify their fixed, variable, or semivariable nature. Financial accounting information which cannot be directly identified with a cost objective may need to be allocated as an indirect cost. Similarly, the methods used to charge personnel costs to accounts for financial accounting purposes may not be sufficient bases for identifying costs to a cost objective for cost accounting purposes.

Reconciliation, the process of identifying and giving appropriate consideration to differences in two or more sets of data, should be made between cost information and official financial and statistical information. This reconciliation is necessary because cost accounting systems or special cost studies normally make some use of the following:

1. Costs appearing in different form from that contained in the financial accounting system.
2. Costs unavailable in the financial accounting system.
3. Statistical data available elsewhere in the institution or from other sources.

The reconciliation of these items is necessary to insure the validity of cost information.

As is true with the presentation of a financial statement, cost information reports should be accompanied by a disclosure statement sufficient to provide the reader with the significant costing standards and policies affecting the determination of the cost information for its intended purpose.

COST DETERMINATION METHODS AND APPROACHES

Cost objectives may represent either (1) specific, unique projects or (2) processes producing similar, repetitive services. The costs of such objectives are determined by one or a combination of two methods, namely, the specific service method or the continuous service method. Generally, under the specific service method, costs are accumulated to a specific service or project, while under the continuous service method they are accumulated to a group of similar units of service. In commercial organizations, these methods are referred to as job order and process costing, respectively. Selection of the appropriate costing method is essential if valid costs are to be determined. The continuous service method costs all units at an average as though the units were all uniform. If the services are unique and not uniform, use of the continuous service method would give invalid results.

Associated with these primary methods are three cost approaches, namely, full costing, variable costing, and standard costing, which can be used with both the specific service and continuous service methods.

Specific Service and Continuous Service Methods

Presented below are the characteristics and uses of each primary method, followed by a description of its applicability to institutions of higher education.

Specific Service Method. As the name implies, this cost determination method is used to collect cost incurred for a specific service, which can be identified separately. It is because each unit is unique that cost must be segregated, rather than being identified as part of a continuous process, wherein an average cost can be derived that is representative of each unit of service. In the specific service method, the costs of different units of service are accumulated individually throughout the period during which service is provided. As a result, costs are compiled by each project or job in each organizational unit.

Examples of specific services are research projects, jobs in print shops, and usage of motor vehicles. Each project or job has unique objectives requiring different amounts of personnel effort, goods and services, and other expenses to achieve the result intended when the project was conceived. For this reason the specific service method is used, which identifies costs of each project.

Continuous Service Method. The continuous

service method is useful when the activities being costed consist of similar units of service. In this instance, the service being costed represents a number of uniform units the cost of which can be aggregated to arrive at an average cost per unit for a particular period. Service may be provided by a number of separate organizational units performing standard activities. Costs may be accumulated through various processes or organizational units until all services are completed.

The method for attributing cost under the continuous service method is comparable to the specific service method in that the cost resulting from expenditures or requisitions of supplies is determined on somewhat the same basis. A difference that does exist, however, is that the cost incurred is accumulated by process or organizational entity rather than by individual project.

An example of the use of the continuous service method is a department such as history, providing instructional services to majors in that discipline. Typically, the department also simultaneously provides instructional services to majors of other disciplines such as English and chemistry. Instructional services provided to these different majors are the same when they attend the same courses. Essentially, courses are designed to provide instructional services to students, according to a defined curriculum. Because of these characteristics, a continuous service cost method may be applied to determine a cost per unit of service provided to each student.

Selection of Method. As a general rule, the following guidelines may be employed to select the method to attribute cost:

1. Cost incurred by an organizational unit to provide a uniform service for a particular period should be accumulated as a single cost objective by the continuous service method.
2. Cost incurred by an organizational unit to provide more than one uniform service for a particular period should be accumulated as more than one cost objective by the continuous service method.
3. Cost incurred by an organizational unit with different services that can be separately identified should be accumulated by the specific service method.

4. Cost incurred by an organizational unit to provide one or more uniform services and one or more different services can be accumulated concurrently or in sequence by both the continuous service method and specific service method, respectively.

Cost Approaches

Full, variable, and standard costing, as previously indicated, are approaches to cost determination that are used in conjunction with either of the primary methods discussed previously. Selection of the cost approach is determined by the purpose for which cost information is to be used.

Full Costing. Full costing is defined as the accumulation of all direct and all indirect costs attributed to units of service. The full costing approach permits the user of cost information to examine the total cost of units of service as well as direct and indirect components of cost that make up the full cost. The full costing approach requires that all direct costs and an appropriate share of indirect costs incurred by an organizational unit (such as an academic department) be included as the cost of units of service. Other indirect costs incurred by the institution also must be considered when determining full cost. These include indirect support activity costs, such as the cost of the president's office and operation and maintenance of plant, which cannot be attributed directly to the units of service being costed.

Full costs also include depreciation expense. Depreciation expense is that portion of the cost of limited-life capital assets (buildings and equipment) which expires during a period. In higher education, financial accounting standards do not require recognition of depreciation; however, if an institution chooses to determine full costs, provision should be made for depreciation expense. There are instances when an institution, in accordance with its costing purposes, may desire to exclude expired capital costs, but the results would not represent full costs.

Full costs also should include direct benefits of a material nature provided by an outside organization, such as pension expense incurred by a state, but not recorded in an institution's financial records.

In colleges and universities, information derived from the full costing approach may be used to compare and examine periodically the cost and revenue per unit of service provided. Full cost information may assist in (1) determining whether tuition, fees, appropriation requests, and revenues from other sources warrant adjustment and (2) evaluating whether funds expended produced the benefits anticipated. Full-cost procedures should be used for cost determination of sponsored projects.

Variable Costing. Variable costing recognizes as the cost of services provided only those costs which are variable, that is, those costs which change when changes occur in service volume or mix. Costs that remain constant, regardless of the number of units of service provided, are referred to as fixed costs.

Full costing encompasses the assignment of all costs, regardless of their variability to the units of service provided, whereas variable costing assigns only those costs that vary with volume or mix. Variable costs include those direct and indirect costs that vary with the number of units of service provided or within a range of activity.

In using the variable costing approach, costs incurred by an organizational unit are classified as either fixed or variable. For instance, if a program were to be added or eliminated, it would be necessary to determine how the costs of faculty salaries, departmental administrative salaries, and supplies would vary as a result of an increasing or decreasing number of units of service to be provided. Aggregate faculty salary cost may increase because additional sections may be required for a new program. If a program is eliminated, faculty cost may or may not decrease, depending on tenure conditions and on existing contractual obligations to nontenured faculty members. In the case of departmental administration, salary cost may be fixed because an anticipated increase or decrease in units of service may not require a change in administrative effort. On the other hand, cost of supplies may vary depending on the number of units of service. Determining the expected variability of these elements of cost is important in examining the financial implications of decisions being considered.

Variable costing is of particular import to an institution when the typical "what if" questions are asked. For instance, the financial impact of different alternatives under consideration might involve the following questions:

1. What if an academic program is expanded or contracted?
2. What if faculty salaries are raised?
3. What if average class size is increased or decreased?
4. What if the number of chemistry and history courses are reduced, with a corresponding increase in the number of English courses?
5. What if enrollments increase or decrease?

Standard Costing. Standard costing uses predetermined unit costs, which are compared with actual unit costs to identify variances. For example, in analyzing operation and maintenance of plant, variances from standard costs assist in focusing attention on variations from plan or budget and in determining corrective action to be taken. Standard costing is also useful in preparing plans and budgets for both management and those performing the work.

INDIRECT COST ALLOCATION

This section describes the considerations involved when indirect costs are to be allocated to cost objectives.

Indirect Cost Pools

Indirect cost pools are established for the purpose of allocating costs on a common allocation basis to a group of cost objectives benefiting from or causing the incurrence of the indirect cost. Indirect costs may be aggregated into pools by (1) organizational unit or cost center; (2) expenditure object, such as fuel and electricity; or (3) other categories. The number and composition of indirect cost pools relate to the characteristics of an individual institution. Factors used in determining indirect cost pool classifications include the purposes for which cost information is to be used, characteristics of the cost objectives being costed, complexity of the organization, and degree of accuracy needed.

Equitable Allocations

Cost accumulated in indirect cost pools should be allocated to cost objectives in an equitable manner. An equitable allocation basis relates to the benefits received by the cost objective or to the activities of the cost objective that logically and reasonably caused the cost to occur.

Selection of Allocation Bases

The bases selected for allocating indirect costs should be quantitative measures that can be applied in a practical manner. Such measures may be total direct costs, direct salaries and wages, square feet of space occupied, population of students and/or faculty served, or others as appropriate for the particular cost pool being allocated. The measure selected can be developed as part of a system designed to collect statistical data throughout the period or as a result of a special study.

The measure selected for distributing indirect cost should be one that will result in the most equitable allocation of indirect cost to the cost objective within the realm of practicability. After considering the purpose of cost determination, the most equitable method may not be the most reasonable in terms of both time and cost involved in collecting and tabulating quantitative data. For this reason the most practical cost distribution base should be employed, provided the result will not be materially different from a more complex alternative.

Common Cost

In processes in which two or more services are provided simultaneously, common costs occur in providing these services. In order to allocate equitably the common cost incurred in a single process to the services provided, a determination of the interrelationship between or among the two or more services involved in a given cost objective must be made. When the services are of similar importance, the process may be referred to as a joint service. Alternatively, when one service is incidental to the other, the process is one of primary-secondary service. This distinction and analysis should be made so that cost incurred in the process can be distributed equitably to the joint services or the primary-secondary services.

Joint Services. Joint services have one or more of the following characteristics:

1. The services are complementary in the sense that providing one results in providing the other.
2. The services are substitute in the sense that increasing one decreases the other.
3. The services are independent in the sense that there is no relationship between or among them except that it is less costly to provide them together rather than separately.

Allocation of cost to each of the joint services is based on a method that treats each service equitably by proportional distribution of cost. For instance, joint service cost may be allocated to the resulting services on the basis of units of each service.

One of the most difficult problems in determining joint service costs is the inseparable nature of many joint services. For example, the research function is an integral part of the instruction function, particularly at the graduate and professional levels. Medical schools have a very complex joint service problem arising from the inseparable nature of instruction, research, and patient care. In such situations, any separation of cost for joint services usually will be subjective.

Primary-Secondary Services. Primary services (main services) are the principal services of the process being costed. Secondary services (by-product services) are produced with a primary service and by the same process. The distinguishing characteristic of a secondary service is its minor importance in relation to the primary service.

Allocation of costs applicable to secondary services is handled in one of two basic ways.

1. No cost allocation is made to the secondary service, and revenue derived therefrom, if any, either is used to reduce the cost of primary service or is treated as other revenue, with no reduction in the cost of primary service.
2. Appropriate costs are allocated to the secondary service.

An example of primary-secondary services would be the academic services of a forestry school and the related forest products available for disposal. Such products are often sold to outside users, but are not a primary reason for the institution to have the forestry school. In this case, no cost would have to be allocated to the secondary service, with earned revenue either used to reduce the cost of primary services or treated as other revenue. As an alternative, a portion of the total operating cost of the forestry school may be allocated to the secondary service.

COST ANALYSIS

Once the purposes of obtaining cost information have been identified and costs have been determined, cost analysis can be performed. The act of performing cost analysis involves the examination and evaluation of costs and related statistical information in order to determine the implications of past, present, and future actions. Although cost analysis can consider past and present actions alone, one of its major uses is that of providing cost information concerning alternative opportunities available and assisting in the selection of those alternatives considered appropriate.

In performing cost analysis in higher education, it may be important in certain cases to differentiate between expenditures financed from restricted funds and those financed from unrestricted funds. This distinction must often be considered when using cost information because restricted funds can be used only for specific purposes and can be terminated at a specific time or at the completion of an activity. Where these factors are of some significance to institutions having large amounts of sponsored projects or restricted grants, it may be useful for unrestricted and restricted costs to be separately identified throughout the cost determination process. For more information on restricted and unrestricted funds, refer to the chapter "Current Funds."

While there are innumerable analyses that may be made of cost information, three basic categories of cost analysis are full cost analysis, cost-volume-revenue analysis, and controllable cost analysis. The particular category of cost analysis to be applied is a chief factor in the selection of one of three costing approaches— full, variable, and standard costing.

Full Cost Analysis

Full cost analysis involves the process of examining and evaluating the total cost attributable to a cost objective. This type of cost analysis may be useful in establishing funding and price structures in higher education for such items as tuition and fees, appropriation requests, and recovery of grant and contract costs. It also may be used in examining and evaluating the historical cost performance of activities and in cost benefit analysis. In utilizing full cost analysis, it is generally useful to consider the component parts of full costs.

It should be noted that the use of average cost per unit of service in full cost analysis is limited for projecting future costs because cost variations resulting from volume changes do not follow the average. More than likely, future average costs will indeed be different from the present level, as the mix changes and the number of units provided increases or decreases. When costs are to be used for projections, it is necessary to consider the fixed and variable nature of the cost components.

Cost-Volume-Revenue Analysis (Differential Analysis)

Cost-volume-revenue analysis involves the relationship among the cost of service, number of units of service provided, and revenue derived from providing such service. This type of analysis presents the financial results anticipated for particular levels of activities or alternatives being considered. Emphasis is placed on examining cost, volume, and revenue, which can be different for alternative activities and for varying levels of units of service provided. For instance, instructional cost in a college or university is affected by changes in student requirements, course offerings, section size, cost of goods and services purchased, and teaching loads. Revenue is affected by the number of students enrolled, tuition and fee rates, and other factors. Since all costs do not vary with volume, analysis is required to identify variable and fixed costs. The variable costing approach to cost determination described earlier is used to perform this type of analysis. Cost-volume-revenue analysis assists in determining the effect of alternatives on revenue and cost.

Differential cost-revenue analysis (often referred to as incremental analysis) is a type of cost-volume-revenue analysis that assists in making choices among various volume alternatives. Differential costs and revenues are costs and revenues expected to change as a result of changes being considered in existing institutional activities. They are the summation of a series of marginal costs and revenues. Marginal cost and revenue refer to the change resulting from the addition of one unit of service.

Emphasis in differential analysis is directed toward examining those cost and revenue elements that will change and the changes in the amount of cost and revenue that will occur as a result of selecting one alternative over another. Similar useful analysis can be performed by relating changes in cost to changes in volume without reference to revenue changes.

Controllable Cost Analysis

Controllable cost analysis, which uses information normally derived from an institution's financial accounting records, involves the examination of those costs that are the assigned responsibility of the manager of an organizational entity. In institutions of higher education, as in other organizations, controllable costs are related to organizational entities so that accountability for the use of resources is identified with a manager.

In this analysis, actual costs are compared to projected (budgeted) or standard costs to determine variances. Analysis may indicate that variances were caused by the actions of a manager, and thus it may be determined that the manager should adjust subsequent expenditures to insure conformance to budgeted cost. Where variances resulted from circumstances beyond that manager's control, the causes may be attributed to: (1) volume changes, such as an increase or decrease from that planned in the number of students requiring room and board; (2) institutional policy decisions requiring a different level of service than originally intended; or (3) the environmental effect on cost, such as that experienced with rapidly changing utility rates. Variances caused by these factors may necessitate an adjustment in the manager's budgeted cost so as to establish a new level of controllable cost, which the manager is responsible for achieving.

COSTING ISSUES

Cost data of various kinds are being used more than ever by colleges and universities for internal management purposes. Furthermore, external agencies, such as state legislatures and local government bodies, increasingly are turning to cost-based formulas to determine the level of funding to be provided to institutions. An important question for both internal and external parties is: How can more and improved cost information be provided in a way that will improve the decision-making process in higher education? Before this question can be answered conclusively, a considerable amount of research should be performed.

This section describes the more significant cost determination issues facing higher education. Some of these issues require extensive definition, testing, and validation of results before they can be resolved.

Quality and Efficiency

There is considerable interest in finding ways to appraise the quality of educational programs in higher education; however, there are no generally accepted measures of quality. Some factors that may affect the quality of educational programs have been identified as the academic ability of students, the effectiveness of faculty, the financial support for programs, and the availability of physical facilities. While there may be a relationship between cost and quality, it is not appropriate to measure quality by using cost information.

There is also interest in measuring the efficiency of educational programs; however, no acceptable measures are available. Some institutions attempt to use average class size data, student credit-hours-taught data, and classroom utilization data as measures of efficiency.

Judgment is often introduced as a substitute for quantifiable measures of quality and efficiency. Such judgment can be based on prior experiences, defined educational priorities, student and faculty demands, and other factors influencing decisions concerning educational programs. It is inappropriate for users of cost information to assume that the higher the cost of a particular program, the higher its quality; or the lower the cost of a program, the greater its efficiency. The cost of a program cannot be assumed to be a measure of its quality or efficiency.

Faculty Time and Effort Reporting

There is a long-standing issue in determining costs in higher education, which involves the appropriate distribution of faculty time or effort to the instruction, research, and public service functions. This distribution is necessary to attribute compensation cost to those functions benefiting from faculty activities.

The first aspect of this issue involves the use of time or the use of effort information as the basis for making a cost distribution. Time involves the number of hours expended, while effort involves the intensity of activity. If the distribution of faculty compensation is based on time information, cost results probably will be different from what they would be if the distribution were based on effort information.

Another aspect in faculty time or effort reporting involves the question of common cost. This difficulty can best be illustrated by the example of a professor who has a sponsored research project and in the conduct of research also provides instructional assistance to a graduate student enrolled in one of his courses. The issue is one of distributing the professor's time or effort to determine the cost of instruction and the cost of research when they occur simultaneously. A possible resolution of this issue lies in reaching consensus on a procedure for an equitable assignment of faculty time or effort. Such a resolution may well be subjective, however, and would require acceptance by a number of concerned groups, including those outside the institution who provide funds.

Costing Units

While it is possible to measure the inputs of higher education activities, there is no general agreement on the definition of measures of output for instruction, research, and public service. In the absence of acceptable output measures, many institutions have substituted measures of the process for costing units.

The definitions of costing units may vary within an institution and from institution to institution, which results in variations in unit cost information. For instance, within a university a general definition of the semester credit-hour may be established, but a particular school in the same university may decide to use a different credit-hour definition for its own purposes. Similarly, the definition of the student credit-hour can vary among institutions depending on whether they are counted at registration, after the drop/add period, or at the end of the semester. These costing unit difficulties will have to be resolved in order to report cost information in a uniform manner.

Formula Funding

Much attention has focused on the development of unit cost information as the basis of formula funding from government agencies. Many state legislatures and local government bodies are asking basic questions such as: How much funding is required for higher education and how should funds be allocated, recognizing that institutions provide different programs and services?

A number of states and local governments have attempted to resolve such questions by developing allocation formulas that involve numerous factors, including unit cost information. The equitableness of allocations resulting from these formulas depends on how well the formulas approximate the real funding needs of the institution, as well as the accuracy and validity of the data used in these formulas. It must be recognized that programs with similar titles may have significantly different costs because of differences in terms of purpose, scope, quality, and efficiency. Analysis of program differences, including cost and non-cost aspects, should be a factor in the development and use of a formula if the resulting distribution of funds is to be equitable.

Interinstitutional Comparisons and Analyses of Cost Information

Some institutional administrators and certain external agency representatives have suggested that interinstitutional comparisons and analyses of cost information are useful for evaluating programs and related activities and for allocating resources both within and among institutions. In using cost in this manner, however, it is evident that there are differences among institutions of higher education that affect the validity of cost information for comparison purposes. These differences may be classified as methodological or functional. When performing a cost study for purposes of interinstitutional cost comparisons and analyses, it is necessary to attempt to eliminate methodological cost determination differences so that the resulting cost information highlights only functional differences.

Methodological differences result from costing procedures that are not uniformly applied. Typical examples of methodological differences are the following:

1. The judgments exercised in collecting, estimating, and allocating costs differ since they often depend on the interpretation of complex situations and on the unique characteristics of individual institutions. For instance, experience has indicated that there are no generally accepted bases suitable for all allocations of indirect cost.
2. The definition of direct and indirect cost can be different from institution to institution, depending on the ability of an institution to identify cost as direct.
3. The methods used to accumulate and analyze cost may differ from institution to institution.

Functional differences principally result from differences in programs and related support activities. Identifying the actual cause of such differences among institutions requires an analysis of the characteristics and content of programs being compared. The following are examples of functional differences affecting the comparison and analysis of cost information:

1. Missions, goals, and objectives differ among institutions.
2. Quality and efficiency of the educational process differ among institutions.
3. Organizational structure, activities, and units of service costed differ from institution to institution.
4. Constituents served by institutions have different needs and, therefore, require different education services.
5. Different geographical locations of institutions cause cost for similar items to vary.
6. Distinct differences exist between those institutions which are well established and those which are developing.
7. Economies of scale may be available to a larger institution and not to a smaller one.
8. Variations in costs occur because of differences in the availability of funds.

If methodological differences can be eliminated and true functional differences identified, the question remains as to how cost information should be used internally by management and externally by government agencies. Can adequate analysis of the relationship of differences in cost to functional differences be developed to permit valid and equitable decisions? Comparative analysis is less difficult when dealing with like institutions, but becomes progressively more difficult as comparisons are made among dissimilar institutions. Much study is required to prove the utility of interinstitutional cost information.

Costing Standards

The term "costing standards" as used here refers to principles that should be applied in determining cost. Costing standards constitute the framework or foundation on which costing is performed. Because costing standards are basic definitions of how costs should be determined, they provide a better understanding of the meaning and applications of costing.

Costing standards facilitate a more consistent determination of cost; however, the application of these standards will not insure uniform determination of cost information, because judgmental and other factors are involved in the costing process. Costing standards provide criteria for the selection of costing alternatives that are valid in terms of their justification of cost accumulation and allocation within a conceptual foundation of cost accounting theory.

The development of costing standards is an evolving process and additional standards may be added from time to time as more study is given to this complex subject.

Costing Standard #1

THE PURPOSES FOR WHICH COST
INFORMATION IS TO BE USED SHOULD
DETERMINE THE FRAMEWORK WITHIN
WHICH COST INFORMATION IS DEVELOPED

Costs are determined to satisfy specific purposes for which cost information is needed. A clear definition of these purposes is needed in order to specify the cost determination approach to be used.

Costing Standard #2

COST INFORMATION SHOULD BE BASED ON
THE ACCRUAL METHOD OF ACCOUNTING

Two methods of determining cost are the cash basis method and the accrual basis method. The cash basis method of accounting recognizes expenditures when cash is paid, whereas accrual accounting recognizes expenditures when materials are used and services are performed. To provide valid and consistent cost, the accrual method of accounting should be used, applying the concept of materiality.

Costing Standard #3

COST DATA SHOULD BE RECONCILABLE TO
OFFICIAL FINANCIAL ACCOUNTING DATA

Reconciliation to official financial accounting records is necessary to insure the validity of cost records. (Reconciliation is the process of identifying and giving appropriate consideration to differences in two or more sets of data.)

Costing Standard #4

NONFINANCIAL DATA SHOULD BE
RECONCILABLE TO OFFICIAL
INSTITUTIONAL RECORDS

Reconciliation of nonfinancial data to the official records of the institution is necessary to insure the validity of cost data when such nonfinancial data are used in the cost determination process. (Reconciliation is the process of identifying and giving appropriate consideration to differences in two or more sets of data.)

Costing Standard #5

DEFINITIONS USED IN COST
DETERMINATIONS SHOULD BE APPLIED
UNIFORMLY

Uniform definitions should be employed during the cost determination process and from period to period to achieve reliable cost information.

Costing Standard #6

COST INFORMATION AND RELATED COSTING
UNITS SHOULD COVER THE SAME PERIOD

Cost determination for a particular period should be related to the units of service provided during that same period.

Costing Standard #7

COST INFORMATION SHOULD BE
CONSISTENTLY DETERMINED

Cost information used in any cost study must be consistently determined for all periods included and for all organizational units included. Cost data will not be comparable unless consistently determined. Consistency depends on uniform definitions, methods, and interpretations as well as judgments exercised in the cost determination process.

Costing Standard #8

COST SHOULD BE ATTRIBUTED TO A COST
OBJECTIVE BASED ON A CAUSAL OR
BENEFICIAL RELATIONSHIP

Meaningful and dependable cost determinations require that costs be assigned to cost objectives according to identifiable relationships that logically and reasonably cause the cost to occur or that result in benefits received by the cost objective.

Costing Standard #9

INDIRECT COST SHOULD BE ALLOCATED
BASED ON QUANTITATIVE MEASURES THAT
CAN BE APPLIED IN A PRACTICAL MANNER

The bases of allocation of indirect cost should involve the use of those quantitative measures which best represent the relationship of cost to the cost objective, with the result that indirect costs are equitably distributed. There are instances when the most equitable distribution may not be the most practical, both in terms of time and related expense involved in collecting and tabulating quantitative measures. In such cases, the most practical measure should be selected, provided the results are not materially different.

Costing Standard# 10

COMMON COST INCURRED TO PROVIDE TWO
OR MORE SERVICES SHOULD BE ALLOCATED
IN AN EQUITABLE MANNER

Allocation of common costs to joint services, which are cost objectives, should be based on a logical relationship of the several services to one another and to the nature and circumstances of the costs incurred. It should be recognized that separate costing of jointly produced services is subjective and the bases available to allocate joint costs are arbitrary.

Costing Standard #11

CAPITAL COST OF A COST OBJECTIVE
SHOULD REFLECT THE APPLICABLE
EXPIRED CAPITAL COST OF THE PERIOD

Capital cost of a cost objective should reflect applicable expired cost determined on the basis of the estimated useful life of the asset being depreciated.

Costing Standard #12

COST INFORMATION SHOULD BE
ACCOMPANIED BY A DISCLOSURE
STATEMENT

Explanatory disclosures necessary to provide the user with a clear understanding of the previously established, intended use of cost information should accompany the reporting of such information. Disclosures should encompass the costing method and approach used, the cost definition used, the types of cost included, identification of cost objectives and costing units, and other information pertinent to the cost determination effort.

appendix b

background documents used in constructing costing illustrations

Student Credit Hours by Division for Institution A			
	Credit Hours		
	19X6- 19X7	**19X7- 19X8**	**19X8- 19X9**
Division of Arts and Humanities	13,989	14,430	14,841
Division of Natural Sciences	8,964	9,377	8,780
Division of Business Administration	5,143	5,433	5,859
Division of Education	4,303	4,353	4,382
Division of Social Sciences	9,937	10,587	11,015
Total	42,336	44,180	44,877

By Department for the Division of Social Sciences			
Economics Department	1,689	1,800	1,872
History Department	1,789	1,906	1,983
Political Science Department	795	847	881
Other Departments	5,664	6,034	6,279
Total	9,937	10,587	11,015

Statement of Current Funds, Revenues, and Expenditures

Institution A	19X9			Total for 19X8
Year Ended June 30, 19X9	**Unrestricted**	**Restricted**	**Total**	
Revenues				
Tuition and Fees	$7,458,500		$ 7,458,500	$ 6,981,200
Federal Grants	14,600	$ 72,600	87,200	74,200
Private Gifts and Grants	532,400	252,400	784,800	700,000
Endowment Income	391,300	273,600	664,900	593,800
Sales and Services of Education Activities	32,700		32,700	31,800
Sales and Services of Auxiliary Enterprises	1,544,900		1,544,900	1,467,700
Other Sources	327,000		327,000	299,900
Total Current Revenues	10,301,400	598,600	10,900,000	10,148,600
Expenditures and Mandatory Transfers				
Educational and General:				
Instruction	4,457,000	143,000	4,600,000*	4,383,000
Research	19,000	131,000	150,000*	151,950
Public Service	60,000		60,000*	55,100
Academic Support	495,000	5,000	500,000*	454,000
Student Services	594,800	5,200	600,000*	544,800
Institutional Support	930,000		930,000*	806,300
Operation and Maintenance of Plant	1,065,679	34,200	1,099,879*	985,500
Scholarships	590,600	217,800	808,400	768,000
Mandatory Transfers:				
Principal and Interest	21,500		21,500	21,500
Loan Fund Matching Grant	7,270		7,270	7,270
Total Educational and General	8,240,849	536,200	8,777,049	8,177,420
Auxiliary Enterprises:				
Operations	1,188,394	900	1,189,294	1,108,422
Mandatory Transfers for:				
Principal and Interest	190,687		190,687	197,933
Renewals and Replacements	20,019		20,019	18,400
Total Auxiliary Enterprises	1,399,100	900	1,400,000*	1,324,755
Total Expenditures and Mandatory Transfers	$9,639,949	$537,100	$10,177,049	$ 9,502,175

*Ties to figures 3.1 and 3.2 in chapter 3 and figures 6.1 and 6.2a and b in chapter 6.

glossary

The following definitions are derived from generally accepted cost accounting terminology and are in compliance with those used in NACUBO's *College & University Business Administration* and *Administrative Service*. Other sources used in developing the glossary include *Accountants' Cost Handbook* (1960), edited by Robert Dickey, and *A Dictionary for Accountants* (1975), by Eric Kohler.

ACTUAL USAGE. An indirect cost allocation base that reflects the amount of service provided by a support activity. One example of actual usage is the number of purchase orders processed by the purchasing office for each benefiting cost center.

ALLOCATION. A method used to apportion support costs to benefiting cost centers. See chapter 2 for discussion of allocation bases and chapter 3 for description of indirect cost allocation methods.

ALLOCATION BASE OR PARAMETER. A proxy or measure of benefits received. It is used to allocate the cost of support activities to benefiting cost objectives and centers.

ASSIGNABLE SQUARE FEET. An allocation parameter based on the sum of the areas in all rooms that can be used by building occupants to carry out their functions. Excluded are circulation, custodial, mechanical, and structural areas.

BREAK-EVEN POINT. The volume point at which revenue and costs are equal.

BUDGETING. The process whereby the plans of an institution are translated into an itemized, authorized, and systematic plan of operation, expressed in dollars, for a given period.

CHARGEBACK SYSTEM. A system that assigns the cost of support activities to benefiting cost centers by (1) tying costs to specific requests for services; (2) establishing rates for service; and (3) charging for services.

CHART OF ACCOUNTS. A systematic classification of financial information applicable to a specific institution. The chart of accounts is designed to be compatible with the institution's organizational structure, and its form and content are arranged to agree with the financial reports to be presented.

COMMON COSTS. Costs that occur when two or more services are provided simultaneously.

CONTRIBUTED GOODS AND SERVICES. The monetary value of goods and services contributed or donated to an organization.

CONTROL OR BUDGET CONTROL. The process by which incurred costs are compared to budgeted costs.

COST ACCOUNTING. That branch of accounting concerned with accumulating, classifying, allocating, summarizing, interpreting, and reporting the cost of personnel, goods and services, and other expenses incurred during a specific period. The primary difference between cost accounting and financial accounting is that the former involves obtaining unit cost information while the latter involves obtaining costs primarily by organizational unit and function (see appendix A). According to Horngren (1977): "The field of financial accounting is concerned mainly with how accounting can serve *external* decision makers, such as stockholders, creditors, governmental agencies, and others. The field of managerial (cost) accounting is concerned mainly with how accounting can serve internal decision makers, such as managers."

COST CENTER. The smallest unit of activity or area of responsibility into which an operating organization is divided for control and accountability purposes and to which costs are assigned or allocated.

COST OBJECTIVE. Any activity to which costs can be attributed. It can be a service provided by an organizational unit, a project, a responsibility center, a function, a program, or any other identifiable activity. Cost objectives can be composed of one or more cost centers.

DEPRECIATION. A charge to current operations in the income statement that distributes in a systematic and logical manner the cost of a tangible asset (or group of assets), less estimated residual value, over the estimated service life of the asset(s).

DIRECT COSTS. Those expenses that are readily identifiable with a specific cost objective or center, generally through the institution's financial records.

EVALUATION. An after-the-fact examination of the results of specific activities, which assists in determining whether activities conducted were as effective as anticipated, whether institutional resources were appropriate to support these activities, whether support should be reduced, or whether the activity should be eliminated.

FACULTY ACTIVITY REPORTING SYSTEMS. A method of determining the percentage of a faculty member's effort devoted to a number of specified activities, such as teaching, research, and course and curriculum development.

FINAL COST OBJECTIVES. Those activities whose outcomes are related directly to the accomplishment of the primary missions of the institution but which do not demonstrate a vital support function for other programs within the institution. Such activities include but are not limited to instruction, research, public service, and auxiliary enterprises.

FIXED COST. An element of cost that remains constant over a period of time regardless of the number of units of service provided.

FULL COST. A combination of all applicable direct and indirect costs plus depreciation of facilities and capital equipment.

FULL-TIME EQUIVALENT (FTE) FACULTY. A means of expressing part-time faculty in terms of full-time. Involves identification of the percentage of time a faculty member was employed, contracted, or assigned during a given period.

FULL-TIME EQUIVALENT (FTE) STAFF. A means of expressing part-time staff in terms of full-time. FTE is generally based on the percentage of time a staff member worked during a given period of time (generally a fiscal year).

FULL-TIME EQUIVALENT (FTE) STUDENT. A means of expressing part-time students in terms of full-time. The formula for calculating FTE students varies from institution to institution, but it is generally based on credit hours. For example, an institu-

tion may define full-time as 12 credit hours, and a student who takes three credit hours as .25 FTE.

HISTORICAL COST. The monetary value of economic resources released to pay faculty and staff salaries, to acquire materials and services, and to utilize facilities. Historical cost results from an expenditure and involves the disbursement of cash or the incurrence of a liability.

IMPUTED COST. Potential resources that would have been available to an institution, but that have been foregone because one alternative was chosen over another. Imputed cost does not consider the past, present, or eventual disbursement of cash or its equivalent, but rather is concerned with measuring the costs of alternative opportunities.

INDIRECT COSTS. Those costs not readily identifiable with a specific cost objective or center. They reflect the cost of support services provided to benefiting cost objectives or centers, are incurred for more than one cost objective or center, and are not readily related in a direct way to any single cost objective or center.

INDIRECT COST POOLS. Groupings of costs identified with two or more cost objectives but not identified specifically with any final cost objective.

JOINT SERVICE COST. The common cost of services employed in the output of two or more simultaneously produced or otherwise closely related operations or services.

MANDATORY TRANSFERS. All transfers from the current funds group that must be made to other fund groups to fulfill a binding legal obligation of the institution.

OBJECT OF EXPENDITURE. The initial designation of an expenditure that identifies that which is received in return for the expenditure. Examples are personnel compensation, supplies and expenses, and capital expenditures.

OMB CIRCULAR A-21. The Office of Management and Budget (OMB) circular designed to provide principles and directions for determining the costs applicable to research and development, training, and other sponsored work performed by colleges and universities under grants, contracts, and other agreements with the federal government.

REPLACEMENT COST. A cost that would be incurred at present or in the future to construct or acquire physical facilities or to purchase comparable services and materials to replace those obtained in the past.

SINGLE-PURPOSE INSTITUTION. An institution whose primary activity is instruction. Such an institution can range from a small four-year college to a multicampus community college.

SPECIFIC SERVICE METHOD. A cost determination method used to collect costs incurred for a specific separately identifiable service. Examples of specific services are research projects, jobs in print shops, and use of motor vehicles.

STANDARD COST. A predetermined cost used as a target or basis of comparison with actual cost when units of service are provided.

SUPPORT ACTIVITIES. Those activities that provide services necessary to the successful operation of other programs within an institution but that do not contribute directly to the primary mission of the institution. Examples are plant operation and maintenance, institutional support, student services, and academic support.

STUDENT CREDIT HOUR. An allocation base that represents one student engaged in an activity for which an hour of credit is awarded.

STUDENT HEADCOUNT. An allocation base that represents the unduplicated number of students as of an official census date.

TIERED APPROACH. A method of collecting and analyzing institutional costs by groupings and levels of cost.

TIER ONE COSTS. All direct costs that are attributable to a cost objective or center. Such costs include salaries and wages, employee benefits, supplies and operating expenses, travel, contractual services, and noncapitalized equipment.

TIER THREE COSTS. All tier two costs plus a depreciation or use charge on facilities and capital equipment. Tier three costs represent the *full* costs associated with cost objectives or centers.

TIER TWO COSTS. All tier one costs plus indirect costs that are attributable to a cost objective or center.

TOTAL COMPENSATION. An allocation base that is the total dollar amount, including gross salaries and employee benefits, paid directly to or on behalf of all personnel.

UNAVOIDABLE INDIRECT COSTS. Indirect costs that would be incurred even if an in-house support service were to be discontinued.

UNIT COST. The cost of a single item or unit of service.

USE CHARGE. An overall rate that an institution can apply to either the total cost of all its buildings and land improvements or to individual capital assets in order to determine the costs associated with depreciation of its facilities and capital equipment.

Other Commonly Used Cost Accounting Terms

The following terms are found frequently in the literature on cost accounting. Definitions for each of these terms can be found in appendix A.

Continuous service method
Controllable cost analysis
Costing standards
Costing units
Cost-volume-revenue analysis
Differential analysis
Equitable allocations
Expense
Faculty time and effort reporting
Financial accounting
Formula funding
Full costing
Incremental costs
Interinstitutional comparisons
Joint service
Primary-secondary service
Projected costs
Semivariable costs
Specific service method
Standard costing
Variable cost
Variable costing

references

Adams, Carl R., Russell L. Hankins, and Roger G. Schroeder. *The Literature of Cost and Cost Analysis in Higher Education/Monograph 1*. Minneapolis: Graduate School of Business Administration, University of Minnesota, 1977.

Association of Research Libraries. *Fees for Service Kit 74*. Washington, D.C., 1981.

_____. *Library Material Cost Studies Kit 60*. Washington, D.C., 1980.

Bowen, Howard Rothman. *The Costs of Higher Education*. San Francisco: Jossey-Bass, 1980.

Cloud, Sherrill, comp. *A Glossary of Standard Terminology for Postsecondary Education, 1979-80*. Boulder: National Center for Higher Education Management Systems (NCHEMS).

Council on Independent Colleges (CIC, formerly CASC). *User Manual for the Instructional Program Module*. Washington, D.C., 1978.

Densmore, Glen, and Charles Bourne. *A Cost Analysis and Utilization Study of the Stanford University Library System*. Stanford: Stanford University Libraries, 1965.

Dickey, Robert I. *Accountants' Cost Handbook*. 2d ed. New York: Wiley, 1960.

Gamso, Gary. *An Approach to Cost Studies in Small Colleges*. Boulder: National Center for Higher Education Management Systems (NCHEMS), 1978.

Horngren, Charles T. *Cost Accounting—A Managerial Emphasis*. 4th ed. Englewood Cliffs, N.J.: Prentice-Hall, 1977.

Kohler, Eric L. *A Dictionary for Accountants*. 5th ed. Englewood Cliffs, N.J.: Prentice-Hall, 1975.

Leimkuhler, Ferdinand F., and Michael D. Cooper. *Cost Accounting and Analysis for University Libraries*. Berkeley: University of California, 1970.

National Association of College and University Business Officers (NACUBO). *Administrative Service*. Washington, D.C., 1982.

_____. *College & University Business Administration*. Washington, D.C., 1982.

_____. *Contracting for Services*. Washington, D.C., 1982.

_____. *Costing for Policy Analysis*. Washington, D.C., 1980.

NACUBO/NCHEMS. *Procedures for Determining Historical Full Costs, Technical Report 65*. 2d ed. Washington, D.C., 1977.

Robinson, Daniel D., Howard W. Ray, and Frederick J. Turk. "Cost Behavior Analysis for Planning in Higher Education." NACUBO *Professional File*, vol. 9, no. 5 (May 1977).

Stewart, Ian R., and John S. Ostrom. "Responsibility Center Management: Risks and Rewards." *Business Officer* (April 1980): 14-16.

Topping, James R. *Cost Analysis Manual*. Boulder: National Center for Higher Education Management Systems at Western Interstate Commission for Higher Education (NCHEMS at WICHE), 1974.